Recollected
Essays 1965–1980

Wendell Berry

North Point Press
San Francisco 1981

*The author wishes to acknowledge his gratitude to
each of these publishers for their permission to re-
print these essays:* THE RISE (1968) first published by
The University of Kentucky Library Press; THE
LONG-LEGGED HOUSE (1969) first published by
Harcourt, Brace and World; THE HIDDEN WOUND
(1970) first published by Houghton Mifflin Com-
pany; A CONTINUOUS HARMONY (1972) first pub-
lished by Harcourt, Brace and Jovanovich; THE
UNFORESEEN WILDERNESS (1977) first published by
The University Press of Kentucky; THE UNSETTLING
OF AMERICA (1977) first published by Sierra Club
Books; "The Making of a Marginal Farm" first pub-
lished by *The Smithsonian* in 1980; "A Native Hill"
and "The Unforeseen Wilderness" first published by
The Hudson Review.

To Jimmy Perry
kinsman, neighbor and friend

Table of Contents

Foreword

Unconsciously perhaps from the beginning, and more and more consciously during the last sixteen or seventeen years, my work has been motivated by a desire to make myself responsibly at home both in this world and in my native and chosen place. As I have slowly come to understand it, this is a long term desire, proposing the work not of a lifetime but of generations.

I have chosen to republish the pieces that follow because I still approve of them in general as serving that desire, and I still approve the drift or direction that seems to me to govern them. However, I have not been able to return to them without misgivings, and without a consequent effort to remedy what I thought objectionable.

In some of the pieces, I have removed passages that I now consider wrongly motivated, or less to the point or

x

less good than I once thought. In several places I have
added footnotes, disagreeing with or qualifying or elaborating earlier statements. And I have made many small
changes which may or may not have altered the meaning,
but which I hope have improved the writing.

Finally, I would like to alert the reader to my conviction that this is a piece of unfinished business, and that
more time and work will reveal further need of correction.

Wendell Berry
Port Royal, Kentucky
February 1981

from

The Long-Legged House

I

The Rise

We put the canoe in about six miles up the Kentucky River from my house. There, at the mouth of Drennon Creek, is a little colony of summer camps. We knew we could get down to the water there with some ease. And it proved easier than we expected. The river was up maybe twenty feet, and we found a path slanting down the grassy slope in front of one of the cabins. It went right into the water, as perfect for launching the canoe and getting in as if it had been worn there by canoeists.

To me that is the excitement of a rise: the unexpectedness, always, of the change it makes. What was difficult becomes easy. What was easy becomes difficult. By water, what was distant becomes near. By land, what was near becomes distant. At the water line, when a rise is on, the world is changing. There is an irresistible sense of adventure in the difference. Once the river is out of its banks, a vertical few inches of rise may widen the surface by many feet over the bottomland. A sizable lagoon will appear in the middle of a cornfield. A drain in a pasture will become a canal. Stands of beech and oak will take on the look of a cypress swamp. There is something Venetian about it. There is a strange excitement in going in a boat where one would ordinarily go on foot—or where, ordinarily, birds would be flying. And so the first excitement of our trip was that little path; where it might go in a time of low water was unimaginable. Now it went down to the river.

Because of the offset in the shore at the creek mouth, there was a large eddy turning in the river where we put in, and we began our drift downstream by drifting upstream. We went up inside the row of shore trees, whose tops now waved in the current, until we found an opening among the branches, and then turned out along the channel. The current took us. We were still settling ourselves as if in preparation, but our starting place was already diminishing behind us.

There is something ominously like life in that. One would always like to settle oneself, get braced, say "Now I am going to begin"—and then begin. But as the necessary quiet seems about to descend, a hand is felt at one's back, shoving. And that is the way with the river when a current is running: once the connection with the shore is broken, the journey has begun.

We were, of course, already at work with the paddles. But we were ahead of ourselves. I think that no matter how deliberately one moved from the shore into the sudden violence of a river on the rise, there would be bound to be several uneasy minutes of transition. It is another world, which means that one's senses and reflexes must begin to live another kind of life. Sounds and movements that from the standpoint of the shore might have come to seem even familiar now make a new urgent demand on the attention.

There is everything to get used to, from a wholly new perspective. And from the outset one has the currents to deal with.

It is easy to think, before one has ever tried it, that nothing could be easier than to drift down the river in a canoe on a strong current. That is because when one thinks of a river one is apt to think of *one* thing—a great singular flowing that one puts one's boat into and lets go. But it is not like that at all, not after the water is up and the current swift. It is not one current, but a braiding together of several, some going at different speeds, some even in different directions. Of course, one *could* just let go, let the boat be taken into the continuous mat of drift—leaves, logs, whole trees, cornstalks, cans, bottles, and such—in the channel, and turn and twist in the eddies there. But one does not have to do that long in order to sense the helplessness of a light canoe when it is sideways to the current. It is out of control then, and endangered. Stuck in the mat of drift, it can't be maneuvered. It would turn over easily; one senses that by a sort of ache in the nerves, the way bad footing is sensed. And so we stayed busy, keeping the canoe between the line of half-submerged shore trees and the line of drift that marked the channel. We weren't trying to hurry—the currents were carrying us as fast as we wanted to go—but it took considerable labor just to keep straight. It was like riding a spirited horse not fully bridle-wise: We kept our direction *by intention*; there could be no dependence on habit or inertia; when our minds wandered the river took over and turned us according to inclinations of its own. It bore us like a consciousness, acutely wakeful, filling perfectly the lapses in our own.

But we did grow used to it, and accepted our being on it as one of the probabilities, and began to take the mechanics of it for granted. The necessary sixth sense had come to us, and we began to notice more than we had to.

There is an exhilaration in being *accustomed* to a boat on dangerous water. It is as though into one's consciousness of the dark violence of the depths at one's feet there rises the idea of the boat, the buoyancy of it. It is always with a sort of triumph that the boat is realized—that it goes *on top of the water*, between breathing and drowning. It is an ancient-feeling triumph; it must have been one of the first ecstasies. The analogy of riding a spirited horse is fairly satisfactory; it is mastery over something resistant—a buoyancy that is not natural and inert like that of a log, but desired and vital and to one's credit. Once the boat has fully entered the consciousness it becomes an intimate extension of the self; one feels as competently amphibious as a duck. And once we felt accustomed and secure in the boat, the day and the river began to come clear to us.

It was a gray, cold Sunday in the middle of December. In the woods on the north slopes above us we could see the black trunks and branches just faintly traced with snow, which gave them a silvery, delicate look—the look of impossibly fine handwork that nature sometimes has. And they looked cold. The wind was coming straight up the river into our faces. But we were dressed warmly, and the wind didn't matter much, at least not yet. The force that mattered, that surrounded us, and inundated us with its sounds, and pulled at or shook or carried everything around us, was the river.

To one standing on the bank, floodwater will seem to be flowing at a terrific rate. People who are not used to it will commonly believe it is going three or four times as fast as it really is. It is so all of a piece, and so continuous. To one drifting along in a boat this exaggerated impression of speed does not occur; one is going the same speed as the river then and is not fooled. In the Kentucky when the water is high a current of four or five miles an hour is about usual, I would say, and there are times in a canoe that make that seem plenty fast.

What the canoeist gets, instead of an impression of the river's speed, is an impression of its power. Or, more exactly, an impression of the *voluminousness* of its power. The sense of the volume alone has come to me when, swimming in the summertime, I have submerged mouth and nose so that the plane of the water spread away from the lower eyelid; the awareness of its bigness that comes then is almost intolerable; one feels how falsely assuring it is to look down on the river, as we usually do. The sense of the power of it came to me one day in my boyhood when I attempted to swim ashore in a swift current, pulling an overturned rowboat. To check the downstream course of the boat I tried grabbing hold of the partly submerged willows along the shore with my free hand, and was repeatedly pulled under as the willows bent, and then torn loose. My arms stretched between the boat and the willow branch might have been sewing threads for all the holding they could do. It was the first time I realized that there could be circumstances in which my life would count for nothing, absolutely nothing—and I have never needed to learn that again.

Sitting in a canoe, riding the back of the flooding river as it flows down into a bend, and turns, the currents racing and crashing among the trees along the outside shore, and flows on, one senses the volume and the power all together. The sophistications of our age do not mitigate the impression. To some degree it remains unimaginable, as is suggested by the memory's recurrent failure to hold on to it. It can never be remembered as wild as it is, and so each new experience of it bears some of the shock of surprise. It would take the mind of a god to watch it as it changes and not be surprised.

These long views that one gets coming down it show it to move majestically. It is stately. It has something of the stylized grandeur and awesomeness of royalty in Sophoclean tragedy. But as one watches, there emanates from it, too, an insinuation of darkness, implacability, horror. And the nearer look tends to confirm this. Contained and borne in the singular large movements are hundreds of smaller ones: eddies and whirlpools, turnings this way and that, cross-currents rushing out from the shores into the channel. One must simplify it in order to speak of it. One probably simplifies it in some way in order to look at it.

There is something deeply horrifying about it, roused. Not, I think, because it is inhuman, alien to us; some of us at least must feel a kinship with it, or we would not loiter around it for pleasure. The horror must come from our sense that, so long as it remains what it is, it is not subject. To say that it is indifferent would be wrong. That would imply a malevolence, as if it could be aware of us if only it wanted to. It is more remote from our concerns than indifference. It is serenely and silently not subject—to us or to anything else except the other natural forces that are also beyond our control. And it is apt to stand for and represent to us all in nature and in the universe that is not subject. That is its horror. We can make use of it. We can ride on its back in boats. But it won't stop to let us get on and off. It is not a passenger train. And if we make a mistake, or risk ourselves too far to it, why then it will suffer a little wrinkle on its surface, and go on as before.

That horror is never fully revealed, but only sensed piecemeal in events, all different, all shaking, yet all together falling short of the full revelation. The next will be as unexpected as the last.

A man I knew in my boyhood capsized his motorboat several miles upriver from here. It was winter. The river was high and swift. It was already nightfall. The river carried him a long way before he drowned. Farmers sitting in their houses in the bottoms heard his cries passing down in the darkness, and failed to know what to make of them. It is hard to imagine what they could have done if they had known.

I can't believe that anyone who has heard that story will ever forget it. Over the years it has been as immediate to me as if I had seen it all—almost as if I had *known* it all: the capsized man aching and then numb in the cold water, clinging to some drift log in the channel, and calling, seeing the house lights appear far off across the bottoms and dwindle behind him, the awful power of the flood and his hopelessness in it finally dawning on him—it is amazingly real; it is happening to him. And the families in their lighted warm kitchens, eating supper maybe, when the tiny desperate outcry comes to them out of the darkness, and they look up at the window, and then at each other.

"Shhh! Listen! What was that?"

"By God, it sounded like somebody hollering out there on the river."

"But it *can't* be."

But it makes them uneasy. Whether or not there *is* somebody out there, the possibility that there *may* be reminds them of their lot; they never know what may be going by them in the darkness. And they think of the river, so dark and cold.

The history of these marginal places is in part the history of drownings—of fishermen, swimmers, men fallen from boats. And there is the talk, the memory, the inescapable *feeling* of dragging for the bodies—that terrible fishing for dead men lost deep in the currents, carried downstream sometimes for miles.

Common to river mentality, too, are the imaginings: step-offs, undertows, divers tangled in sunken treetops, fishermen hooked on their own lines.

And yet it fascinates. Sometimes it draws the most fearful to it. Men must test themselves against it. Its mystery must be forever tampered with. There is a story told here of a strong big boy who tried unsuccessfully to cross the river by walking on the bottom, carrying an iron kettle over his head for a diving bell. And another story tells of a young man who, instead of walking under it, thought he would walk *on* it, with the help of a gallon jug tied to each foot. The miracle failing, of course, the jugs held his feet up, and his head under, until somebody obliged him by pulling him out. His pride, like Icarus', was transformed neatly into his fall—the work of a river god surely, hubris being as dangerous in Henry County as anywhere else.

To sense fully the power and the mystery of it, the eye must be close to it, near to level with the surface. I think that is the revelation of George Caleb Bingham's painting of trappers on the Missouri. The painter's eye, there, is very near the water, and so he sees the river as the trappers see it from their dugout—all the space coming down to that vast level. One feels the force, the aliveness, of the water under the boat, close under the feet of the men. And there they are, isolated in the midst of it, with their box of cargo and their pet fox—men and boat and box and animal all so strangely and poignantly coherent on the wild plain of the water, a sort of island.

But impressive as the sights may be, the river's wildness is most awesomely announced to the ear. Along the channel, the area of the most concentrated and the freest energy, there is silence. It is at the shore line, where obstructions are, that the currents find their voices. The water divides around the trunks of the trees, and sucks and slurs as it closes together again. Trunks and branches are ridden down to the surface, or suddenly caught by the rising water, and the current pours over them in a waterfall. And the weaker trees throb and vibrate in the flow, their naked branches clashing and rattling. It is a storm of sound, changing as the shores change, increasing and diminishing, but never ceasing. And between these two storm lines of commotion there is that silence of the middle, as though the quiet of the deep flowing rises into the air. Once it is recognized, listened to, that silence has the force of a voice.

After we had come down a mile or two we passed the house of a fisherman. His children were standing on top of the bank, high at that place, waiting for him to come in off the river. And on down we met the fisherman himself, working his way home among the nets he had placed in the quieter water inside the rows of shore trees. We spoke and passed, and were soon out of sight of each other. But seeing him there changed the aspect of the river for us, as meeting an Arab on a camel might change the aspect of the desert. Problematic and strange as it seemed to us, here was a man who made a daily thing of it, and went to it as another man would go to an office. That race of violent water, which would hang flowing among the treetops only three or four days, had become familiar country to him, and he sunk his nets in it with more assurance than men sink wells in the earth. And so the flood bore a pattern of his making, and he went his set way on it.

And he was not the only creature who had made familiarity with the risen water. Where the drift had matted in the shore eddies, or caught against trees in the current, the cardinals and chickadees and titmice foraged as confidently as on dry land. The rise was an opportunity for them, turning up edibles they would have found with more difficulty otherwise. The cardinals were more brilliant than ever, kindling in the black-wet drift in the cold wind.

The Kentucky is a river of steep high banks, nearly everywhere thickly grown with willows and water maples and elms and sycamores. Boating on it in the summer, one is enclosed in a river-world, moving as though deep inside the country. One sees only the river, the high walls of foliage along the banks, the hilltops that rise over the trees first on one side and then the other. And that is one of the delights of this river. But one of the delights of being out on a winter rise is in seeing the country, and in seeing it from a vantage point that one does not usually see it from. The rise, that Sunday, had lifted us to the bank tops and higher, and through the naked trees we could look out across the bottoms. It was maybe like boating on a canal in Holland, though we had never done that. We could see the picked cornfields, their blanched yellow seeming even on that cloudy day to give off a light. We could see the winter grain spiking green over the summer's tobacco patches, the thickly wooded hollows and slews, the backs of houses and farm buildings usually seen only by the people who live there.

Once, before the man-made floods of modern times, and before the automobile, all the river country turned toward the river. In those days our trip would probably have had more witnesses than it did. We might have been waved to from house windows, and from barn doors. But now the country has turned toward the roads, and we had what has come to be the back view of it. We went by mostly in secret. Only one of the fine old river houses is left on this side of the river in the six miles of our trip, and it is abandoned and weathering out; the floods have been in it too many times in the last thirty-five years, and it is too hard to get back to from the road. We went by its blank windows as the last settlers going west passed the hollow eyes of the skulls of their predecessors' oxen.

The living houses are all out along the edges of the valley floor, where the roads are. And now that all the crops had been gathered out of the bottoms, men's attention had mostly turned away. The land along the river had taken on a wildness that in the summer it would not have. We saw a pair of red-tailed hawks circling low and unafraid, more surprised to see us than we were to see them.

Where the river was over the banks a stretch of comparatively quiet water lay between the trees on the bank top and the new shore line. After a while, weary of the currents, we turned into one of these. As we made our way past the treetops and approached the shore we flushed a bobwhite out of a brush pile near the water and saw it fly off downstream. It seemed strange to see only one. But we didn't have to wait long for an explanation, for presently we saw the dogs, and then the hunters coming over the horizon with their guns. We knew where their bird had gone, but we didn't wait to tell them.

These men come out from the cities now that the hunting season is open. They walk in these foreign places, unknown to them for most of the year, looking for something to kill. They wear and carry many dollars' worth of equipment, and go to a great deal of trouble, in order to kill some small creature that they would never trouble to know alive, and that means little to them once they have killed it. If those we saw had killed the bobwhite they would no doubt have felt all their expense and effort justified, and would have thought themselves more manly than before. It reminds one of the extraordinary trouble and expense governments go to in order to kill men—and consider it justified or not, according to the "kill ratio." The diggers among our artifacts will find us to have been honorable lovers of death, having been willing to pay exorbitantly for it. How much better, we thought, to have come upon the *life* of the bird as we did, moving peaceably among the lives of the country that showed themselves to us because we were peaceable, than to have tramped fixedly, half oblivious, for miles in order to come at its death.

We left the hunters behind and went down past a

green grainfield where cattle were grazing and drinking at the waterside. They were not disturbed that the river had come up over part of their pasture, no more troubled by the height of today's shore line than they were by the height of yesterday's. To them, no matter how high it was, so long as the ground was higher it was as ordinary as a summer pond. Surely the creatures of the fifth day of Creation accepted those of the sixth with equanimity, as though they had always been there. Eternity is always present in the animal mind; only men deal in beginnings and ends. It is probably lucky for man that he was created last. He would have got too excited and upset over all the change.

Two mallards flew up ahead of us and turned downriver into the wind. They had been feeding in the flooded corn rows, reminding us what a godsend the high water must be for ducks. The valley is suddenly full of little coves and havens, so that they can scatter out and feed safer and more hidden, and more abundantly too, than they usually can, never having to leave the river for such delicacies as the shattered corn left by the pickers. A picked cornfield under a few inches of water must be the duck Paradise —Paradise being, I assume, more often achieved by ducks than by men.

If one imagines the shore line exactly enough as the division between water and land, and imagines it rising—it comes up too slowly for the eye usually, so one *must* imagine it—there is a sort of magic about it. As it moves upward it makes a vast change, far more than the eye sees. It makes a new geography, altering the boundaries of worlds. Above it, it widens the freehold of the birds; below it, that of the fish. The land creatures are driven back and higher up. It is a line between boating and walking, gill and lung, standing still and flowing. Along it, suddenly and continuously, all that will float is picked up and carried away: leaves, logs, seeds, little straws, bits of dead grass.

And also empty cans and bottles and all sorts of buoyant trash left behind by fishermen and hunters and picnickers, or dumped over creek banks by householders who sometimes drive miles to do it. We passed behind a house built on one of the higher banks whose backyard was an avalanche of kitchen trash going down to the river. Those people, for all I know, may be champion homebodies, but their garbage is well-traveled, having departed for the Gulf of Mexico on every winter rise for years.

It is illuminating and suitably humbling to a man to recognize the great power of the river. But after he has recognized its power he is next called upon to recognize its limits. It can neither swallow up nor carry off all the trash that people convenience themselves by dumping into it. It can't carry off harmlessly all the sewage and pesticides and industrial contaminants that we are putting into it now, much less all that we will be capable of putting into it in a few years. We haven't accepted—we can't really believe—that the most characteristic product of our age of scientific miracles is junk, but that is so. And we still think and behave as though we face an unspoiled continent, with thousands of acres of living space for every man. We still sing "America the Beautiful" as though we had not created in it, by strenuous effort, at great expense, and with dauntless self-praise, an unprecedented ugliness.

The last couple of miles of our trip we could hear off in the bottoms alongside us the cries of pileated woodpeckers, and we welcomed the news of them. These belong to the big trees and big woods, and more than any other birds along this river they speak out of our past. Their voices are loud and wild, the cries building strongly and then trailing off arrhythmically and hesitantly as though reluctant to end. Though they never seemed very near, we could hear them clearly over the commotion of the water. There were probably only a pair or two of them, but their voices kept coming to us a long time, creating beyond the present wildness of the river, muddy from the ruin of mountain-sides and farmlands, the intimation of another wildness that will not overflow again in *our* history.

The wind had finally made its way into our clothes, and our feet and hands and faces were beginning to stiffen a little with the cold. And so when home came back in sight we thought it wasn't too soon. We began to slant across the currents toward the shore. The river didn't stop to let us off. We ran the bow out onto the path that goes up to my house, and the current rippled on past the stern as though it were no more than the end of a stranded log. We were out of it, wobbling stiff-legged along the midrib on our way to the high ground.

With the uproar of the water still in our ears, we had as we entered the house the sense of having been utter-ly outside the lives we live as usual. My warm living room was a place we seemed to have been away from a long way. It needed getting used to.

The Long-
Legged House

1

Sometime in the twenties, nobody knows exactly
when any more, Curran Mathews built a cabin of two
small rooms near Port Royal between the Kentucky River
and the road, on a narrow strip of land belonging to my
mother's father. Curran Mathews was my grandmother's
bachelor brother. He died of cancer when I was a boy and
I have come to know him better since his death than I did
while he was alive. At the time he died I knew him mostly
as a sort of wanderer visiting in the family households, an
inspired tinkerer with broken gadgetry and furniture, a man
of small disciplines and solutions without either a home
or a profession, and a teller of wonderful bedtime stories.

At that time the family still owned the building in
Port Royal in which James Mathews, my great-grandfather, an immigrant from Ireland, had made shoes and run

an undertaking business. There was a little partitioned-off space at the back of this building that Curran used as a workshop. He was good with tools, and a thorough workman—though I don't believe he ever made any money in that way, or ever intended to. I loved that little shop, and the smells of it, and spent some happy hours there. It smelled of varnish, and was filled with tools and objects of mysterious use. It was tucked away there, as if secretly, out of the way of the main coming and going of the town, looking out across the back lots into a pasture. And everything about it partook of the excitement I felt in this man, home from his wanderings, with his precise ways and peculiarly concentrated silences. I sat in the open doorway there one afternoon, a rich plot of sunlight on the floor around me, Curran quietly at work in the room at my back; I looked up at the ridge beyond the town, the open, still sunlit country of the summer afternoon, and felt a happiness I will never forget.

As for the bedtime stories, they were inexhaustible and always lasted a fine long while past bedtime. He was a reader of adventure stories, and a restless man who spent a large part of his life in distant places. And his stories fed on his reading and on his travels. They could keep going night after night for weeks, and then he would go off someplace. By the time he got back he would have "forgot" the story, and we would have to tell it to him up to where he left off, and then after grunting a little with effort he would produce the next installment. Some of these were straight out of books—I discovered later that he had told us, almost page by page, the first of the *Tarzan* stories; and some were adapted from Zane Grey. But others are harder to account for. I remember that the best one was a sort of Swiftian yarn about a boy who was kidnaped by the fairies, and escaped, and was captured and then adopted by a tribe of Indians, and escaped, and so on and on through a summer in which bedtime was, for a change, looked forward to.

He had a family side, and another side. The family side I knew, I suppose, well enough. The other side I still pick up the hearsay of in conversations here and there. The other side is wild, extravagant, funny in the telling, and for me always more than a little troubling and sad. There was something he needed that he never found. That other side of his life he lived alone. Though some of his doings are legendary among people who remember him, I believe he kept quiet about them himself, and I think I will do the same.

He built the cabin on the river because he thought it would improve his health to live more in the open. His health had never been good. He had permanently injured his leg in a buggy accident in his youth—he disguised his limp so well that he was taken into the army during World War I. And there seems reason to think that the disease that finally killed him had begun years back in his life.

But health must have been only the ostensible reason; the best reason for the cabin he built here must be that it was in his nature to have a house in the woods and to return now and again to live in it. For there was in him something quiet-loving and solitary and kin to the river and the woods. My mother remembers summer evenings in her girlhood when they would drive his old car five or six miles out in the country to a railroad section pond, where as it grew dark they would sit and listen for a certain bullfrog to croak—and when the frog croaked at last they would drive back to Port Royal. He did that, of course, partly for the entertainment of his young niece; but partly, too, he was entertaining himself. Given the same niece and the same need for entertainment, another man would not have thought of that.

And so his building of the cabin on the riverbank had a certain logic. The state road had not yet been built up the river on our side—that would have to wait for the Depression and the W.P.A. There was only a sort of rocked wagon-track going up through the bottoms, winding around the heads of slew-hollows, fording the creeks; farm fences crossed it, and one could not travel it without opening and closing gates. Only a few hundred yards down the river from the site of the cabin was Lane's Landing, the port of Port Royal, with its coal tipple and general store, but even so Curran Mathew's wooded stretch of riverbank was far more remote and isolated then than it is now. The voices of the frogs were here—there must have been summer nights when he sat awake a long time, listening to them. And there were other wild voices, too, that I know he heard, because I have heard them here myself. Through a notch in the far bank a little stream poured into the river, a clear moist sound, a part of the constancy of the place. And up in the thickets on the hillside there would be a cowbell, pastoral music, *tinkle-tink tink tink tinkle,* a sort of rhythmless rhythm late into the night sometimes, and nearby, when all else would be still. It was a place where a man, staying by himself, could become deeply quiet. It would have been a quiet that grew deeper and wider as the days passed, and would have come to include many things, both familiar and unexpected. If the stories about him are correct, and they doubtless are, Curran Mathews was not always alone here, and not always quiet. But there were times when he was both. He is said to have owned an old fiddle that he played at these times.

He did most of the building himself. And I imagine that those were days of high excitement. Except for the floors and the one partition, the lumber came out of an old log house that was built up on the hilltop by my grandfather's great-grandfather, Ben Perry. It surely must have been one of the first houses built in this part of the country. In my childhood the main part of it was still standing, and was known then as the Aunt Molly Perry House, after the last member of the family to live in it. It was in bad shape when I knew it, and hogs were being fed in it. Now there is nothing left but the well and the stones of the chimneys. The lot where it stood is still known, though, as the Old House Lot, and it is a lovely place, looking out over the woods into the river valley. Some of the old locusts that stood in the yard are still there, and in the spring the little white starry flowers of old-time dooryards still bloom in the grass. It is a place I like, and like to go to and sit down. I am not oppressed by it as I would be by an ancient and venerated family seat, full of old records and traditions and memories. I figure a ponderous amount of my historical inheritance took place there—it is one of the main routes on my way here—but none of it was written down, and most of it has been forgotten. Last summer for a while I pastured a mare and colt up there in the Old House Lot, and where my forebears had sat down to meals three times a day for generations, the horses grazed and thought nothing of it, it being only daylight and grass to them. I sat sometimes on the piled stones of the old chimneys, watching them graze, and it seemed to me that my line had issued out of the ground there like a spring, as regardless of itself, in the historical sense anyhow, and as little able to memorialize itself, as water—and had trickled off into oblivion.

But the house—or, anyhow, part of it—had a very pleasing resurrection. I think of Curran Mathews coming there one summer morning, full of the excitement of his vision of a cabin on the riverbank, to begin work. I can see him carefully prizing off the boards of the kitchen L—broad poplar and walnut boards cut to irregular thicknesses in some crude sawmill; and fine handmade tongue-and-groove paneling out of, I think, the dining room. The nails would probably have rusted tight in their holes, and it would have been slow, nagging work, getting boards off without splitting them, but Curran was a man capable of great persistence and patience when he wanted to be, and he got it done, and drew out the old hand-forged square-headed nails, and loaded his lumber, and hauled it down the hill to the riverbank where he intended to settle a new place. Figuring backward from my own experiences here later, I think I partly know what was on his mind then. He was striking out beyond the bounds of the accepted, beyond the ordinary and common things that most people respect—as any man does who sets a willing foot into the woods—and there would have been an exhilaration in that. As soon as he marked out the dimensions of his house on the ground the place would have begun to look different to him, would have begun to have an intimacy for him that it could never have had before. Earlier, any place he stood was more or less equal to any other place he stood; he would move on to another place. But once those boundaries were marked on the ground, there would have begun to be a permanent allegiance. Here was the tree that would stand by the door. This limb would reach across the porch. Looking out here would give a fine view of the water. Here was where the steppingstones must come down the slope. When he began clearing the ground he was an eager man, and he felt an eagerness that is felt only by men who are doing what they want passionately to do, and who are not justifying it in an account book. All this I have experienced myself, much of it in the same place and in the same way that he experienced it, and I know it must be so. But there is a great deal, too, that I don't know, and never will. What did he think in the nights he spent here alone? What desires and dreams came to him in his solitudes? Had he read Thoreau, I wonder—or any of the other writers and poets who have so shaped my life? I doubt it, and feel in that a large difference between us.

He built a cabin of two rooms, a bedroom and a kitchen. The bedroom opened onto a small screened porch, and an open porch went the rest of the way across the front and along the upriver side, railed with locust poles. He painted it with a green paint that in my time took on a bluish cast, weathered and natural-looking, a color I never saw anywhere else. It has somehow come to be associated in my mind with the lichens that grow here on the trunks of the trees, but it was more vivid. He planted a few shrubs around it, some of which are still living: two spiraeas and a bush honeysuckle whose translucent red berries I remember wanting badly to eat when I was a child. Though I could eat them now if I wanted to, I never have, certain they would taste worse than they look.

A few years ago I was given an old dim photograph of Curran from back in the days when he lived actively here on the river. It shows him at the top of a flight of steps he had just finished digging into the steep bank below the cabin. He is bent slightly forward, holding a shovel in his hands, looking up the slope. He is wearing an old limber-brimmed felt hat. You can barely see his face. Behind him his new steps go down to the river, where, under the lacy top of an overhanging willow, a boat rests lightly on the water.

I have no memory of the cabin as it stood on its original site. Before I was three years old, the flood of 1937 picked it up from where Curran had built it and carried it several feet downriver and up the bank, where it lodged against some trees, and was then anchored and given new underpinnings. But I knew it early, and my first memories of it, trivial as they are, involve a delight that I associate with no other place. The cabin had come to be known simply as the Camp—or, when one wanted to be very specific, Curran's Camp. Throughout my childhood "going down to the Camp" was to be going to the most exciting place. In my very early years it was often used as a family gathering place in the summers. We children had an Uncle Herbert who got to be known as Uncle River because we hardly ever saw him except at the Camp. And I had another uncle, Uncle Doc, with whom it was a ritual for me to go down the long flight of stone steps to the river to watch for boats—which usually never appeared, but whose mere possibility was charming enough. And I remember being put to bed there for a nap on the promise that when I woke up I could have a dish of chocolate pudding. I needed to be bribed, of course, for I knew even then that those were indispensable times. And Clio, the bitter Muse, has had her way even with that, for I remember the nap but have forgot the pudding.

Throughout my childhood there were trips to the Camp—some memorable, some forgotten. Those visits put the place deeply into my mind. It was a place I often thought about. I located a lot of my imaginings in it. Very early, I think, I began to be bound to the place in a relation so rich and profound as to seem almost mystical, as though I knew it before birth and was born for it. It remained so attractive to me, for one reason, because I had no bad associations with it. It was the family's wilderness place, and lay beyond the claims and disciplines and obligations that motivated my grownups. From the first I must have associated it with freedom. And I associated it with Curran, who must have associated it with freedom. It always had for me something of the charming strangeness of that man's life, as though he had carried it with him in his travels out in the West—as indeed I know he had, in his mind. Like Curran's life, the Camp seemed open to experiences not comprehended in the regularities of the other grown people. That is only to suggest the intensity and the nature of the bond; such feelings, coming from so far back in childhood, lie deeper than the reasons that are thought of afterward. But given the bond, it was no doubt inevitable that I would sooner or later turn to the place on my own, without the company of the grownups.

The first such visit I remember was during the flood of March, 1945. With my brother and a friend, I slipped away one bright Saturday and hitchhiked to Port Royal. We walked down to the Camp from there. It is one of the clearest days I have in my memory. The water was up over the floor of the Camp, and we spent a good while there, straddling out along the porch railings over the water—a dangerous business, of course, but we were in danger the rest of that day. There is something about a flooded house that is endlessly fascinating. Mystery again. One world being supplanted by another. But to a boy on a bright spring day it is without horror. I remember well the fascination I felt: the river pouring by, bright in the sun, laced with the complex shadows of the still naked trees, its currents passing the porch posts in little whirlpools the size of half dollars. The world suddenly looked profoundly alive and full of new interest. I had a transfiguring sense of adventure. The world lay before me, and Saturday lay before the world.

We left the Camp after a while and walked on up the river to where several johnboats were tied, and helped ourselves to the biggest one, a white one, built long and wide and heavy, as a boat must be when it is used for net fishing. We unfastened its mooring chain and pushed off. For oars we had an oak board about four feet long and an old broom worn off up to the bindings, but that seemed the paltriest of facts. We were free on the big water. Once we broke with the shore and disappeared into the bushes along the backwater, we were farther beyond the reach of our parents than we had ever been, and we knew it—and if our parents had known it, what a dark day it would have been for them! But they didn't. They were twelve miles away in New Castle, their minds on other things, assuming maybe that we had just gone to somebody's house to play basketball. And we had the world to ourselves—it would be years before we would realize how far we were from knowing what to do with it. That clumsy boat and our paddles seemed as miraculous as if we were cave men paddling the first dugout.

We paddled up to the Cane Run bridge and found the water over the road. Another wonder! And since it was unthinkable to refuse such an opportunity, we boated over the top of the road and entered the creek valley. We worked our way up through the treetops for some way, and broke out into a beautiful lake of the backwater, the sun on it and all around it the flooded woods. It was quiet—nobody around anywhere, and nobody likely to be. The world expanded yet again. It would have taken an airplane to find us. From being mere boys—nine, ten and eleven years old, I believe—we were enlarged beyond our dreams.

We went up the long backwater and into the woods. The woods is still there and I often go there these days to walk or to sit and look. It is a large stand of trees, and there is some big timber in it. I know it well now, but then I had only been there a few times to gather ferns with the rest of the family, and it was still new to me. The woods stands on a series of narrow low ridges divided by deep hollows. On the day of our adventure the backwater was in all these hollows, and we could go far into the woods without ever setting foot on the ground. That was another wondrous opportunity, and the hollows were numerous and long, allowing for endless variation and elaboration. The first wildflowers were blooming among the dead leaves above the water line, and I remember how green and suggestive the pads of moss looked in the warm water light, that time of the year. I gathered some and wrapped it in my handkerchief and put it in the boat, as if to take that place and the day with me when I left. We found a groundhog basking on a point of land, and got out and gave chase, thinking we had him cornered, only to see him take to the water and swim away. It never had occurred to me that ground-hogs could swim, and I felt like a naturalist because of the discovery.

But it had to end, and it ended hard. When we started back the wind had risen, and drove strong against our boat. Our crude paddles lost their gleeful aura of makeshift, and turned against us. We moved like the hands of a clock, and only by the greatest effort. I don't think it occurred to any of us to worry about getting out, or even about being late, but being thwarted that way, pitted so against the wind and the water, had terror in it. Before we got safely back it had become a considerable ordeal— which, as soon as we *were* safely back, began to look like the best adventure of all. We tied the boat and walked up to the road, feeling like Conquerors, weary as Conquerors.

And there my grandparents were, waiting anxiously for us. We had been spied upon, it turned out. We had been seen taking the boat. Phone calls had been made. And my grandparents had driven down—in great fear, I'm sure—to see what was to be done. When we finally came off the river they were ready to give us up for drowned. They told us that. And suddenly we felt a good deal relieved to know we weren't.

That was the second bad flood to hit the Camp. These were modern floods, and man-made. Too many of the mountain slopes along the headwater streams had been denuded by thoughtless lumbering and thoughtless farming. Too little humus remained in the soil to hold the rains. After this second flood more of the old houses built near the river in earlier times would be abandoned. And in that spring of 1945 the war was about to end. Before long the country, as never before, would be full of people with money to spend. Men's demands upon nature were about to begin an amazing increase that would continue until now. The era when Curran Mathews conceived and built the Camp was coming to an end.

And two springs later Curran lay dying in the town of Carrollton at the mouth of the river. He had gone to spend his last days in the home of two of my aunts. From his bedroom in Carrollton the windows looked out across backyards and gardens toward the bluff over the valley of the Ohio. He couldn't see the river, but as always in a river town it would have been present to his mind, part of his sense of the place, the condition of everything else. The valley of the river that had been home to him all his life, and where his cabin stood in its woods patch on the bank, lay across town, behind him. He knew he wouldn't see it again.

That spring he watched the lengthening of the buds and the leafing out of a young beech near his window. And after the leaves had come he continued to watch it—the lights and moods and movements of it. He spoke often to my aunts of its beauty. I learned of this only a year or so ago. It has made his illness and death real to me, as they never were before. It has become one of the most vivid links in my kinship with him. How joyous the young tree must have been to him, who could have had so little joy then in himself. That he watched it and did not turn away from it must mean that he found joy in it, affirmed the life in it, even though his own life was painfully going out.

In those years of the war and of Curran's illness the Camp fell into disuse and neglect. The screens rotted; leaves piled up on the porch, and the boards decayed under them; the weeds and bushes grew up around it; window glasses were broken out by rock-throwers; drunks and lovers slipped in and out through the windows. And then one evening in early summer—it must have been the year after Curran's death, when I was nearly fourteen—I came down by myself just before dark, and cooked a supper on the riverbank below the house, and spent the night in a sleeping bag on the porch. I don't remember much about that night, and don't remember at all what reason I had for coming. But that night began a conscious relation between me and the Camp, and it has been in my mind and figured in my plans ever since.

I must have come, that first time, intending to stay for a while, though I can't remember how long. The next morning as I was finishing breakfast a car pulled in off the road and an old man got out, saying he had come to fish. Did I mind? Maybe I felt flattered that my permission had been asked. No, I didn't mind, I said. In fact, I'd fish with him. He was a friendly white-haired old man, very fat, smiling, full of talk. Would he like to fish from a boat? I asked him. I'd go get one. He said that would be fine, and I went down along the bank to the landing and got one—again, I think, by the forthright method of "borrowing"—and brought it back. It was a good big boat, but I had managed to find only a broken oar to paddle with. He got in with his equipment and we set off. We fished the whole day together. Not much was said. I don't remember that we ever introduced ourselves. But it was a friendly day. I was slow in moving us between fishing spots with my broken oar and I remember how he sat in the middle seat and hunched us along like a kid in a toy car. It helped a great deal. We fished until the late afternoon and caught—or, rather, *he* caught—a sizable string of little perch and catfish. When he left he gave me all the catch. He fished, he said, for the love of it. I don't yet know who he was. I never saw him again. In the evening, after I had taken the boat home and had started cleaning the fish on the porch, my friend Pete stopped by with his father. They had been working on their farm up the river that day, and were on their way home. Pete liked the look of things and decided to stay on with me. And that began a partnership that lasted a long time.

The next morning we began scraping out the dried mud that the last high water had deposited on the floors—and suddenly the place entered our imagination. We quit being campers and became settlers. Twenty or so years before, the same metamorphosis must have taken place in the mind of Curran Mathews. A dozen or two strokes, flaking up the sediment from the floor—and we had got an idea, and been transformed by it: we'd clean her out and fix her up.

And that is what we did. We gave it a cleaning, and then scrounged enough furnishings and food from our families to set up in free and independent bachelorhood on the river. The idea was to be well enough supplied that we wouldn't need to go back home for a while. That way, if somebody wanted to impose work or church on us they would have to come get us. That was another realization the Camp had suddenly lit up for us: We were against civilization, and wanted as little to do with it as possible. On the river we came aware of a most inviting silence: the absence of somebody telling us what to do and what not to do. We swam and fished and ate and slept. We could leave our clothes in the cabin and run naked down the bank and into the water. We could buy cigars and lie around and smoke. We could go out on the porch in the bright damp shadowy mornings and pee over the railing. We made a ritual of dispensing with nonessentials; one of us would wash the dishes with his shirttail, and the other would dry them with his. We were proud of that, and thought it had style.

For several years we came to the Camp every chance we got, and made good memories for ourselves. We will never live days like those again, and will never live happier ones. I suppose it was growing up that put an end to them—college, jobs, marriages and families of our own. We began to have a stake in civilization, and could no longer just turn our backs on it and go off. Back in our free days we used to tell people—a good deal to their delight, for we were both sons of respected lawyers—that we intended to be bootleggers. I think the foreknowledge of our fate lay in that. For to contrive long to be as free and careless as we were in those days we would have had to become bootleggers, or something of the kind. Ambition and responsibility would take us a different way.

During those years when I would come down to the Camp with Pete, I would also fairly often come alone. Pete, who was older than I was, would be having a date. Or he would have to stay home and work at a time when I could get free. And at times I came alone because I wanted to. I was melancholic and rebellious, and these moods would often send me off to the river.

Those times were quiet and lonely, troubled often by the vague uneasiness and dissatisfaction of growing up. The years I spent between childhood and manhood seem as strange to me now as they did then. Clumsy in body and mind, I knew no place I could go to and feel certain I ought to be there. I had no very good understanding of what I was rebelling against: I was going mostly by my feelings, and so I was rarely calm. And I didn't know with enough certainty what I wanted to be purposeful about getting it. The Camp offered no escape from these troubles, but it did allow them the dignity of solitude. And there were days there, as in no other place, when as if by accident, beyond any reason I might have had, I was at peace, and happy. And those days that gave me peace suggested to me the possibility of a greater, more substantial peace—a decent, open, generous relation between a man's life and the world—that I have never achieved; but it must have begun to be then, and it has come more and more consciously to be, the hope and the ruling idea of my life.

I remember one afternoon when I tied my boat to a snag in the middle of the river outside the mouth of Cane Run, and began fishing. It was a warm sunny afternoon, quiet all around, and I had the river to myself. There is some uncanny charm about a boat that I have always been keenly aware of, and tied there that afternoon in midstream, a sort of island, it made me intensely alive to the charm of it. It seemed so intact and dry in its boatness, and I so coherent and satisfied in my humanness. I fished and was happy for some time, until I became *conscious* of what a fine thing I was doing. It came to me that this was one of the grand possibilities of my life. And suddenly I became uneasy, even distressed. What I had been at ease with, in fact and without thinking, had become, as a possibility, too large. I hadn't the thoughts for it. I hadn't the background for it. My cultural inheritance had prepared me to exert myself, work, move, "get someplace." To be idle, simply to live there in the sunlight in the middle of the river, was something I was not prepared to do deliberately. I tried to stay on, forcing myself to do what I now *thought* I ought to be doing, but the spell was broken. That I had nothing to do but what I wanted to do, and what I was in fact doing, had become utterly impotent as an idea. I had to leave. I would have to live to twice that age before I could do consciously what I wanted so much then to do. And even now I can do it only occasionally.

I read a good deal during those stays I made at the river. I read *Walden* here then—though I can't remember whether it was for the first or second time. And I was beginning to read poetry with some awareness that it interested me and was important to me—an awareness I had not yet come by in any classroom. I had a paperback anthology of English and American poems, and I would lie in bed at night and read it by the light of a kerosene lamp. One night I lay there late and read for the first time Gray's "Elegy Written in a Country Churchyard." It seemed to me to be a fine thing, and I thought I understood it and knew why it was fine. That was a revealing experience. While I read a dog was howling somewhere down the river, and an owl was calling over in the Owen County bottom, and my father's old nickel-plated Smith and Wesson revolver lay in the bedding under my head. I loved this place and had begun to understand it a little—but I didn't love it and understand it well enough yet to be able to trust it in the dark. That revolver belonged on top of the bookcase at home, but nobody ever thought of it, and I could borrow it and bring it back without fear that it would be missed.

What I remember best from those years are the days in early summer when I would first come down to the Camp to clean the place up. By the time school would be out the weeds there on the damp riverbank would have already grown waist-high. I would come down with ax and scythe, preparatory to some stay I intended to make, and drive back the wilderness. I would mow the wild grass and horseweeds and nettles and elderberries, and chop down the tree sprouts, and trim obstructive branches off the nearby trees. It would be hard to describe the satisfaction this opening up would give me. I would sit down now and again to rest and dry the sweat a little, and look at what I had done. I would meditate on the difference I had made, and my mind would be full of delight. It was some instinctive love of wildness that would always bring me back here, but it was by the instincts of a farmer that I established myself. The Camp itself was not imaginable until the weeds were cut around it; until that was done I could hardly bring myself to enter it. A house is not simply a building, it is also an enactment. That is the first law of domesticity, even the most meager. The mere fact must somehow be turned into meaning. Necessity must be made a little ceremonious. To ever arrive at what one would call home even for a few days, a decent, thoughtful approach must be made, a clarity, an opening.

Only after I had mowed and trimmed around it, so

that it stood clear of its surroundings, or rather clearly within them, could I turn to the house. The winter's leaves would have to be swept off the porch, the doors opened, the shutters opened, daylight filling the rooms for the first time in months, the sashes drawn back in their slots, the walls and floors swept. And then, finished, having earned the right to be there again, I would go out on the porch and sit down. Tired and sweaty, the dust of my sweeping still flavoring the air, I would have a wonderful sense of order and freedom. The old recognitions would come back, the familiar sights and sounds slowly returning to their places in my mind. It would seem inexpressibly fine to be living, a joy to breathe.

During the last of my college years and the year I spent as a graduate student, the Camp went through another period of neglect. There were distractions. I had begun to be preoccupied with the girl I was going to marry. In a blundering, half-aware fashion I was becoming a writer. And, as I think of it now, school itself was a distraction. Although I have become, among other things, a teacher, I am skeptical of education. It seems to me a most doubtful process, and I think the good of it is taken too much for granted. It is a matter that is overtheorized and overvalued and always approached with too much confidence. It is, as we skeptics are always discovering to our delight, no substitute for experience or life or virtue or devotion. As it is handed out by the schools, it is only theoretically useful, like a randomly mixed handful of seeds carried in one's pocket. When one carries them back to one's own place in the world and plants them, some will prove unfit for the climate or the ground, some are sterile, some are not seeds at all but little clods and bits of gravel. Surprisingly few of them come to anything. There is an incredible waste and clumsiness in most efforts to prepare the young. For me, as a student and as a teacher, there has always been a pressing

anxiety between the classroom and the world: how can you get from one to the other except by a blind jump? School is not so pleasant or valuable an experience as it is made out to be in the theorizing and reminiscing of elders. In a sense, it is not an experience at all, but a hiatus in experience.

My student career was over in the spring of 1957, and I was glad enough to be done with it. My wife and I were married in May of that year. In the fall I was to take my first teaching job. We decided to stay through the summer at the Camp. For me, that was a happy return. For Tanya, who was hardly a country girl, it was a new kind of place, confronting her with hardships she could not have expected. We were starting a long way from the all-electric marriage that the average modern American girl supposedly takes for granted. If Tanya had been the average modern American girl, she probably would have returned me to bachelorhood within a week—but then, of course, she would have had no interest in such a life, or in such a marriage, in the first place. As it was, she came as a stranger into the country where I had spent my life, and made me feel more free and comfortable in it than I had ever felt before. That is the most graceful generosity that I know.

For weeks before the wedding I spent every spare minute at the Camp, getting it ready to live in. I mowed around it, and cleaned it out, and patched the roof. I replaced the broken windowpanes, and put on new screens, and whitewashed the walls, and scrounged furniture out of various family attics and back rooms. As a special wedding gift to Tanya I built a new privy—which never aspired so high as to have a door, but did sport a real toilet seat.

All this, I think, was more meaningful and proper than I knew at the time. To a greater extent than is now common, or even possible for most men, I had by my own doing prepared the house I was to bring my wife to, and in preparing the house I prepared myself. This was the place

that was more my own than any other in the world. In it, I had made of loneliness a good thing. I had lived days and days of solitary happiness there. And now I changed it, to make it the place of my marriage. A complex love went into those preparations—for Tanya, and for the place too. Working through those bright May days, the foliage fresh and full around me, the river running swift and high after rain, was an act of realization: as I worked, getting ready for the time when Tanya would come to live there with me, I understood more and more what the possible meanings were. If it had gone differently—if it had followed, say, the prescription of caution: first "enough" money, and then the "right" sort of house in the "right" sort of place—I think I would have been a poorer husband. And my life, I know, would have been poorer. It wasn't, to be sure, a permanent place that I had prepared; we were going to be there only for the one summer. It was, maybe one ought to say, no more than a ritual. But it was a meaningful and useful ritual.

In the sense that is most meaningful, our wedding did not begin until the ceremony was over. It began, it seems to me, the next morning when we went together to the Camp for the first time since I started work on it. I hesitate to try to represent here the pleasure Tanya may have felt on this first arrival at our house, or the pride that I felt—those feelings were innocent enough, and probably had no more foundation than innocence needs. The point is that, for us, these feelings were substantiated by the Camp; they had its atmosphere and flavor, and partook of its history. That morning when Tanya first came to it as my wife, its long involvement in my life was transformed, given a richness and significance it had not had before. It had come to a suddenly illuminating promise. A new life had been added to it, as a new life had been added to my life. The ramshackle old house and my renewal of it particular-

ized a good deal more for us than we could have realized then. We began there.

It would be a mistake to imply that two lives can unite and make a life between them without discord and pain. Marriage is a perilous and fearful effort, it seems to me. There can't be enough knowledge at the beginning. It must endure the blundering of ignorance. It is both the cause and the effect of what happens to it. It creates pain that it is the only cure for. It is the only comfort for its hardships. In a time when divorce is as accepted and conventionalized as marriage, a marriage that lasts must look a little like a miracle. That ours lasts—and in its own right and its own way, not in pathetic and hopeless parody of some "expert" notion—is largely, I believe, owing to the way it began, to the Camp and what it meant and came to mean. In coming there, we avoided either suspending ourselves in some honeymoon resort or sinking ourselves into the stampede for "success." In the life we lived that summer we represented to ourselves what we wanted—and it was *not* the headlong pilgrimage after money and comfort and prestige. We were spared that stress from the beginning. And there at the Camp we had around us the elemental world of water and light and earth and air. We felt the presences of the wild creatures, the river, the trees, the stars. Though we had our troubles, we had them in a true perspective. The universe, as we could see any night, is unimaginably large, and mostly empty, and mostly dark. We knew we needed to be together more than we needed to be apart.

That summer has no story; it has not simplified itself enough in my memory to have the consistency of a story and maybe it never will; the memories are too numerous and too diverse, and too deeply rooted in my life.

One of the first things I did after we got settled was to put some trotlines in the river. On a dark rainy night in early June we had stayed up until nearly midnight, making strawberry preserves, and I decided on an impulse to go and raise my lines. Working my way along the line in pitch dark a few minutes later, I pulled out of the middle of the river a catfish that weighed twenty-seven pounds. Tanya had already gone to bed, and had to get up again to hear me congratulate myself in the presence of the captive. And so, indelibly associated with the early days of my marriage is a big catfish. Perhaps it is for the best.

The night of the Fourth of July of that year there came one of the worst storms this part of the country ever knew. For hours the rain spouted down on our tin roof in a wild crashing that did not let up. The Camp had no inner walls or ceilings; it was like trying to sleep inside a drum. The lightning strokes overlapped, so that it would seem to stay light for minutes at a stretch, and the thunder kept up a great knocking at the walls. After a while it began to seem unbelievable that the rain did not break through the roof. It was an apocalyptic night. The next morning we went out in bright sunshine to find the river risen to the top of its banks. There was a lasting astonishment in looking at it, and a sort of speculative fear; if that storm had reached much farther upstream we would have had to swim out of bed. Upstream, we could see several large trees that Cane Run had torn out by the roots and hurled clear across the river to lodge against the Owen County bank. The marks of that rain are still visible here.

And I remember a quiet night of a full moon when we rowed the boat up into the bend above the mouth of Cane Run, and let the slow current bring us down again. I sat on the rower's seat in the middle of the boat, and Tanya sat facing me in the stern. We stayed quiet, aware of the quietness in the country around us, the sky and the water and the Owen County hills all still in the white stare of the moon. The wooded hill above the Camp stood dark over us. As it bore us, the current turned us as though in the slow spiral of a dance.

Summer evenings here on the river have a quietness and a feeling of completion about them that I have never known in any other place, and I have kept in mind the evenings of that summer. The wind dies about sundown, and the surface of the river grows smooth. The reflections of the trees lie inverted and perfect on it. Occasionally a fish will jump, or a kingfisher hurry, skreaking, along the fringe of willows. In the clearing around the house the phoebes and pewees call from their lookout perches, circling out and back in their hunting flights as long as the light lasts. Out over the water the swallows silently pass and return, dipping and looping, climbing and dipping and looping, sometimes skimming the surface to drink or bathe as they fly. The air seems to come alive with the weaving of their paths. As I sat there watching from the porch those evenings, sometimes a profound peacefulness would come to me, as it had at other times, but now it came of an awareness not only of the place, but of my marriage, a completeness I had not felt before. I was there not only because I wanted to be, as always before, but now because Tanya was there too.

But most of all I like to remember the mornings. We would get up early, and I would go out on the river to raise my lines the first thing. There is no light like that on the river on a clear early morning. It is fresh and damp and full of glitters. The bright linear reflections off the waves wobble up the tree trunks and under the leaves. It was fishing that paid well, though not always in fish. When I came back to the Camp, Tanya would have a big breakfast waiting.

After we ate I would carry a card table out into a corner of the little screened porch, and sit down to write. I would put in the morning there, conscious always as I worked of the life of the river. Fish would jump. A kingfisher would swing out over the water, blue and sudden in the water light, making his harsh ratcheting boast to startle the world. The green herons would pass intently up and down, low to the water, just outside the willows. Or one would stop to fish from a snag or a low-bending willow, a little nucleus of stillness; sitting at my own work on the other side of the river I would feel an emanation of his intent silence; he was an example to me. And in the trees around the Camp all the smaller birds would be deep in their affairs. It might be that a towboat—the *Kentuckian* or the old *John J. Kelly,* that summer—would come up, pushing bargeloads of sand to Frankfort. Or there would be somebody fishing from the other bank, or from a boat. And the river itself was as intricately and vigorously alive as anything on it or in it, always shifting its lights and its moods.

That confirmed me in one of my needs. I have never been able to work with any pleasure facing a wall, or in any other way fenced off from things. I need a window or a porch, or even the open outdoors. I have always had a lively sympathy for Thoreau's idea of a hypaethral book, a roofless book. Why should I shut myself up to write? Why not write and live at the same time?

There on the porch of the Camp that summer I wrote the first poetry that I still feel represented by—a long poem rather ostentatiously titled "Diagon," about the river—and did some of the most important reading I have ever done.

In the spring of that year I had read attentively through the poems of Andrew Marvell, and had felt a strong kinship with him. The poem of his that interested me most was not one of the familiar short poems, but the strange, imperfect long one entitled "Upon Appleton House, to my Lord *Fairfax.*" This is a complimentary piece, evidently very deliberately undertaken, and in long stretches it is amply boring. But in his description of the countryside Marvell's imagination seems abruptly to break out of the limitations of subject and genre, and he wrote some stunning poetry. It has remained for me one of the most exciting poems I know—not just in spite of its faults, but to a considerable extent because of them. Its landscape is most *particularly* observed—as rarely happens in English nature poetry; the scene is of interest itself, not just as the manifestation of something transcendent or subjective. The grass is grass, and one feels the real rankness and tallness of it. Equally, the killed bird is real; its blood is on the scythe's edge, and we feel the mower's regret of the useless death. What natural things manifest, if observed closely enough, is their nature, and their nature is to change. Marvell's landscape is in constant metamorphosis, and so metaphor is peculiarly necessary to its poetry—it is continuously being carried beyond what it was. The comparative image is not imposed from without by the poet, but is seen by the poet to be implicit in the nature of the thing: it is in the nature of a meadow to be like a sea.

It is not difficult to see how serviceable and clarifying I found those lines from "Upon Appleton House." They showed me the poet's vision breaking out of its confines into the presence of its subject. I feel yet the exhilaration and release when Marvell turns from his elaborate overextended compliment to the noble family, and takes up a matter that really interested him; the full powers of his imagination and intelligence become suddenly useful to him, and necessary:

> And now the Abbyss I pass
> Of that unfathomable Grass. . . .

He is talking about a river valley of farms and woodlands such as I had known all my life, and now had before me as I wrote and read through that summer. As a child I had even believed, on what I then considered the best advice, in the metamorphosis of horsehairs that Marvell alludes to in the last stanza of his description of the meadows. I would put hairs from tails and manes into the watering trough at night, confident that by morning they would be turned to snakes. But I was a poor scientist, and in the mornings always forgot to look—and so kept the faith.

With Marvell's work in my mind, I began that summer of my marriage the surprisingly long and difficult labor of *seeing* the country I had been born in and had lived my life in until then. I think that this was peculiarly important and necessary to me; for whereas most American writers—and even most Americans—of my time are displaced persons, I am a placed person. For longer than they remember, both sides of my family have lived within five or six miles of this riverbank where the old Camp stood and where I sit writing now. And so my connection with this place comes not only from the intimate familiarity that began in babyhood, but also from the even more profound and mysterious knowledge that is inherited, handed down in memories and names and gestures and feelings, and in tones and inflections of voice. For reasons that could perhaps be explained, I never lost affection for this place, as American writers have almost traditionally lost affection for their rural birthplaces. I have loved this country from the beginning, and I believe I was grown before I ever really confronted the possibility that I could live in another place. As a writer, then, I have had this place as my fate. For me, it was never a question of *finding* a subject, but rather of learning what to do with the subject I had had from the beginning and could not escape. Whereas most of this country's young writers seem able to relate to no place at all, or to several, I am related absolutely to one.

And this place I am related to had never had a writer of any kind. It was, from a writer's point of view, undiscovered country. I have found this to be both an opportunity and a disadvantage. The opportunity is obvious. The disadvantage is that of solitude. Everything is to be done. No beginnings are ready-made. One has no proof that the place can be written about, no confidence that it can produce such a poet as one would like to be, and there is a hesitance about local names and places and histories because they are so naked of associations and assigned values—none of which difficulties would bother a poet beginning in Concord, say, or the Lake District. But here I either had to struggle with these problems or not write. I was so intricately dependent on this place that I did not begin in any meaningful sense to be a writer until I began to see the place clearly and for what it was. For me, the two have been the same.

That summer I was only beginning, and my poem "Diagon" came out of the excitement of that first seeing, and the first inklings that there might be viable meanings in what I knew. I was seeing consciously the lights and colors and forms of my own world for the first time:

> The sun sets vision afloat,
> Its hard glare down
> All the reaches of the river,
> Light on the wind waves
> Running to shore. Under the light
> River and hill divide. Two dead
> White trees stand in the water,
> The shimmering river casts
> A net of light around them,
> Their snagged shapes break through.

It is a descriptive poem mostly, and I have worried at times because in my work I have been so often preoccupied with description. But I have begun to think of that as necessary. I had to observe closely—be disciplined by the look and shape and feel of things and places—if I wanted to escape the blindness that would have made my work sound like an imitation of some Kentucky politician's imitation of the Romantic poets.

Sustaining and elaborating the effect of Marvell were the poems of William Carlos Williams, whose work I had known before but read extensively and studiously during that summer of 1957. I had two books of his, the *Collected Earlier Poems,* and his newest one, *Journey to Love.* I saw how his poems had grown out of his life in his native city in New Jersey, and his books set me free in my own life and my own place as no other books could have. I'll not forget the delight and hopefulness I felt in reading them. They relieved some of the pressure in the solitude I mentioned earlier. Reading them, I felt I had a predecessor, if not in Kentucky then in New Jersey, who confirmed and contemporized for me the experience of Thoreau in Concord.

Another book that deeply affected me that summer was Kenneth Rexroth's *100 Poems from the Chinese,* which immediately influenced my work and introduced me to Oriental poetry, not to mention the happy reading it made. I still think it is one of the loveliest books I know.

All these—my new marriage, the Camp, the river, the reading and writing—are intimately associated in my mind. It would be impossible to do more than imply the connections. Those were probably the three most important months in my life, as well as the happiest. When the summer was over it was a sharp sorrow to have to go. I remember us loading our borrowed household things into and onto our old Jeep station wagon and driving off up the river road on a brilliant day, the fields in the bottoms all yellow with fall flowers. And I remember the troubling sense that what we were going to would be more ordinary than what we were leaving behind. And it was.

2

It has been almost exactly a year since I began this history. My work was interrupted by the spring weather, when gardening and other outside concerns took me away from writing. But now it is winter again. Yesterday snow fell all day and covered the ground. This morning, though the sun came up clear, the thermometer read four above—a good morning to sit in the Camp in the warmth of the stove and the brisk snow light from the big window over the table. It is a morning for books and notebooks and the inviting blank pages of writing paper.

For people who live in the country there is a charming freedom in such days. One is free of obligations to the ground. There is no outside work that one ought to do, simply because, with the ground frozen deep and covered with snow, no such work is possible. Growth has stopped; there is plenty of hay and grain in the barn; the present has abated its urgencies. And the mind may again turn freely to the past and look back on the way it came. This morning has been bearing down out of the future toward this bit of riverbank forever. And for perhaps as long my life has been approaching from the opposite direction. The approach of a man's life out of the past is history, and the approach of time out of the future is mystery. Their meeting is the present, and it is consciousness, the only time life is alive. The endless wonder of this meeting is what causes the mind, in its inward liberty of a frozen morning, to turn back and question and remember. The world is full of places. Why is it that I am here?

What has interested me in telling the history of the Camp is the possibility of showing how a place and a person can come to belong to each other—or, rather, how a person can come to belong to a place, for places really belong to nobody. There is a startling reversal of our ordinary sense of things in the recognition that we are the belongings of the world, not its owners. The social convention of ownership must be qualified by this stern fact, and by the humility it implies, if we are not to be blinded altogether to where we are. We may deeply affect a place we own for good or ill, but our lives are nevertheless included in its life; it will survive us, bearing the results. Each of us is a part of a succession. I have come here following Curran Mathews. Who was here or what was done before he came, I do not know. I know that he had predecessors. It is certain that at some time the virgin timber that once stood here was cut down, and no doubt somebody then planted corn among the stumps, and so wore out the ground and allowed the trees to return. Before the white men were the Indians, who generation after generation bequeathed the country to their children, whole, as they received it. The history is largely conjecture. The future is mystery altogether: I do not know who will follow me. These realizations are both aesthetic and moral; they clear the eyes and prescribe an obligation.

At the point when my story was interrupted, my life no longer seemed to be bearing toward this place, but away from it. In the early fall of 1957 Tanya and I left the Camp, and through the following year I taught at Georgetown College. In the spring of 1958 our daughter Mary was born, and in the fall we left Kentucky for the West Coast. The Camp was closed and shuttered. Even though it had taken a new and lasting hold on my mind, it had entered another time of neglect. Three years would pass before I would come back to it. Toward the end of that summer of 1958 my friend Ed McClanahan and I made a canoe trip down the river and spent a night in the Camp, sleeping on the floor. For me, that night had the sadness of a parting. I was about to leave the state; the past was concluded, and the future, not yet begun, was hardly imaginable. The Camp was empty, dark, full of finished memories, already falling back into the decay of human things that humans have abandoned. I was glad when the morning came, and we loafed on down along the shady margin of the river, watching the muskrats and the wood ducks.

I did not go back to the Camp again until the May of 1961. After two years on the West Coast, we had spent another year in Kentucky, this time on the farm, and again we had a departure ahead of us; late in the summer we would be going to Europe for a year. In order to prepare myself for this experience I began spending some mornings and rainy days at the Camp. My intention at first was to do some reading that would help me to understand the life of the places I would be seeing in Europe. But as I might have expected it was not Europe that most held my attention on those days, but the Camp and the riverbank and the river. It soon became clear that I was not so much preparing for an important experience as *having* an important one. I had been changed by what had happened to me and what I had learned during the last three years, and I was no sooner back at the Camp, with the familiar trees around me and the river in front of me again, than I began to see it differently and in some ways more clearly than I had before. Through that summer I wrote a sort of journal, keeping account of what I saw.

I first went back to the Camp that year on a rainy Monday, May 8. Heavy rains had begun the Saturday before, and the river was in flood. The water was under the house, within about a foot and a half of the floor. I had come to read, but mostly I sat and looked. How can one read history when the water is rising? The presence of the present had become insistent, undeniable, and I could not look away; the past had grown still, and could be observed at leisure in a less pressing time. The current was driving drift logs against the legs of the cabin beneath my chair. The river flexed and throbbed against the underpinnings like a great muscle, its vibrations too set in my nerves to permit thinking of anything else.

The river had become a lake, but a lake *flowing,* a continuous island of drift going down the channel, moving swiftly and steadily but forever twisting and eddying within itself; and along the edges the water was picking up little sticks and leaves and bits of grass as it rose. The house's perspective on the river had become the same as that of a boat. I kept an uneasy sense of its nearness, knowing that it was coming nearer; in an hour and a quarter it rose five inches. And there was a sort of permanent astonishment at its massiveness and flatness and oblivious implacable movement.

That day a new awareness of the Camp came to me, an awareness that has become a part of my understanding of all houses. It was a boat—a futile, ill-constructed, doomed boat—a boat such as a child might make on a hilltop. It had been built to stand there on the bank according to the rules of building on solid ground. But now the ground was under water, and the water was rising. The house would have the river to contend with. It would be called on to be a boat, as it had been called on before—as in the 1937 flood it had been called on, and had made its short voyage downstream and up the bank until it lodged among the trees. It was a boat by necessity, but not by nature, which is a recipe for failure. It was built with kinder hopes, to fare in a gentler element than water. All houses are not failed boats, but all are the failed, or failing, vehicles of some alien element; of wind, or fire, or time. When I left that night the river was only a foot beneath the floor, and still rising.

It rose two feet into the Camp, cresting sometime Wednesday. It was out of the house again by Thursday afternoon, and I opened the doors to dry the mud. On Sunday I was at work at a table on the screened porch, sitting in a chair where I could have sat in a boat a few days before, looking down into a landscape that still bore everywhere the marks of overflowing. As far as I could see, up and down and across the valley, there was the horizon of the flood, a level in the air below which everything was stained the dull gray-brown of silt, and the tree branches were hung with tatters of drift, as though the flood was still there in ghostly presence. Above that horizon the spring went on uninterrupted, the new clear green of the leaves unfolding. It was as though I sat with my feet in one world and my head in another. And so with the mud still drying on the floors, I resumed my connection with the Camp.

Other creatures had worse luck getting started that spring than I did. On the Monday of the rise I watched a pair of prothonotary warblers hovering and fluttering around their nest hole near the top of a box elder snag. The snag stood on the bank directly below the porch of the Camp, its top about level with the floor. And so that night when the river crept into the Camp it had already filled the warblers' nest. When I came back after the water went down the birds were back. They nested again in the same hole. And then sometime around the middle of June the snag blew over. Since then I believe that no pair has nested near the Camp, though they nest around the slew across the river and I often see them feeding here.

That spring a pair of phoebes nested under the eaves in front of the house just above the door to the screened porch. A dead elm branch reaching over the porch made them a handy place to sit and watch for insects. I would often pause in my writing or reading to watch them fly out, pick an insect out of the air, and return to the branch. Sometimes I could hear their beaks snap when they made a catch.

A pair of starlings was nesting in a woodpecker hole in a maple down the bank in front of my writing table and a pair of crested flycatchers in another hollow maple a few yards upstream. Titmice were in a woodpecker hole in the dead locust near the kitchen door. High up in an elm, in the fork of a branch hanging over the driveway, pewees built their neat cup of a nest and covered the outside with lichens.

Wood thrushes lived in the thicker woods upriver. They never came near the house while I was there, but their music did, as though their feeling toward me was both timid and generous. One of the unforgettable voices of this place is their exultant fluting rising out of the morning shadows.

On two separate days, while I sat at work, a hummingbird came in through a hole in the rotted porch screen to collect spiderwebs for his nest. He would stand in the air, deliberate as a harvester, and gather the web in his beak with a sort of winding motion.

Later, in July, I would often watch a red-bellied woodpecker who hunted along the tree trunks on this side of the river to feed his young in a hollow snag on the far side. He would work his way slowly up the trunks of the sycamores, turning his head to the side, putting his eye close to the trunk to search under the loose bark scales. And then he would fly to the far side of the river, where his snag jutted up over the top of a big willow. With the binoculars I could see him perch at his hole and feed his nestlings.

For the first time in all my staying at the Camp I had a pair of binoculars, and they enlarged and intensified my awareness of the place. With their help I began to know the warblers. At a distance these little birds usually look drab, and the species are hardly distinguishable, but the binoculars show them to be beautifully colored and marked, and wonderfully various in their kinds. There is always something deeply enticing and pleasing to me in the sight of them. Perhaps because I was only dimly aware of them for so long, I always see them at first with a certain unexpectedness, and with the sense of gratitude that one feels for any goodness unearned and almost missed. In their secretive worlds of treetop and undergrowth, they seem among the most remote of the wild creatures. They see little of us, and we see even less of them. I think of them as being aloof somehow from common life. Certain of the most beautiful of them, I am sure, have lived and died for generations in some of our woods without being recognized by a human being.

But the binoculars not only give access to knowledge of lives that are usually elusive and distant; they make possible a peculiar imaginative association with those lives. While opening and clarifying the remote, they block out the immediate. Where one is is no longer apparent. It is as though one stood at the window of a darkened room, lifted into a world that cannot be reached except by flying. The treetops are no longer a ceiling, but a spacious airy zone full of perching places and nervously living lights and shadows. One sees not just the bird, but something of how it is to *be* the bird. One's imagination begins to reach and explore into the sense of how it would be to be without barriers, to fly over the river, to perch at the frailest, most outward branchings of the trees.

In those days I began the long difficult realization of the complexity of the life of this place. Until then—at the level of consciousness, at least—I had thoughtlessly accepted the common assumption of my countrymen that the world is merely an inert surface that man lives on and uses. I don't believe that I had yet read anything on the subject of ecology.* But I had read Thoreau and Gilbert White and a little of Fabre, and from seeing natural history displays I

*I had read, in the previous winter, Marston Bates' *The Forest and the Sea.*

knew the concept of the habitat group. And that summer, I remember, I began to think of myself as living within rather than upon the life of the place. I began to think of my life as one among many, and one kind among many kinds. I began to see how little of the beauty and the richness of the world is of human origin, and how superficial and crude and destructive—even self-destructive—is man's conception of himself as the owner of the land and the master of nature and the center of the universe. The Camp with its strip of riverbank woods, like all other places of the earth, stood under its own widening column of sky, in the neighborhood of the stars, lighted a little within the darkness. It was more unknown than known. It was populated by creatures whose ancestors were here long before my ancestors, and who had been more faithful to it than I had been, and who would live as well the day after my death as the day before.

Seen as belonging there with other native things, my own nativeness began a renewal of meaning. The sense of belonging began to turn around. I saw that if I belonged here, which I felt I did, it was not because anything here belonged to me. A man might own a whole county and be a stranger in it. If I belonged *in* this place it was because I belonged *to* it. And I began to understand that so long as I did not know the place fully, or even adequately, I belonged to it only partially. That summer I began to see, however dimly, that one of my ambitions, perhaps my governing ambition, was to belong fully to this place, to belong as the thrushes and the herons and the muskrats belonged, to be altogether at home here. That is still my ambition. But now I have come to see that it proposes an enormous labor. It is a spiritual ambition, like goodness. The wild creatures belong to the place by nature, but as a man I can belong to it only by understanding and by virtue. It is an ambition I cannot hope to succeed in wholly, but I have come to believe that it is the most worthy of all.

Whenever I could during that summer I would come to the Camp—usually on Sundays, and on days when it was too wet for farm work. I remember the fine feeling I would have, starting out after breakfast with a day at the river ahead of me. The roadsides would be deep in the fresh clear blue of chicory flowers that in the early morning sun appeared to give off a light of their own. And then I would go down into the fog that lay deep in the valley, and begin work. Slowly the sun would burn through the fog, and brighten the wet foliage along the riverbanks in a kind of second dawn. When I got tired of reading or writing I would cut weeds around the house, or trim the trees to open up the view of the river. Or I would take a walk into the woods.

And as before, as always, there was the persistent consciousness of the river, the sense of sitting at the edge of a great opening passing through the country from the Appalachians to the Gulf of Mexico. The river is the ruling presence of this place. Here one is always under its influence. The mind, no matter how it concentrates on other things, is never quite free of it, is always tempted and tugged at by the nearness of the water and the clear space over it, ever widening and deepening into the continent. Its life, in the long warm days of summer when the water is low, is as leisurely and self-preoccupied as the life of a street in a country town. Fish and fishermen pass along it, and so do the kingfishers and the herons. Rabbits and squirrels and groundhogs come down in the late afternoon to drink. The birds crisscross between shores from morning to night. The muskrats graze the weed patches or browse the overhanging willows or carry whole stalks of green corn down out of the fields to the water's edge. Molting wood ducks skulk along the banks, hiding under the willows and behind the screens of grapevines. But of all the creatures, except the fish, I think the swallows enjoy the river most. Whole flocks of barn swallows and bank swal-

lows and rough wings will spend hours in the afternoon
and evening circling and dipping over the water, feeding,
bathing, drinking—and rejoicing, too, as I steadfastly believe, for I cannot imagine that anything could fly as splen-
didly as the swallows and not enjoy it.

One afternoon as I was sitting at my worktable on
the porch a towboat came up with two barges loaded with
sand. A man and a boy sat on the edge of the bow of the
head barge, their feet hanging over the water. They were
absorbed in their talk, remote from observance, the river
world wholly surrounding and containing them, like the
boatmen in the paintings of George Caleb Bingham. For
the moment they belonged to movement and I to stillness;
they were bound in kinship with the river, which is always
passing, and I in kinship with the trees, which stand still. I
watched them out of sight, intensely aware of them and of
their unawareness of me. It is an eloquent memory, full of
the meaning of this river.

And on those days, as on all the days I have spent
here, I was often accompanied by the thought of Curran
Mathews. When I am here, I am always near the thought of
him, whether I think about him or not. For me, his memory
will always be here, as indigenous and congenial as the
sycamores. As long as I am here, I think, he will not be entirely gone. Shortly after the May flood of that year of 1961
I was walking in the weeds on the slope above the original
site of the Camp, and I came unexpectingly on a patch of
flowers that he had planted there thirty years before. They
were trillium, lily of the valley, woodland phlox, Jacob's-
ladder, and some ferns. Except for the lily of the valley,
these flowers are native to the woods of this area—though
they apparently had not returned to this stretch of the
riverbank since it was cleared and plowed. And so in digging them up and bringing them here, Curran was assisting
amiably in the natural order. They have remained through

all the years because they belong here; it is their nature to live in such a place as this. And his pleasure in bringing them here is an addition to them that does not hamper them at all. All their lives they go free of him. Because the river had carried the Camp some distance from the old site, leaving the flowers out of the way of our usual comings and goings, I had never seen them before. They appeared at my feet like some good news of Curran, fresh as if he had spoken it to me, tidings of a day when all was well with him.

Another insistent presence that summer was that of time. The Camp was rapidly aging and wearing out. It had suffered too much abandonment, had been forgotten too much, and the river had flowed into it too many times. Its floors were warped and tilted. The roof leaked where a falling elm branch had punched through the tin. Some of the boards of the walls had begun to rot where the wet weeds leaned against them. What was purposive in it had begun to be overtaken by the necessary accidents of time and weather. Decay revealed its kinship with the earth, and it seemed more than ever to belong to the riverbank. The more the illusion of permanence fell away from it, the easier it fit into the flux of things, as though it entered the fellowship of birds' nests and of burrows. But as a house, it was a failed boat. As a place to sit and work, it was a flimsy, slowly tilting shelf. As a shelter, it was like a tree.

And the day was coming when I would leave again. And again I did not know when I would be back. But this time I did consciously intend to come back. Tanya and I had even begun to talk of building a house someday there on the riverbank, although the possibility seemed a long way off, and the plan was more to comfort ourselves with than to act on. But the plan, because it represented so deep a desire, was vivid to us and we believed in it. Near the original site of the Camp were two fine sycamores, and we thought of a house standing on the slope above them, looking down between them at the river. As a sort of farewell gesture, and as a pledge, I cut down some box elders and elms whose branches had begun to grow obstructively into the crowns of the sycamores. And so, before leaving, I made the beginning of a future that I hoped for and dimly foresaw.

On the twelfth of March the following spring, a letter came to us in Florence, Italy, saying that the river was in the Camp again. Far away as I was, the letter made me strangely restless and sad. I could clearly imagine the look of it. The thought of inundation filled me: the river claiming its valley, making it over again and again—the Camp, my land creature, inhabited by water. The thought, at that distance, that what I knew might be changed filled me and held me in abeyance, as the river filled and held the Camp.

After the year in Europe we lived in New York, and I taught at New York University. We had a second child by then, a boy. In the winter of 1963, I accepted a teaching job at the University of Kentucky to begin in the fall of the following year. That suited us. Our hopes and plans had already turned us back toward Kentucky. We had already spent several years living in other places, and after a second year in New York we would be ready to think of settling down at home.

We returned to Kentucky when school was out that year to spend the summer. And encouraged by the prospect that my relation to the place might soon be permanent, I planned to rebuild the Camp. For one reason, I would be needing a place set aside to do my work in. Another reason, and the main one, was that I needed to preserve the Camp as an idea and a possibility here where it had always been. So many of the good days of my life had been lived here that I could not willingly separate myself from it.

At first I considered repairing the Camp as it stood.

But as I looked it over it appeared to be too far gone to be worth the effort and money I would have to spend on it. Besides, it was too near the river; as the watershed deteriorated more and more through misuse, the spring rises had begun to come over the floors too often. Much as I still valued it, the old house had become a relic, and there were no more arguments in its favor. And so on the sixth of June, 1963, I began the work of tearing it down and clearing a place farther up the bank to build it back again. That afternoon I took out the partition between the two rooms, and then cut down the elm that stood where the new building was to be.

The next afternoon I cleared the weeds and bushes off the building site, and with that my sadness at parting with the old house began to give way to the idea of the new. I was going to build the new house several feet higher up the slope than the old one, and to place it so that it would look out between the two big sycamores. Unlike a wild place, a human place gone wild can be strangely forbidding and even depressing. But that afternoon's work made me feel at home here again. My plans suddenly took hold of me, and I began to visualize the new house as I needed it to be and as I thought it ought to look. My work had made the place inhabitable, had set my imagination free in it. I began again to belong to it.

During the next several days I worked back and forth between the old and the new, tearing down and preparing to build. The tearing down was slow work, for I wanted to save and reuse as much of the old lumber as I could, and the floods had rusted all the nails tight in their holes. The sediment of the flood of 1937 still lay on the tops of the rafters. And on the sheeting under the tin of the roof I found the wallpaper the boards had worn when they stood in the walls of the old family house up on the top of the hill. I squared the outlines of the new house on the slope—measuring off a single room twelve by sixteen feet, and a porch eight by eight feet—and dug the holes for the posts it would stand on.

By June 18 I was ready to begin building, and that day two carpenters, friends of mine I had hired to help me, came early in the morning, and we began work. By the night of the twenty-fifth the new house was up, the roof and siding were on, and from that day I continued the work by myself. The old Camp provided the roof, the floor, and three walls of the new, as well as the two doors and some windows. This dependence on the old materials determined to a considerable extent the shape of the new house, for we would shorten or lengthen the dimensions as we went along in accordance with the lengths of the old boards. And so the new house was a true descendant of the old, as the old in its time was the descendant of one still older.

That summer I was deep into the writing on a long book called *A Place on Earth*. And as soon as the heavier work on the house was done and I no longer needed the carpenters, I returned to work on the book, writing in the mornings and continuing work on the house in the afternoons. I nailed battens over the cracks between the boards, braced the underpinnings, made screens and screen doors and shutters and steps, painted the roof and the outside walls. At the end of the summer I had a satisfactory nutshell of a house, green-roofed and brown-walled, that seemed to fit well enough into the place. Standing on its long legs, it had a peering, aerial look, as though built under the influence of trees. But it was heron-like, too, and made for wading at the edge of the water.

The most expensive member of the new house was a big window, six feet by four and a half feet, with forty panes. This was the eye of the house, and I put it in the wall facing the river and built a long worktable under it. In addition, three window sashes from the old Camp were set into each of the end walls. And so the house became a container of shifting light, the sunlight entering by the little windows in the east wall in the morning, and by those in the west wall in the afternoon, and the steadier light from the northward-staring big window over the worktable.

When I began tearing down the old Camp a pair of phoebes was nesting as usual under one of the eaves. Four eggs were already in the nest. I took an old shutter and fixed a little shelf and a sort of porch roof on it, and nailed it to a locust tree nearby, and set the nest with its eggs carefully on it. As I feared, the old birds would have nothing to do with it. The nest stayed where I had put it for another year or so, a symbol of the ended possibilities of the old Camp, and then it blew away.

As I wrote through the mornings of the rest of that summer, a green heron would often be fishing opposite me on the far bank. An old willow had leaned down there until it floated on the water, reaching maybe twenty feet out from the bank. The tree was still living, nearly the whole length of it covered with leafy sprouts. It was dead only at the outer end, which bent up a few inches above the surface of the river. And it was there that the heron fished. He stooped a little, leaning a little forward, his eyes stalking the river as it flowed down and passed beneath him. His attention would be wonderfully concentrated for minutes at a stretch, he would stand still as a dead branch on the trunk of his willow, and then he would itch and have to scratch among his feathers with his beak. When prey swam within his reach, he would crouch, tilt, pick it deftly out of the water, sit back, swallow. Once I saw him plunge headlong into the water and flounder out with his minnow—as if the awkward flogging body had been literally yanked off its perch by the accurate hunger of the beak. When a boat passed he did not fly, but walked calmly back into the shadows among the sprouts of the willow and stood still.

Another bird I was much aware of that summer was the sycamore warbler. Nearly every day I would see one feeding in the tall sycamores in front of the house, or when I failed to see the bird I would hear its song. This is a bird of the tall trees, and he lives mostly in their highest branches. He loves the sycamores. He moves through their crowns, feeding, and singing his peculiar quaking seven-note song, a voice passing overhead like the sun. I am sure I had spent many days of my life with this bird going about his business high over my head, and I had never been aware of him before. This always amazes me; it has happened to me over and over; for years I will go in ignorance of some creature that will later become important to me, as though we are slowly drifting toward each other in time, and then it will suddenly become as visible to me as a star. It is at once almost a habit. After the first sighting I see it often. I become dependent on it, and am uneasy when I do not see it. In the years since I first saw it here and heard its song, the sycamore warbler has come to hold this sort of power over me. I never hear it approaching through the white branches of its trees that I don't stop and listen; or I get the binoculars and watch him as he makes his way from one sycamore to another along the riverbank, a tiny gray bird with a yellow throat, singing from white branch to white branch, among the leaf lights and shadows. When I hear his song for the first time in the spring, I am deeply touched and reassured. It has come to be the most characteristic voice of this place. He is the Camp's emblem bird, as the sycamore is its emblem tree.

From the old Camp the new Camp inherited the fate of a river house. High up as I had built it, I hadn't been able to move it beyond the reach of the river; there was not room enough here below the road to do that. Like the old house, the new was doomed to make its way in the water—to be a failed boat, and survive by luck. The first spring after it was built the river rose more than two feet over the floor. When the water went down, my Uncle Jimmy hosed out the silt and made the place clean again, and when I came back from New York later in the spring it looked the way it had before. But the idea of it had changed. If it had been built in the hope that the river would never rise into it and in the fear that it would, it now lived in the fact that the river had and in the likelihood that it would again. Like all river houses, it had become a stoical house. Sitting in it, I never forget that I am within the reach of an awesome power. It is a truthful house, not indulging the illusion of the permanence of human things. To be here always is not its hope. Long-legged as it is, it is responsive to the natural vibrations. When the dog scratches under the table there is a tremor in the rafters.

Our return from New York in early June of 1964 changed our lives. We were coming back to Kentucky this time with the intention of staying and making a home. Our plans were still unsettled, but our direction was clear. For the first time, we were beginning to have a foreseeable future. From then on, my relation to my native country here might be interrupted occasionally, but it would not be broken. For the summer, we would stay on the farm and I would spend the days working at the Camp, as before.

The previous summer, when I had moved the phoebes' nest from under the eaves of the old Camp before tearing it down, I had said to myself that it would be a good omen if the birds should nest the next year at the new Camp. And they did, building their mossy nest under the roof of the porch. I felt honored by this, as though my work had been received into the natural order. The phoebes had added to its meaning. Later in the summer a pair of

Carolina wrens also nested under the porch roof. Instead of one room, I had begun to have a house of apartments where several different kinds of life went on together. And who is to say that one kind is more possible or natural here than another? My writing and the family life of the phoebes go along here together, in a kind of equality.

In that summer of 1964 one of my first jobs was to insulate the Camp, and to wall and ceil it on the inside with six-inch tongue and groove. Once that was done, I resumed my mornings of writing. The afternoons I often spent working around the Camp, or reading, or walking in the woods. As fall approached I had a bottle-gas heater and a two-burner cooking stove installed, which made the Camp ready for cold weather use and for what is known as batching.

We still were unsure what shape our life in Kentucky was going to take, and so we had rented a furnished house in Lexington for the winter. Since I was still at work on my book, the plan was that I would do my teaching at the university on Tuesdays, Wednesdays, and Thursdays, and then drive down to the Camp to write during the other four days. Difficult as this was, it seemed the best way of assuring the quiet and the concentration that I needed for my work. But as a sort of by-product, it also made for the most intense and prolonged experience of the Camp and the river that I had ever known. In many ways that was to be a most critical time for me. Before it was over it would make a deep change in my sense of myself, and in my sense of the country I was born in.

From the beginning of September, when school started, until the first of May, when it was over, I would leave Lexington after supper Thursday night and stay at the Camp through Monday afternoon. Occasionally I would stay for some meeting or other at the university on into Thursday night, and those late drives are the ones I remember best. I would leave the university and drive across Lexington and the suburbs, and then the sixty miles through the country and down along the river to the Camp. As I went, the roads would grow less traveled, the night quieter and lonelier, the darkness broken by fewer lights. I would reach the Camp in the middle of the night, the country quiet and dark all around when I turned off the car engine and the headlights. I would hear an owl calling, or the sound of the small stream on the far bank tumbling into the river. I would go in, light the lamp and the stove, read until the room warmed, and then sleep. The next morning I would be at work on my book at the table under the window. It was always a journey from the sound of public voices to the sound of a private quiet voice rising falteringly out of the roots of my mind, that I listened carefully in the silence to hear. It was a journey from the abstract collective life of the university and the city into the intimate country of my own life. It is only in a country that is well-known, full of familiar names and places, full of life that is always changing, that the mind goes free of abstractions, and renews itself in the presence of the creation, that so persistently eludes human comprehension and human law. It is only in the place that one belongs to, intimate and familiar, long watched over, that the details rise up out of the whole and become visible: the hawk stoops into the clearing before one's eyes; the wood drake, aloof and serene in his glorious plumage, swims out of his hiding place.

One clear morning as the fall was coming on I saw a chipmunk sunning on a log, as though filling himself with light and warmth in preparation for his winter sleep. He was wholly preoccupied with the sun, for though I watched him from only a few steps away he did not move. And while he mused or dozed rusty-golden sycamore leaves bigger than he was were falling all around him.

With the approach of winter the country opened. Around the Camp the limits of seeing drew back like the

eyelids of a great eye. The foliage that since spring had enclosed it slowly fell away, and the outlook from its windows came to include the neighboring houses. It was as
though on every frosty night the distances stole up nearer.

On the last morning of October, waking, I looked
out the window and saw a fisherman in a red jacket fishing
alone in his boat tied against the far bank. He sat deeply
quiet and still, unmoved as a tree by my rising and the
other events that went on around him. There was something heron-like in his intent waiting upon what the day
might bring him out of the dark. In his quietness and patience he might have been the incarnation of some river
god, at home among all things, awake while I had slept.

One bright warm day in November it was so quiet
that I could hear the fallen leaves ticking, like a light rain,
as they dried and contracted, scraping their points and
edges against each other. That day I saw the first sapsuck-
ers, which are here only in the winter.

Another day I woke to see the trees below the house
full of birds: chickadees, titmice, juncos, bluebirds, jays.
They had found a red screech owl asleep in a hollow in one
of the water maples. It was a most noisy event, and it lasted
a long time. The bluebirds would hover, fluttering like
sparrow hawks, over the owl's hole, looking in. The titmice
would perch on the very lip of the hole and scold and then,
as if in fear of their own bravery, suddenly startle away.
They all flew away and came back again two or three
times. Everybody seemed to have a great backlog of invective to hurl down upon the head of the owl, who apparently paid no attention at all—at least when I climbed up and
looked in he paid no attention to me.

I believe that the owl soon changed his sleeping
place; when I next looked in he was gone. But for days
afterward the birds of the neighborhood pretended he was
still there, and would stop in passing to enact a sort of rit-

ual of outrage and fright. The titmice seemed especially susceptible to the fascination of that hole. They would lean over it, yell down into it, and then spring away in a spasm of fear. They seemed to be scaring themselves for fun, like children playing around a deserted house. And yet for both birds and children there must be a seriousness in such play; they mimic fear in order to be prepared for it when it is real.

While I was eating breakfast the morning after the birds' discovery of the owl, I heard several times a voice that I knew was strange to this place. I was reading as I ate, and at first I paid little attention. But the voice persisted, and when I put my mind to it I thought it must be that of a goose. I went out with the binoculars, and saw two blue geese, the young of that year, on the water near the far bank. Though the morning was clear and the sun well up, there was a light fog blowing over the river, thickening and thinning out and thickening again, making it difficult to see, but I made out their markings clearly enough. While I watched they waded out on shore at a place where the bank had slipped, preened their feathers, and drank, and after about fifteen minutes flew away.

That afternoon I found them again in the same slip where I had seen them in the morning. I paddled the canoe within twenty feet of them, and then they only flew out onto the water a short distance away. I thought that since these birds nest to the north of Hudson Bay and often fly enormous distances in migration, I might have been the first man these had ever seen. Not wanting to call attention to them and so get them shot, I went on across the river and walked into the bottom on the far side. I spent some time there, looking at the wood ducks and some green-winged teal on the slews, and when I returned to the canoe a little before five the geese were gone. But my encounter with them cast a new charm on my sense of the place. They made me realize that the geography of this patch of river-bank takes in much of the geography of the world. It is under the influence of the Arctic, where the winter birds go in summer, and of the tropics, where the summer birds go in winter. It is under the influence of forests and of crop-lands and of strip mines in the Appalachians, and it feels the pull of the Gulf of Mexico. How many nights have the migrants loosened from their guide stars and descended here to rest or to stay for a season or to die and enter this earth? The geography of this place is airy and starry as well as earthy and watery. It has been arrived at from a thousand other places, some as far away as the poles. I have come here from great distances myself, and am resigned to the knowledge that I cannot go without leaving it better or worse. Here as well as any place I can look out my window and see the world. There are lights that arrive here from deep in the universe. A man can be provincial only by being blind and deaf to his province.

In December the winter cold began. Early in the mornings when it would be clear and cold the drift logs going down the channel would be white with frost, not having moved except as the current moved all night, as firmly embedded in the current, almost, as in the ground. A sight that has always fascinated me, when the river is up and the water swift, is to see the birds walking about, calm-ly feeding, on the floating logs and the mats of drift as they pass downward, slowly spinning in the currents. The ducks, too, like to feed among the drift in the channel at these times. I have seen mallards drift down, feeding among the uprooted tree trunks and the cornstalks and the rafted brush, and then fly back upstream to drift down again.

A voice I came to love and listen for on the clear cold mornings was that of the Carolina wren. He would be quick and busy, on the move, singing as he went. Unlike the calls of the other birds, whose songs, if they sang at all, would be faltering and halfhearted in the cold, the wren's song would come big and clear, filling the air of the whole neighborhood with energy, as though he could not bear to live except in the atmosphere of his own music.

Toward the end of that December a gray squirrel began building a nest in a hollow sycamore near the house. He seemed unable or unwilling to climb the trunk of the sycamore; in all the time I watched him he never attempted to do so. He always followed the same complicated route to his nest: up a grapevine, through the top of an elm and then, by a long leap, into the sycamore. On his way down this route offered him no difficulties, but the return trip, when he carried a load of sycamore leaves in his mouth, seemed fairly risky. The big leaves gave him a good deal of trouble; he frequently stopped and worked with his forepaws to make the load more compact. But because he persisted in carrying as big loads as he could, his forward vision seemed usually to be blocked altogether. I believe that his very exacting leaps were made blind, by memory, after a bit of nervous calculation beforehand. When he moved with a load of leaves, apparently because of the obstruction of his vision, he was always extremely wary, stopping often to listen and look around.

I remember one night of snow, so cold that the snow squeaked under my feet when I went out. The valley was full of moonlight; the fields were dazzling white, the woods deep black, the shadows of the trees printed heavily on the snow. And it was quiet everywhere. As long as I stood still there was not a sound.

That winter a pair of flickers drilled into the attic and slept there. Sometimes at night, after I went to bed, I could hear them stirring. But contrary to my sense of economy—though, I suppose, in keeping with theirs—they did not make do with a single hole, but bored one in one gable and one in the other. I shared my roof with them until the cold weather ended, and then evicted them. Later I put up a nesting box for them, which was promptly taken over by starlings.

One sunny morning of high water in April while I sat at work, keeping an eye on the window as usual, there were nineteen coot, a pair of wood ducks, and two pairs of blue-winged teal feeding together near the opposite bank. They fed facing upstream, working against the current, now and then allowing themselves to be carried down-stream a little way, then working upstream again. After a while the four teal climbed out onto a drift log caught in the bushes near the shore. For some time they sat sunning and preening there. And then the log broke loose and began to drift again. The four birds never moved. They rode it down the river and out of sight. They accepted this accident of the river as much as a matter of fact as if it had been a purpose of theirs. Able both to swim and to fly, they made a felicity of traveling by drift log, as if serendipity were merely a way of life with them.

On the tenth of April, I woke at about six o'clock, and the first sound I heard was the song of the sycamore warbler, returned from the South. With that my thoughts entered spring. I went into the woods and found the blood-root in bloom. Curran's flowers were coming up on the slope beside the house. In the warm evening I noticed other spring music: the calling of doves, and the slamming of newly hung screen doors.

During that winter I had spent many days and nights of watchfulness and silence here. I had learned the power of silence in a place—silence that is the imitation of absence, that permits one to be present as if absent, so that the life of the place goes its way undisturbed. It proposes an ideal of harmlessness. A man should be in the world as though he were not in it,* so that it will be no worse because of his life. His obligation may not be to make "a better world," but the world certainly requires of him that he make it no worse. That, at least, was man's moral circumstance before he began his ruinous attempt to "improve" on the creation; now, perhaps, he is under an obligation to leave it better than he found it, by undoing some of the effects of his meddling and restoring its old initiatives—by making his absence the model of his presence.

But there was not only the power of silence; there was the power of attentiveness, of permanence of interest. By coming back to Kentucky and renewing my devotion to the Camp and the river valley, I had, in a sense, made a marriage with the place. I had established a trust, and within the assurance of the trust the place had begun to reveal its life to me in moments of deep intimacy and beauty. I had been a native; now I was beginning to belong. There is no word—certainly not *native* or *citizen*—to suggest the state I mean, that of belonging willingly and gladly and with some fullness of knowledge to a place. I had ceased to be a native as men usually are, merely by chance and legality, and had begun to be native in the fashion of the birds and animals; I had begun to be born here in mind and spirit as well as in body.

For some months after our return to Kentucky we assumed that we would settle more or less permanently in Lexington, near the university, and perhaps have a place here in the country to come to for the summers. We had thought of building a couple of more rooms onto the Camp for that purpose, and we had thought of buying a piece of woods out of reach of the river and building there. But in November of that first winter the Lane's Landing property, adjoining the Camp on the downriver side, came up for

*Impossible. The problem calls for *practical* solutions.

sale, and we were able to buy it. We would, we told ourselves, fix it up a little, use it in the summers, and perhaps settle there permanently some day. The previous owners moved out in February, and I began spending some of my afternoons there, working to get ready for the carpenters who would work there later on. But on the weekends Tanya and the children would often come down from Lexington, and we would walk over the place, and through the rooms of the house, talking and looking and measuring and planning. And soon we began to see possibilities there that we could not resist. Our life began to offer itself to us in a new way, in the terms of that place, and we could not escape it or satisfy it by anything partial or temporary. We made up our minds to live there. By the morning in April when I first heard the sycamore warbler, we had begun a full-scale overhaul of the house, and I had planted two dozen fruit trees. Early in July, with work completed on only three of the rooms, we moved in. After eight years, our lives enlarged in idea and in concern, our marriage enlarged into a family, we had come back to where we had begun. The Camp, always symbolically the center of our life, had fastened us here at last.

It has been several years now since I first consciously undertook to learn about the natural history of this place. My desire to do this grew out of the sense that the human life of the country is only part of its life, and that in spite of the extreme *effects* of modern man's presence on the land, his relation to it is largely superficial. In spite of all his technical prowess, nothing he has built or done has the permanence, or the congeniality with the earth, of the nesting instincts of the birds.

As soon as I felt a necessity to learn about the non-human world, I wished to learn about it in a hurry. And then I began to learn perhaps the most important lesson that nature had to teach me: that I could not learn about

her in a hurry. The most important learning, that of experience, can be neither summoned nor sought out. The most
worthy knowledge cannot be acquired by what is known as
study—though that is necessary, and has its use. It comes in
its own good time and in its own way to the man who will
go where it lives, and wait, and be ready, and watch. Hurry
is beside the point, useless, an obstruction. The thing is to
be attentively present. To sit and wait is as important as to
move. Patience is as valuable as industry. What is to be
known is always there. When it reveals itself to you, or
when you come upon it, it is by chance. The only condition
is your being there and being watchful.

Though it has come slowly and a little at a time, by
bits and fragments sometimes weeks apart, I realize after so
many years of just being here that my knowledge of the life
of this place is rich, my own life part of its richness. And at
that I have only made a beginning. Eternal mysteries are
here, and temporal ones too. I expect to learn many things
before my life is over, and yet to die ignorant. My most in-
spiring thought is that this place, if I am to live well in it,
requires and deserves a lifetime of the most careful attention. And the day that will finally enlighten me, if it ever
comes, will come as the successor of many days spent here
unenlightened or benighted entirely. "It requires more than
a day's devotion," Thoreau says, "to know and to possess
the wealth of a day."

At the same time my days here have taught me the
futility of living for the future. Men who drudge all their
lives in order to retire happily are the victims of a cheap
spiritual fashion invented for their enslavement. It is no
more possible to live in the future than it is to live in the
past. It is impossible to imagine "how it will be," and to
linger over that task is to prepare a disappointment. The
tomorrow I hope for may very well be worse than today.
There is a great waste and destructiveness in our people's

desire to "get somewhere." I myself have traveled several thousand miles to arrive at Lane's Landing, five miles from where I was born, and the knowledge I gained by my travels was mainly that I was born into the same world as everybody else.

Days come to me here when I rest in spirit, and am involuntarily glad. I sense the adequacy of the world, and believe that everything I need is here. I do not strain after ambition or heaven. I feel no dependence on tomorrow. I do not long to travel to Italy or Japan, but only across the river or up the hill into the woods.

And somewhere back of all this, in a relation too intricate and profound to trace out, is the life that Curran Mathews lived here before me. Perhaps he, too, experienced holy days here. Perhaps he only sensed their possibility. But if he had not come here and made a firm allegiance with this place, it is likely that I never would have. I am his follower and his heir. "For an inheritance to be really great," René Char says, "the hand of the deceased must not be seen." The Camp is my inheritance from Curran Mathews, and though certain of his meanings continue in it, his hand is not on it. As an inheritance, he touched it only as a good man touches the earth—to cherish and augment it. Where his hand went to the ground one forgotten day flowers rise up spring after spring.

Now it is getting on toward the end of March. Just as the grass had started to grow and the jonquils were ready to bloom, we had a foot of snow and more cold. Today it is clear and thawing, but the ground is still white. Though the redbird sings his mating song, it is still winter, and my thoughts keep their winter habits. But soon there will come a day when, without expecting to, I will hear the clear seven-note song of the sycamore warbler passing over the Camp roof. Something will close and open in my mind like a page turning. It will be another spring.

A Native Hill

Pull down thy vanity, it is not man
Made courage, or made order, or made grace,
    Pull down thy vanity, I say pull down.
Learn of the green world what can be thy place. . .
                                Ezra Pound, *Canto LXXXI*

1

The hill is not a hill in the usual sense. It has no "other side." It is an arm of Kentucky's central upland known as The Bluegrass; one can think of it as a ridge reaching out from that center, progressively cut and divided, made ever narrower by the valleys of the creeks that drain it. The town of Port Royal in Henry County stands on one of the last heights of this upland, the valleys of two creeks, Gullion's Branch and Cane Run, opening on either side of it into the valley of the Kentucky River. My house backs against the hill's foot where it descends from the town to the river. The river, whose waters have carved the hill and so descended from it, lies within a hundred steps of my door.

Within about four miles of Port Royal, on the upland and in the bottoms upriver, all my grandparents and great-grandparents lived and left such memories as their descendants have bothered to keep. Little enough has been remembered. The family's life here goes back to my mother's great-great-grandfather and to my father's great-grandfather, but of those earliest ones there are only a few vague word-of-mouth recollections. The only place antecedent to this place that has any immediacy to any of us is the town of Cashel in County Tipperary, Ireland, which one of my great-grandfathers left as a boy to spend the rest of his life in Port Royal. His name was James Mathews, and he was a shoemaker. So well did he fit his life into this place that he is remembered, even in the family, as having belonged here. The family's only real memories of Cashel are my own, coming from a short visit I made there five years ago.

And so such history as my family has is the history of its life here. All that any of us may know of ourselves is to be known in relation to this place. And since I did most of my growing up here, and have had most of my most meaningful experiences here, the place and the history, for me, have been inseparable, and there is a sense in which my own life is inseparable from the history and the place. It is a complex inheritance, and I have been both enriched and bewildered by it.

*

I began my life as the old times and the last of the old-time people were dying out. The Depression and World War II delayed the mechanization of the farms here, and one of the first disciplines imposed on me was that of a teamster. Perhaps I first stood in the role of student before my father's father, who, halting a team in front of me, would demand to know which mule had the best head, which the best shoulder or rump, which was the lead mule, were they hitched right. And there came a time when I knew, and took a considerable pride in knowing. Having a boy's usual desire to play at what he sees men working at, I learned to harness and hitch and work a team. I felt distinguished by that, and took the same pride in it that other boys my age took in their knowledge of automobiles. I seem to have been born with an aptitude for a way of life that was doomed, although I did not understand that at the time. Free of any intuition of its doom, I delighted in it, and learned all I could about it.

That knowledge, and the men who gave it to me, influenced me deeply. It entered my imagination, and gave its substance and tone to my mind. It fashioned in me possibilities and limits, desires and frustrations, that I do not expect to live to the end of. And it is strange to think how barely in the nick of time it came to me. If I had been born five years later I would have begun in a different world, and would no doubt have become a different man.

Those five years made a critical difference in my life, and it is a historical difference. One of the results is that in my generation I am something of an anachronism. I am less a child of my time than the people of my age who grew up in the cities, or than the people who grew up here in my own place five years after I did. In my acceptance of twentieth-century realities there has had to be a certain deliberateness, whereas most of my contemporaries had them simply by being born to them.

*

In my teens, when I was away at school, I could comfort myself by recalling in intricate detail the fields I had worked and played in, and hunted over, and ridden through on horseback—and that were richly associated in my mind with people and with stories. I could recall even the casual locations of certain small rocks. I could recall the look of a hundred different kinds of daylight on all those places, the look of animals grazing over them, the postures and attitudes and movements of the men who worked in them, the quality of the grass and the crops that had grown on them. I had come to be aware of it as one is aware of one's body; it was present to me whether I thought of it or not.

When I have thought of the welfare of the earth, the problems of its health and preservation, the care of its life, I have had this place before me, the part representing the whole more vividly and accurately, making clearer and more pressing demands, than any *idea* of the whole. When I have thought of kindness or cruelty, weariness or exuberance, devotion or betrayal, carelessness or care, doggedness or awkwardness or grace, I have had in my mind's eye the men and women of this place, their faces and gestures and movements.

*

I have pondered a great deal over a conversation I took part in a number of years ago in one of the offices of New York University. I had lived away from Kentucky for several years—in California, in Europe, in New York City. And now I had decided to go back and take a teaching job at the University of Kentucky, giving up the position I then held on the New York University faculty. That day I had been summoned by one of my superiors at the university, whose intention, I had already learned, was to persuade me to stay on in New York "for my own good."

The decision to leave had cost me considerable difficulty and doubt and hard thought—for hadn't I achieved what had become one of the almost traditional goals of American writers? I had reached the greatest city in the nation; I had a good job; I was meeting other writers and talking with them and learning from them; I had reason to hope that I might take a still larger part in the literary life of that place. On the other hand, I knew I had not escaped Kentucky, and had never really wanted to. I was still writing about it, and had recognized that I would probably need to write about it for the rest of my life. Kentucky was my fate—not an altogether pleasant fate, though it had much that was pleasing in it, but one that I could not leave behind simply by going to another place, and that I therefore felt more and more obligated to meet directly and to understand. Perhaps even more important, I still had a deep love for the place I had been born in, and liked the idea of going back to be part of it again. And that, too, I felt obligated to try to understand. Why should I love one place so much more than any other? What could be the meaning or use of such love?

The elder of the faculty began the conversation by alluding to Thomas Wolfe, who once taught at the same institution. "Young man," he said, "don't you know you can't go home again?" And he went on to speak of the advantages, for a young writer, of living in New York among the writers and the editors and the publishers.

The conversation that followed was a persistence of politeness in the face of impossibility. I knew as well as Wolfe that there is a certain *metaphorical* sense in which you can't go home again—that is, the past is lost to the extent that it cannot be lived in again. I knew perfectly well that I could not return home and be a child, or recover the secure pleasures of childhood. But I knew also that as the sentence was spoken to me it bore a self-dramatizing sentimentality that was absurd. Home—the place, the countryside—was still there, still pretty much as I left it, and there was no reason I could not go back to it if I wanted to.

As for the literary world, I had ventured some distance into that, and liked it well enough. I knew that because I was a writer the literary world would always have an importance for me and would always attract my inter-

est. But I never doubted that the world was more important
to me than the literary world; and the world would always
be most fully and clearly present to me in the place I was
fated by birth to know better than any other.

And so I had already chosen according to the most
intimate and necessary inclinations of my own life. But
what keeps me thinking of that conversation is the feeling
that it was a confrontation of two radically different
minds, and that it was a confrontation with significant historical overtones.

I do not pretend to know all about the other man's
mind, but it was clear that he wished to speak to me as a
representative of the literary world—the world he assumed
that I aspired to above all others. His argument was based
on the belief that once one had attained the metropolis, the
literary capital, the worth of one's origins was canceled
out; there simply could be nothing *worth* going back to.
What lay behind one had ceased to be a part of life, and
had become "subject matter." And there was the belief,
long honored among American intellectuals and artists and
writers, that a place such as I came from could be returned
to only at the price of intellectual death; cut off from the
cultural springs of the metropolis, the American countryside is Circe and Mammon. Finally, there was the assumption that the life of the metropolis is *the* experience, the
modern experience, and that the life of the rural towns, the
farms, the wilderness places is not only irrelevant to our
time, but archaic as well because unknown or unconsidered by the people who really matter—that is, the urban
intellectuals.

I was to realize during the next few years how false
and destructive and silly those ideas are. But even then I
was aware that life outside the literary world was not
without honorable precedent: if there was Wolfe, there was
also Faulkner; if there was James, there was also Thoreau.

But what I had in my mind that made the greatest difference was the knowledge of the few square miles in Kentucky that were mine by inheritance and by birth and by the intimacy the mind makes with the place it awakens in.

*

What finally freed me from these doubts and suspicions was the insistence in what was happening to me that, far from being bored and diminished and obscured to myself by my life here, I had grown more alive and more conscious than I had ever been.

I had made a significant change in my relation to the place: before, it had been mine by coincidence or accident; now it was mine by choice. My return, which at first had been hesitant and tentative, grew wholehearted and sure. I had come back to stay. I hoped to live here the rest of my life. And once that was settled I began to *see* the place with a new clarity and a new understanding and a new seriousness. Before coming back I had been willing to allow the possibility—which one of my friends insisted on—that I already knew this place as well as I ever would. But now I began to see the real abundance and richness of it. It is, I saw, inexhaustible in its history, in the details of its life, in its possibilities. I walked over it, looking, listening, smelling, touching, alive to it as never before. I listened to the talk of my kinsmen and neighbors as I never had done, alert to their knowledge of the place, and to the qualities and energies of their speech. I began more seriously than ever to learn the names of things—the wild plants and animals, the natural processes, the local places—and to articulate my observations and memories. My language increased and strengthened, and sent my mind into the place like a live root system. And so what has become the usual order of things reversed itself with me; my mind became the root of my life rather than its sublimation. I came to see myself as growing out of the earth like the other native animals and plants. I saw my body and my daily motions as brief coherences and articulations of the energy of the place, which would fall back into it like leaves in the autumn.

*

In this awakening there has been a good deal of pain. When I lived in other places I looked on their evils with the curious eye of a traveler; I was not responsible for them; it cost me nothing to be a critic, for I had not been there long, and I did not feel that I would stay. But here, now that I am both native and citizen, there is no immunity to what is wrong. It is impossible to escape the sense that I am involved in history. What I am has been to a considerable extent determined by what my forebears were, by how they chose to treat this place while they lived in it; the lives of most of them diminished it, and limited its possibilities, and narrowed its future. And every day I am confronted by the question of what inheritance I will leave. What do I have that I am using up? For it has been our history that each generation in this place has been less welcome to it than the last. There has been less here for them. At each arrival there has been less fertility in the soil, and a larger inheritance of destructive precedent and shameful history.

I am forever being crept up on and newly startled by the realization that my people established themselves here by killing or driving out the original possessors, by the awareness that people were once bought and sold here by my people, by the sense of the violence they have done to their own kind and to each other and to the earth, by the evidence of their persistent failure to serve either the place or their own community in it. I am forced, against all my hopes and inclinations, to regard the history of my people here as the progress of the doom of what I value most in the world: the life and health of the earth, the peacefulness of human communities and households.

And so here, in the place I love more than any other and where I have chosen among all other places to live my life, I am more painfully divided within myself than I could be in any other place.

*

I know of no better key to what is adverse in our heritage in this place than the account of "The Battle of the Fire-Brands," quoted in Collins' *History of Kentucky* "from the autobiography of Rev. Jacob Young, a Methodist minister." The "Newcastle" referred to is the present-day New Castle, the county seat of Henry County. I give the quote in full:

> The costume of the Kentuckians was a hunting shirt, buckskin pantaloons, a leathern belt around their middle, a scabbard, and a big knife fastened to their belt; some of them wore hats and some caps. Their feet were covered with moccasins, made of dressed deer skins. They did not think themselves dressed without their powder-horn and shot-pouch, or the gun and the tomahawk. They were ready, then, for all alarms. They knew but little. They could clear ground, raise corn, and kill turkeys, deer, bears, and buffalo; and, when it became necessary, they understood the art of fighting the Indians as well as any men in the United States.
>
> Shortly after we had taken up our residence, I was called upon to assist in opening a road from the place where Newcastle now stands, to the mouth of Kentucky river. That country, then, was an unbroken forest; there was nothing but an Indian trail passing the wilderness. I met the company early in the morning, with my axe, three days' provisions, and my knapsack. Here I found a captain, with about 100 men, all prepared to labor; about as jovial a company as I ever saw, all good-natured and civil. This was about the last of November, 1797. The day was cold and clear. The country through which the company

passed was delightful; it was not a flat country, but, what the Kentuckians called, rolling ground—was quite well stored with lofty timber, and the undergrowth was very pretty. The beautiful canebrakes gave it a peculiar charm. What rendered it most interesting was the great abundance of wild turkeys, deer, bears, and other wild animals. The company worked hard all day, in quiet, and every man obeyed the captain's orders punctually.

About sundown, the captain, after a short address, told us the night was going to be very cold, and we must make very large fires. We felled the hickory trees in great abundance; made great log-heaps, mixing the dry wood with the green hickory; and, laying down a kind of sleepers under the pile, elevated the heap and caused it to burn rapidly. Every man had a water vessel in his knapsack; we searched for and found a stream of water. By this time, the fires were showing to great advantage; so we warmed our cold victuals, ate our suppers, and spent the evening in hearing the hunter's stories relative to the bloody scenes of the Indian war. We then heard some pretty fine singing, considering the circumstances.

Thus far, well; but a change began to take place. They became very rude, and raised the war-whoop. Their shrill shrieks made me tremble. They chose two captains, divided the men into two companies, and commenced fighting with the firebrands—the log heaps having burned down. The only law for their government was, that no man should throw a brand without fire on it—so that they might know how to dodge. They fought, for two or three hours, in perfect good nature; till brands became scarce, and they began to violate the law. Some were severely wounded, blood began to flow freely, and they were in a fair way of commencing a fight in earnest. At this moment, the loud voice of the captain rang out above the din, ordering every man to retire to rest. They dropped their weapons of warfare, rekindled the fires, and laid down to sleep. We finished our road according to directions, and returned home in health and peace.

*

The significance of this bit of history is in its utter violence. The work of clearing the road was itself violent. And from the orderly violence of that labor, these men turned for amusement to disorderly violence. They were men whose element was violence; the only alternatives they were aware of were those within the comprehension of main strength. And let us acknowledge that these were the truly influential men in the history of Kentucky, as well as in the history of most of the rest of America. In comparison to the fatherhood of such as these, the so-called "founding fathers" who established our political ideals are but distant cousins. It is not John Adams or Thomas Jefferson whom we see night after night in the magic mirror of the television set; we see these builders of the road from New Castle to the mouth of the Kentucky River. Their reckless violence has glamorized all our trivialities and evils. Their aggressions have simplified our complexities and problems. They have cut all our Gordian knots. They have appeared in all our disguises and costumes. They have worn all our uniforms. Their war whoop has sanctified our inhumanity and ratified our blunders of policy.

To testify to the persistence of their influence, it is only necessary for me to confess that I read the Reverend Young's account of them with delight; I yield a considerable admiration to the exuberance and extravagance of their fight with the firebrands; I take a certain pride in belonging to the same history and the same place that they belong to—though I know that they represent the worst that is in us, and in me, and that their presence in our history has been ruinous, and that their survival among us promises ruin.

"They knew but little," the observant Reverend says of them, and this is the most suggestive thing he says. It is surely understandable and pardonable, under the circumstances, that these men were ignorant by the standards of formal schooling. But one immediately reflects that the American Indian, who was ignorant by the same standards, nevertheless knew how to live in the country without making violence the invariable mode of his relation to it; in fact, from the ecologist's or the conservationist's point of view, he did it *no* violence. This is because he had, in place of what we would call education, a fully integrated culture, the content of which was a highly complex sense of his dependence on the earth. The same, I believe, was generally true of the peasants of certain old agricultural societies, particularly in the Orient. They belonged by an intricate awareness to the earth they lived on and by, which meant that they respected it, which meant that they practiced strict economies in the use of it.

The abilities of those Kentucky road builders of 1797 were far more primitive and rudimentary than those of the Stone Age people they had driven out. They could clear the ground, grow corn, kill game, and make war. In the minds and hands of men who "know but little"—or little else—all of these abilities are certain to be destructive, even of those values and benefits their use may be intended to serve.

On such a night as the Reverend Young describes, an Indian would have made do with a small shelter and a small fire. But these road builders, veterans of the Indian War, "felled the hickory trees in great abundance; made great log-heaps . . . and caused [them] to burn rapidly." Far from making a small shelter that could be adequately heated by a small fire, their way was to make no shelter at all, and heat instead a sizable area of the landscape. The idea was that when faced with abundance one should consume abundantly—an idea that has survived to become the basis of our present economy. It is neither natural nor civilized, and even from a "practical" point of view it is to the last degree brutalizing and stupid.

I think that the comparison of these road builders with the Indians, on the one hand, and with Old World peasants on the other, is a most suggestive one. The Indians and the peasants were people who belonged deeply and intricately to their places. Their ways of life had evolved slowly in accordance with their knowledge of their land, of its needs, of their own relation of dependence and responsibility to it. The road builders, on the contrary, were *placeless* people. That is why they "knew but little." Having left Europe far behind, they had not yet in any meaningful sense arrived in America, not yet having *devoted* themselves to any part of it in a way that would produce the intricate knowledge of it necessary to live in it without destroying it. Because they belonged to no place, it was almost inevitable that they should behave violently toward the places they came to. We *still* have not, in any meaningful way, arrived in America. And in spite of our great reservoir of facts and methods, in comparison to the deep earthly wisdom of established peoples we still know but little.

But my understanding of this curiously parabolic fragment of history will not be complete until I have considered more directly that the occasion of this particular violence was the building of a road. It is obvious that one who values the idea of community cannot speak against roads without risking all sorts of absurdity. It must be noticed, nevertheless, that the predecessor to this first road was "nothing but an Indian trail passing the wilderness"—a path. The Indians, then, who had the wisdom and the grace to live in this country for perhaps ten thousand years without destroying or damaging any of it, needed for their travels no more than a footpath; but their successors, who in a century and a half plundered the area of at least half its topsoil and virtually all of its forest, felt immediately that they had to have a road. My interest is not in the question of whether or not they *needed* the road, but in the fact that the road was then, and is now, the most character-istic form of their relation to the country.

The difference between a path and a road is not only the obvious one. A path is little more than a habit that comes with knowledge of a place. It is a sort of ritual of familiarity. As a form, it is a form of contact with a known landscape. It is not destructive. It is the perfect adaptation, through experience and familiarity, of movement to place; it obeys the natural contours; such obstacles as it meets it goes around. A road, on the other hand, even the most primitive road, embodies a resistance against the land-scape. Its reason is not simply the necessity for movement, but haste. Its wish is to *avoid* contact with the landscape; it seeks so far as possible to go over the country, rather than through it; its aspiration, as we see clearly in the example of our modern freeways, is to be a bridge; its tendency is to translate place into space in order to traverse it with the least effort. It is destructive, seeking to remove or destroy all obstacles in its way. The primitive road advanced by the destruction of the forest; modern roads advance by the de-struction of topography.

That first road from the site of New Castle to the mouth of the Kentucky River—lost now either by obsoles-cence or metamorphosis—is now being crossed and to some extent replaced by its modern descendant known as I-71, and I have no wish to disturb the question of whether or not *this* road was needed. I only want to observe that it bears no relation whatever to the country it passes through. It is a pure abstraction, built to serve the two ab-stractions that are the poles of our national life: commerce and expensive pleasure. It was built, not according to the lay of the land, but according to a blueprint. Such homes and farmlands and woodlands as happened to be in its way are now buried under it. A part of a hill near here that would have caused it to turn aside was simply cut down and disposed of as thoughtlessly as the pioneer road builders would have disposed of a tree. Its form is the form of speed, dissatisfaction, and anxiety. It represents the ultimate in engineering sophistication, but the crudest possible valuation of life in this world. It is as adequate a symbol of our relation to our country now as that first road was of our relation to it in 1797.

*

But the sense of the past also gives a deep richness and resonance to nearly everything I see here. It is partly the sense that what I now see, other men that I have known once saw, and partly that this knowledge provides an imaginative access to what I do not know. I think of the country as a kind of palimpsest scrawled over with the comings and goings of people, the erasure of time already in process even as the marks of passage are put down. There are the ritual marks of neighborhood—roads, paths between houses. There are the domestic paths from house to barns and outbuildings and gardens, farm roads threading the pasture gates. There are the wanderings of hunters and searchers after lost stock, and the speculative or meditative or inquisitive "walking around" of farmers on wet days and Sundays. There is the spiraling geometry of the rounds of implements in fields, and the passing and returning scratches of plows across croplands. Often these have filled an interval, an opening, between the retreat of the forest from the virgin ground and the forest's return to ground that has been worn out and given up. In the woods here one often finds cairns of stones picked up out of furrows, gullies left by bad farming, forgotten roads, stone chimneys of houses long rotted away or burned.

*

Occasionally one stumbles into a coincidence that, like an unexpected alignment of windows, momentarily cancels out the sense of historical whereabouts, giving with an overwhelming immediacy an awareness of the reality of the past.

The possibility of this awareness is always immanent in old homesites. It may suddenly bear in upon one at the sight of old orchard trees standing in the dooryard of a house now filled with baled hay. It came to me when I looked out the attic window of a disintegrating log house and saw a far view of the cleared ridges with wooded hollows in between, and nothing in sight to reveal the date. Who was I, leaning to the window? When?

It broke upon me one afternoon when, walking in the woods on one of my family places, I came upon a gap in a fence, wired shut, but with deep-cut wagon tracks still passing through it under the weed growth and the fallen leaves. Where that thicket stands there was crop ground, maybe as late as my own time. I knew some of the men who tended it; their names and faces were instantly alive in my mind. I knew how it had been with them—how they would harness their mule teams in the early mornings in my grandfather's big barn and come to the woods-rimmed tobacco patches, the mules' feet wet with the dew. And in the solitude and silence that came upon them they would set to work, their water jugs left in the shade of bushes in the fencerows.

As a child I learned the early mornings in these places for myself, riding out in the wagons with the tobacco-cutting crews to those steep fields in the dew-wet shadow of the woods. As the day went on the shadow would draw back under the feet of the trees, and it would get hot. Little whirlwinds would cross the opening, picking up the dust and the dry "ground leaves" of the tobacco. We made a game of running with my grandfather to stand, shoulders scrunched and eyes squinched, in their middles.

Having such memories, I can acknowledge only with reluctance and sorrow that those slopes should never have been broken. Rich as they were, they were too steep. The humus stood dark and heavy over them once; the plow was its doom.

*

Early one February morning in thick fog and spattering rain I stood on the riverbank and listened to a towboat working its way downstream. Its engines were idling, nudging cautiously through the fog into the Cane Run bend. The end of the head barge emerged finally like a shadow, and then the second barge appeared, and then the towboat itself. They made the bend, increased power, and went thumping off out of sight into the fog again.

Because the valley was so enclosed in fog, the boat with its tow appearing and disappearing again into the muffling whiteness within two hundred yards, the moment had a curious ambiguity. It was as though I was not necessarily myself at all. I could have been my grandfather, in his time, standing there watching, as I knew he had.

2

I start down from one of the heights of the upland, the town of Port Royal at my back. It is a winter day, overcast and still, and the town is closed in itself, humming and muttering a little, like a winter beehive.

The dog runs ahead, prancing and looking back, knowing the way we are about to go. This is a walk well established with us—a route in our minds as well as on the ground. There is a sort of mystery in the establishment of these ways. Any time one crosses a given stretch of country with some frequency, no matter how wanderingly one begins, the tendency is always toward habit. By the third or fourth trip, without realizing it, one is following a fixed path, going the way one went before. After that, one may

still wander, but only by deliberation, and when there is
reason to hurry, or when the mind wanders rather than the
feet, one returns to the old route. Familiarity has begun.
One has made a relationship with the landscape, and the
form and the symbol and the enactment of the relationship
is the path. These paths of mine are seldom worn on the
ground. They are habits of mind, directions and turns.
They are as personal as old shoes. My feet are comfortable
in them.

From the height I can see far out over the country,
the long open ridges of the farmland, the wooded notches
of the streams, the valley of the river opening beyond, and
then more ridges and hollows of the same kind.

Underlying this country, nine hundred feet below
the highest ridgetops, more than four hundred feet below
the surface of the river, is sea level. We seldom think of it
here; we are a long way from the coast, and the sea is alien
to us. And yet the attraction of sea level dwells in this country as an ideal dwells in a man's mind. All our rains go in
search of it and, departing, they have carved the land in a
shape that is fluent and falling. The streams branch like
vines, and between the branches the land rises steeply and
then rounds and gentles into the long narrowing fingers of
ridgeland. Near the heads of the streams even the steepest
land was not too long ago farmed and kept cleared. But
now it has been given up and the woods is returning. The
wild is flowing back like a tide. The arable ridgetops reach
out above the gathered trees like headlands into the sea,
bearing their human burdens of fences and houses and
barns, crops and roads.

Looking out over the country, one gets a sense of
the whole of it: the ridges and hollows, the clustered buildings of the farms, the open fields, the woods, the stock
ponds set like coins into the slopes. But this is a surface
sense, an exterior sense, such as you get from looking down

on the roof of a house. The height is a threshold from which to step down into the wooded folds of the land, the interior, under the trees and along the branching streams.

I pass through a pasture gate on a deep-worn path that grows shallow a little way beyond, and then disappears altogether into the grass. The gate has gathered thousands of passings to and fro that have divided like the slats of a fan on either side of it. It is like a fist holding together the strands of a net.

Beyond the gate the land leans always more steeply toward the branch. I follow it down, and then bear left along the crease at the bottom of the slope. I have entered the downflow of the land. The way I am going is the way the water goes. There is something comfortable and fit-feeling in this, something free in this yielding to gravity and taking the shortest way down.

As the hollow deepens into the hill, before it has yet entered the woods, the grassy crease becomes a raw gully, and along the steepening slopes on either side I can see the old scars of erosion, places where the earth is gone clear to the rock. My people's errors have become the features of my country.

It occurs to me that it is no longer possible to imagine how this country looked in the beginning, before the white people drove their plows into it. It is not possible to know what was the shape of the land here in this hollow when it was first cleared. Too much of it is gone, loosened by the plows and washed away by the rain. I am walking the route of the departure of the virgin soil of the hill. I am not looking at the same land the firstcomers saw. The original surface of the hill is as extinct as the passenger pigeon. The pristine America that the first white man saw is a lost continent, sunk like Atlantis in the sea. The thought of what was here once and is gone forever will not leave me as long as I live. It is as though I walk knee-deep in its absence.

The slopes along the hollow steepen still more, and I go in under the trees. I pass beneath the surface. I am enclosed, and my sense, my interior sense, of the country becomes intricate. There is no longer the possibility of seeing very far. The distances are closed off by the trees and the steepening walls of the hollow. One cannot grow familiar here by sitting and looking as one can up in the open on the ridge. Here the eyes become dependent on the feet. To see the woods from the inside one must look and move and look again. It is inexhaustible in its standpoints. A lifetime will not be enough to experience it all. Not far from the beginning of the woods, and set deep in the earth in the bottom of the hollow, is a rock-walled pool not a lot bigger than a bathtub. The wall is still nearly as straight and tight as when it was built. It makes a neatly turned narrow horseshoe, the open end downstream. This is a historical ruin, dug here either to catch and hold the water of the little branch, or to collect the water of a spring whose vein broke to the surface here—it is probably no longer possible to know which. The pool is filled with earth now, and grass grows in it. And the branch bends around it, cut down to the bare rock, a torrent after heavy rain, other times bone dry. All that is certain is that when the pool was dug and walled there was deep topsoil on the hill to gather and hold the water. And this high up, at least, the bottom of the hollow, instead of the present raw notch of the stream bed, wore the same mantle of soil as the slopes, and the stream was a steady seep or trickle, running most or all of the year. This tiny pool no doubt once furnished water for a considerable number of stock through the hot summers. And now it is only a lost souvenir, archaic and useless, except for the bitter intelligence there is in it. It is one of the monuments to what is lost.

Wherever one goes along the streams of this part of

the country, one is apt to come upon this old stonework. There are walled springs and pools. There are the walls built in the steeper hollows where the fences cross or used to cross; the streams have drifted dirt in behind them, so that now where they are still intact they make waterfalls that have scooped out small pools at their feet. And there used to be miles of stone fences, now mostly scattered and sifted back into the ground.

Considering these, one senses a historical patience, now also extinct in the country. These walls were built by men working long days for little wages, or by slaves. It was work that could not be hurried at, a meticulous finding and fitting together, as though reconstructing a previous wall that had been broken up and scattered like puzzle pieces. The wall would advance only a few yards a day. The pace of it could not be borne by most modern men, even if the wages could be afforded. Those men had to move in closer accord with their own rhythms, and nature's, than we do. They had no machines. Their capacities were only those of flesh and blood. They talked as they worked. They joked and laughed. They sang. The work was exacting and heavy and hard and slow. No opportunity for pleasure was missed or slighted. The days and the years were long. The work was long. At the end of this job the next would begin. Therefore, be patient. Such pleasure as there is, is here, now. Take pleasure as it comes. Take work as it comes. The end may never come, or when it does it may be the wrong end.

Now the men who built the walls and the men who had them built have long gone underground to be, along with the buried ledges and the roots and the burrowing animals, a part of the nature of the place in the minds of the ones who come after them. I think of them lying still in their graves, as level as the sills and thresholds of their lives, as though resisting to the last the slant of the ground. And their old walls, too, re-enter nature, collecting lichens and mosses with patience their builders never conceived.

Like the pasture gates, the streams are great collectors of comings and goings. The streams go down, and paths always go down beside the streams. For a while I walk along an old wagon road that is buried in leaves—a fragment, beginningless and endless as the middle of a sentence on some scrap of papyrus. There is a cedar whose branches reach over this road, and under the branches I find the leavings of two kills of some bird of prey. The most recent is a pile of blue jay feathers. The other has been rained on and is not identifiable. How little we know. How little of this was intended or expected by any man. The road that has become the grave of men's passages has led to the life of the woods.

> And I say to myself: Here is your road
> without beginning or end, appearing
> out of the earth and ending in it, bearing
> no load but the hawk's kill, and the leaves
> building earth on it, something more
> to be borne. Tracks fill with earth
> and return to absence. The road was worn
> by men bearing earth along it. They have come
> to endlessness. In their passing
> they could not stay in, trees have risen
> and stand still. It is leading to the dark,
> to mornings where you are not. Here
> is your road, beginningless and endless as God.

Now I have come down within the sound of the water. The winter has been rainy, and the hill is full of dark seeps and trickles, gathering finally, along these creases, into flowing streams. The sound of them is one of the elements, and defines a zone. When their voices return to the hill after their absence during summer and autumn, it is a better place to be. A thirst in the mind is quenched.

I have already passed the place where water began to flow in the little stream bed I am following. It broke into the light from beneath a rock ledge, a thin glittering stream. It lies beside me as I walk, overtaking me and going by, yet not moving, a thread of light and sound. And now from below comes the steady tumble and rush of the water of Camp Branch—whose nameless camp was it named for?—and gradually as I descend the sound of the smaller stream is lost in the sound of the larger.

The two hollows join, the line of the meeting of the two spaces obscured even in winter by the trees. But the two streams meet precisely as two roads. That is, the stream *beds* do; the one ends in the other. As for the meeting of the waters, there is no looking at that. The one flow does not end in the other, but continues in it, one with it, two clarities merged without a shadow.

All waters are one. This is a reach of the sea, flung like a net over the hill, and now drawn back to the sea. And as the sea is never raised in the earthly nets of fishermen, so the hill is never caught and pulled down by the watery net of the sea. But always a little of it is. Each of the gathering strands of the net carries back some of the hill melted in it. Sometimes, as now, it carries so little that the water flows clear; sometimes it carries a lot and is brown and heavy with it. Whenever greedy or thoughtless men have lived on it, the hill has literally flowed out of their tracks into the bottom of the sea.

There appears to be a law that when creatures have reached the level of consciousness, as men have, they must become conscious of the creation; they must learn how they fit into it and what its needs are and what it requires of them, or else pay a terrible penalty: the spirit of the creation will go out of them, and they will become destructive; the very earth will depart from them and go where they cannot follow.

My mind is never empty or idle at the joinings of streams. Here is the work of the world going on. The creation is felt, alive and intent on its materials, in such places. In the angle of the meeting of the two streams stands the steep wooded point of the ridge, like the prow of an up-turned boat—finished, as it was a thousand years ago, as it will be in a thousand years. Its becoming is only incidental to its being. It will be because it is. It has no aim or end except to be. By being, it is growing and wearing into what it will be. The fork of the stream lies at the foot of the slope like hammer and chisel laid down at the foot of a finished sculpture. But the stream is no dead tool; it is alive, it is still at its work. Put your hand to it to learn the health of this part of the world. It is the wrist of the hill.

Perhaps it is to prepare to hear some day the music of the spheres that I am always turning my ears to the music of streams. There is indeed a music in streams, but it is not for the hurried. It has to be loitered by and imagined. Or imagined *toward,* for it is hardly for men at all. Nature has a patient ear. To her the slowest funeral march sounds like a jig. She is satisfied to have the notes drawn out to the lengths of days or weeks or months. Small variations are acceptable to her, modulations as leisurely as the opening of a flower.

The stream is full of stops and gates. Here it has piled up rocks in its path, and pours over them into a tiny pool it has scooped at the foot of its fall. Here it has been dammed by a mat of leaves caught behind a fallen limb. Here it must force a narrow passage, here a wider one. To-morrow the flow may increase or slacken, and the tone will shift. In an hour or a week that rock may give way, and the composition will advance by another note. Some idea of it may be got by walking slowly along and noting the changes as one passes from one little fall or rapid to another. But this is a highly simplified and diluted version of the real thing, which is too complex and widespread ever to be actually heard by us. The ear must imagine an impossible patience in order to grasp even the unimaginableness of such music.

But the creation is musical, and this is a part of its music, as bird song is, or the words of poets. The music of the streams is the music of the shaping of the earth, by which the rocks are pushed and shifted downward toward the level of the sea.

And now I find an empty beer can lying in the path. This is the track of the ubiquitous man Friday of all our woods. In my walks I never fail to discover some sign that he has preceded me. I find his empty shotgun shells, his empty cans and bottles, his sandwich wrappings. In wooded places along roadsides one is apt to find, as well, his overtraveled bedsprings, his outcast refrigerator, and heaps of the imperishable refuse of his modern kitchen. A year ago, almost in this same place where I have found his beer can, I found a possum that he had shot dead and left lying, in celebration of his manhood. He is the true American pioneer, perfectly at rest in his assumption that he is the first and the last whose inheritance and fate this place will ever be. Going forth, as he may think, to sow, he only broadcasts his effects.

As I go on down the path alongside Camp Branch, I walk by the edge of croplands abandoned only within my own lifetime. On my left are the south slopes where the woods is old, long undisturbed. On my right, the more fertile north slopes are covered with patches of briars and sumacs and a lot of young walnut trees. Tobacco of an extraordinary quality was once grown here, and then the soil wore thin, and these places were given up for the more accessible ridges that were not so steep, where row cropping made better sense anyway. But now, under the thicket growth, a mat of bluegrass has grown to testify to the good nature of this ground. It was fine dirt that lay here once, and I am far from being able to say that I could have resisted the temptation to plow it. My understanding of what is best for it is the tragic understanding of hindsight, the awareness that I have been taught what was here to be lost by the loss of it.

We have lived by the assumption that what was good for us would be good for the world. And this has been based on the even flimsier assumption that we could know with any certainty what was good even for us. We have fulfilled the danger of this by making our personal pride and greed the standard of our behavior toward the world—to the incalculable disadvantage of the world and every living thing in it. And now, perhaps very close to too late, our great error has become clear. It is not only our own creativity—our own capacity for life—that is stifled by our arrogant assumption; the creation itself is stifled.

We have been wrong. We must change our lives, so that it will be possible to live by the contrary assumption that what is good for the world will be good for us. And that requires that we make the effort to *know* the world and to learn what is good for it. We must learn to cooperate in its processes, and to yield to its limits. But even more important, we must learn to acknowledge that the creation is full of mystery; we will never entirely understand it. We must abandon arrogance and stand in awe. We must recover the sense of the majesty of creation, and the ability to be worshipful in its presence. For I do not doubt that it is only on the condition of humility and reverence before the world that our species will be able to remain in it.

Standing in the presence of these worn and abandoned fields, where the creation has begun its healing without the hindrance or the help of man, with the voice of the stream in the air and the woods standing in silence on all the slopes around me, I am deep in the interior not only of my place in the world, but of my own life, its sources and searches and concerns. I first came into these places following the men to work when I was a child. I knew the men who took their lives from such fields as these, and their lives to a considerable extent made my life what it is. In what came to me from them there was both wealth and poverty, and I have been a long time discovering which was which.

It was in the woods here along Camp Branch that Bill White, my grandfather's Negro hired hand, taught me to hunt squirrels. Bill lived in a little tin-roofed house on up nearer the head of the hollow. And this was, I suppose more than any other place, his hunting ground. It was the place of his freedom, where he could move without subservience, without considering who he was or who anybody else was. On late summer mornings, when it was too wet to work, I would follow him into the woods. As soon as we stepped in under the trees he would become silent and absolutely attentive to the life of the place. He was a good teacher and an exacting one. The rule seemed to be that if I wanted to stay with him, I had to make it possible for him to forget I was there. I was to make no noise. If I did he would look back and make a downward emphatic gesture with his hand, as explicit as writing: Be quiet, or go home. He would see a squirrel crouched in a fork or lying along the top of a branch, and indicate with a grin and a small jerk of his head where I should look; and then wait, while I, conscious of being watched and demanded upon, searched it out for myself. He taught me to look and to listen and to be quiet. I wonder if he knew the value of such teaching or the rarity of such a teacher.

In the years that followed I hunted often here alone. And later in these same woods I experienced my first obscure dissatisfactions with hunting. Though I could not have put it into words then, the sense had come to me that hunting as I knew it—the eagerness to kill something I did not need to eat—was an artificial relation to the place, when what I was beginning to need, just as inarticulately then, was a relation that would be necessary and meaningful. That was a time of great uneasiness and restlessness for me. It would be the fall of the year, the leaves would be turning, and ahead of me would be another year of school. There would be confusions about girls and ambitions, the wordless hurried feeling that time and events and my own nature were pushing me toward what I was going to be—and I had no notion what it was, or how to prepare.

And then there were years when I did not come here at all—when these places and their history were in my mind, and part of me, in places thousands of miles away. And now I am here again, changed from what I was, and still changing. The future is no more certain to me now than it ever was, though its risks are clearer, and so are my own desires: I am the father of two young children whose lives are hostages given to the future. Because of them and because of events in the world, life seems more fearful and difficult to me now than ever before. But it is also more inviting, and I am constantly aware of its nearness to joy. Much of the interest and excitement that I have in my life now has come from the deepening, in the years since my return here, of my relation to this place. For in spite of all that has happened to me in other places, the great change and the great possibility of change in my life has been in my sense of this place. The major difference is perhaps only that I have grown able to be wholeheartedly present here. I am able to sit and be quiet at the foot of some tree here in this woods along Camp Branch, and feel a deep peace, both in the place and in my awareness of it, that not too long ago I was not conscious of the possibility of. This peace is partly in being free of the suspicion that pursued me for

most of my life, no matter where I was, that there was perhaps another place I *should* be, or would be happier or better in; it is partly in the increasingly articulate consciousness of being here, and of the significance and importance
of being here.

After more than thirty years I have at last arrived at
the candor necessary to stand on this part of the earth that
is so full of my own history and so much damaged by it,
and ask: What *is* this place? What is in it? What is its nature? How should men live in it? What must I do?

I have not found the answers, though I believe that
in partial and fragmentary ways they have begun to come
to me. But the questions are more important than their answers. In the final sense they *have* no answers. They are like
the questions—they are perhaps the same questions—that
were the discipline of Job. They are a part of the necessary
enactment of humility, teaching a man what his importance is, what his responsibility is, and what his place is,
both on the earth and in the order of things. And though
the answers must always come obscurely and in fragments,
the questions must be asked. They are fertile questions. In
their implications and effects, they are moral and aesthetic
and, in the best and fullest sense, practical. They promise a
relationship to the world that is decent and preserving.

They are also, both in origin and effect, religious. I
am uneasy with the term, for such religion as has been
openly practiced in this part of the world has promoted
and fed upon a destructive schism between body and soul,
Heaven and earth. It has encouraged people to believe that
the world is of no importance, and that their only obligation in it is to submit to certain churchly formulas in order
to get to Heaven. And so the people who might have been
expected to care most selflessly for the world have had
their minds turned elsewhere—to a pursuit of "salvation"
that was really only another form of gluttony and self-love,

the desire to perpetuate their lives beyond the life of the
world. The Heaven-bent have abused the earth thoughtlessly, by inattention, and their negligence has permitted
and encouraged others to abuse it deliberately. Once the
creator was removed from the creation, divinity became
only a remote abstraction, a social weapon in the hands of
the religious institutions. This split in public values produced or was accompanied by, as it was bound to be, an
equally artificial and ugly division in people's lives, so that
a man, while pursuing Heaven with the sublime appetite he
thought of as his soul, could turn his heart against his
neighbors and his hands against the world. For these reasons, though I know that my questions *are* religious, I dis-
like having to *say* that they are.

But when I ask them my aim is not primarily to get
to Heaven. Though Heaven is certainly more important
than the earth if all they say about it is true, it is still morally incidental to it and dependent on it, and I can only imagine it and desire it in terms of what I know of the earth.
And so my questions do not aspire beyond the earth. They
aspire *toward* it and *into* it. Perhaps they aspire *through* it.
They are religious because they are asked at the limit of
what I know; they acknowledge mystery and honor its
presence in the creation; they are spoken in reverence for
the order and grace that I see, and that I trust beyond my
power to see.

The stream has led me down to an old barn built
deep in the hollow to house the tobacco once grown on
those abandoned fields. Now it is surrounded by the trees
that have come back on every side—a relic, a fragment of
another time, strayed out of its meaning. This is the last of
my historical landmarks. To here, my walk has had insistent overtones of memory and history. It has been a movement of consciousness through knowledge, eroding and
shaping, adding and wearing away. I have descended like

the water of the stream through what I know of myself, and now that I have there is a little more to know. But here at the barn, the old roads and the cow paths—the formal connections with civilization—come to an end.

I stoop between the strands of a barbed-wire fence, and in that movement I go out of time into timelessness. I come into a wild place. The trees grow big, their trunks rising clean, free of undergrowth. The place has a serenity and dignity that one feels immediately; the creation is whole in it and unobstructed. It is free of the strivings and dissatisfactions, the partialities and imperfections of places under the mechanical dominance of men. Here, what to a housekeeper's eye might seem disorderly is nonetheless orderly and within order; what might seem arbitrary or accidental is included in the design of the whole; what might seem evil or violent is a comfortable member of the household. Where the creation is whole nothing is extraneous. The presence of the creation here makes this a holy place, and it is as a pilgrim that I have come. It is the creation that has attracted me, its perfect interfusion of life and design. I have made myself its follower and its apprentice.

One early morning last spring, I came and found the woods floor strewn with bluebells. In the cool sunlight and the lacy shadows of the spring woods the blueness of those flowers, their elegant shape, their delicate fresh scent kept me standing and looking. I found a delight in them that I cannot describe and that I will never forget. Though I had been familiar for years with most of the spring woods flowers, I had never seen these and had not known they were here. Looking at them, I felt a strange loss and sorrow that I had never seen them before. But I was also exultant that I saw them now—that they were here.

For me, in the thought of them will always be the sense of the joyful surprise with which I found them—the sense that came suddenly to me then that the world is blessed beyond my understanding, more abundantly than I will ever know. What lives are still ahead of me here to be discovered and exulted in, tomorrow, or in twenty years? What wonder will be found here on the morning after my death? Though as a man I inherit great evils and the possibility of great loss and suffering, I know that my life is blessed and graced by the yearly flowering of the bluebells. How perfect they are! In their presence I am humble and joyful. If I were given all the learning and all the methods of my race I could not make one of them, or even imagine one. Solomon in all his glory was not arrayed like one of these. It is the privilege and the labor of the apprentice of creation to come with his imagination into the unimaginable, and with his speech into the unspeakable.

3

Sometimes I can no longer think in the house or in the garden or in the cleared fields. They bear too much resemblance to our failed human history—failed, because it has led to this human present that is such a bitterness and a trial. And so I go to the woods. As I go in under the trees, dependably, almost at once, and by nothing I do, things fall into place. I enter an order that does not exist outside, in the human spaces. I feel my life take its place among the lives—the trees, the annual plants, the animals and birds, the living of all these and the dead—that go and have gone to make the life of the earth. I am less important than I thought, the human race is less important than I thought. I rejoice in that. My mind loses its urgings, senses its nature, and is free. The forest grew here in its own time, and so I will live, suffer and rejoice, and die in my own time. There is nothing that I may decently hope for that I cannot reach by patience as well as by anxiety. The hill, which is a part of America, has killed no one in the service of the American government. Then why should I, who am a fragment of the hill? I wish to be as peaceable as my land, which does no violence, though it has been the scene of violence and has had violence done to it.

How, having a consciousness, an intelligence, a human spirit—all the vaunted equipment of my race—can I humble myself before a mere piece of the earth and speak of myself as its fragment? Because my mind transcends the hill only to be filled with it, to comprehend it a little, to know that it lives on the hill in time as well as in place, to recognize itself as the hill's fragment.

The false and truly belittling transcendence is ownership. The hill has had more owners than its owners have had years—they are grist for its mill. It has had few friends. But I wish to be its friend, for I think it serves its friends well. It tells them they are fragments of its life. In its life they transcend their years.

*

The most exemplary nature is that of the topsoil. It is very Christ-like in its passivity and beneficence, and in the penetrating energy that issues out of its peaceableness. It increases by experience, by the passage of seasons over it, growth rising out of it and returning to it, not by ambition or aggressiveness. It is enriched by all things that die and enter into it. It keeps the past, not as history or as memory, but as richness, new possibility. Its fertility is always building up out of death into promise. Death is the bridge or the tunnel by which its past enters its future.

*

To walk in the woods, mindful only of the *physical* extent of it, is to go perhaps as owner, or as knower, confident of one's own history and of one's own importance. But to go there, mindful as well of its temporal extent, of the age of it, and of all that led up to the present life of it, and of all that may follow it, is to feel oneself a flea in the pelt of a great living thing, the discrepancy between its life and one's own so great that it cannot be imagined. One has come into the presence of mystery. After all the trouble one has taken to be a modern man, one has come back under the spell of a primitive awe, wordless and humble.

*

In the centuries before its settlement by white men, among the most characteristic and pleasing features of the floor of this valley, and of the stream banks on its slopes, were the forests and the groves of great beech trees. With their silver bark and their light graceful foliage, turning gold in the fall, they were surely as lovely as any forests that ever grew on earth. I think so because I have seen their diminished descendants, which have returned to stand in the wasted places that we have so quickly misused and given up. But those old forests are all gone. We will never know them as they were. We have driven them beyond the reach of our minds, only a vague hint of their presence returning to haunt us, as though in dreams—a fugitive rumor of the nobility and beauty and abundance of the squandered maidenhood of our world—so that, do what we will, we will never quite be satisfied ever again to be here.

The country, as we have made it by the pretense that we can do without it as soon as we have completed its metamorphosis into cash, no longer holds even the possibility of such forests, for the topsoil that they made and stood upon, like children piling up and trampling underfoot the fallen leaves, is no longer here.

*

There is an ominous—perhaps a fatal—presumptuousness in living in a place by the *imposition* on it of one's ideas and wishes. And that is the way we white people have lived in America throughout our history, and it is the way our history now teaches us to live here.

Surely there could be a more indigenous life than we have. There could be a consciousness that would establish itself on a place by understanding its nature and learning what is potential in it. A man ought to study the wilderness of a place before applying to it the ways he learned in another place. Thousands of acres of hill land, here and in the rest of the country, were wasted by a system of agriculture that was fundamentally alien to it. For more than a century, here, the steepest hillsides were farmed, by my forefathers and their neighbors, as if they were flat, and as if this was not a country of heavy rains. We haven't yet, in any meaningful sense, arrived in these places that we declare we own. We undertook the privilege of the virgin abundance of this land without any awareness at all that we undertook at the same time a responsibility toward it. That responsibility has never yet impressed itself upon our character; its absence in us is signified on the land by scars.

Until we understand what the land is, we are at odds with everything we touch. And to come to that understanding it is necessary, even now, to leave the regions of our conquest—the cleared fields, the towns and cities, the highways—and re-enter the woods. For only there can a man encounter the silence and the darkness of his own absence. Only in this silence and darkness can he recover the sense of the world's longevity, of its ability to thrive without him, of his inferiority to it and his dependence on it. Perhaps then, having heard that silence and seen that darkness, he will grow humble before the place and begin to take it in—to learn *from it* what it is. As its sounds come into his hearing, and its lights and colors come into his vision, and its odors come into his nostrils, then he may come into *its* presence as he never has before, and he will arrive in his place and will want to remain. His life will grow out of the ground like the other lives of the place, and take its place among them. He will be *with* them—neither ignorant of them, nor indifferent to them, nor against them—and so at last he will grow to be native-born. That is, he must re-enter the silence and the darkness, and be born again.

One winter night nearly twenty years ago I was in the woods with the coon hunters, and we were walking toward the dogs, who had moved out to the point of the bluff where the valley of Cane Run enters the valley of the river. The footing was difficult, and one of the hunters was having trouble with his lantern. The flame would "run up" and smoke the globe, so that the light it gave obscured more than it illuminated, an obstacle between his eyes and the path. At last he cursed it and flung it down into a hollow. Its little light went looping down through the trees and disappeared, and there was a distant tinkle of glass as the globe shattered. After that he saw better and went along the bluff easier than before, and lighter, too.

Not long ago, walking up there, I came across his old lantern lying rusted in the crease of the hill, half buried already in the siftings of the slope, and I let it lie. But I've kept the memory that it renewed. I have made it one of my myths of the hill. It has come to be truer to me now than it was then.

For I have turned aside from much that I knew, and have given up much that went before. What will not bring me, more certainly than before, to where I am is of no use to me. I have stepped out of the clearing into the woods. I have thrown away my lantern, and I can see the dark.

*

The hill, like Valéry's sycamore, is a voyager standing still. Never moving a step, it travels through years, seasons, weathers, days and nights. These are the measures of its time, and they alter it, marking their passage on it as on a man's face. The hill has never observed a Christmas or an Easter or a Fourth of July. It has nothing to do with a dial or a calendar. Time is told in it mutely and immediately, with perfect accuracy, as it is told by the heart in the body. Its time is the birth and the flourishing and the death of the many lives that are its life.

*

The hill is like an old woman, all her human obligations met, who sits at work day after day, in a kind of rapt leisure, at an intricate embroidery. She has time for all things. Because she does not expect ever to be finished, she is endlessly patient with details. She perfects flower and leaf, feather and song, adorning the briefest life in great beauty as though it were meant to last forever.

*

In the early spring I climb up through the woods to an east-facing bluff where the bloodroot bloom in scattered colonies around the foot of the rotting monument of a tree trunk. The sunlight is slanting, clear, through the leafless branches. The flowers are white and perfect, delicate as though shaped in air and water. There is a fragility about them that communicates how short a time they will last. There is some subtle bond between them and the dwindling great trunk of the dead tree. There comes on me a pressing wish to preserve them. But I know that what draws me to them would not pass over into anything I can *do*. They will be lost. In a few days none will be here.

*

Coming upon a mushroom growing out of a pad of green moss between the thick roots of an oak, the sun and the dew still there together, I have felt my mind irresistibly become small, to inhabit that place, leaving me standing vacant and bewildered, like a boy whose captured field mouse has just leaped out of his hand.

*

As I slowly fill with the knowledge of this place, and sink into it, I come to the sense that my life here is inexhaustible, that its possibilities lie rich behind and ahead of me, that when I am dead it will not be used up.

*

Too much that we do is done at the expense of something else, or somebody else. There is some intransigent destructiveness in us. My days, though I think I know better, are filled with a thousand irritations, worries, regrets for what has happened and fears for what may, trivial duties, meaningless torments—as destructive of my life as if I wanted to be dead. Take today for what it is, I counsel myself. Let it be enough.

And I dare not, for fear that if I do, yesterday will infect tomorrow. We are in the habit of contention—against the world, against each other, against ourselves.

It is not from ourselves that we will learn to be better than we are.

*

In spite of all the talk about the law of tooth and fang and the struggle for survival, there is in the lives of the animals and birds a great peacefulness. It is not all fear and flight, pursuit and killing. That is part of it, certainly; and there is cold and hunger; there is the likelihood that death, when it comes, will be violent. But there is peace, too, and I think that the intervals of peace are frequent and prolonged. These are the times when the creature rests, communes with himself or with his kind, takes pleasure in being alive.

This morning while I wrote I was aware of a fox squirrel hunched in the sunlight on a high elm branch beyond my window. The night had been frosty, and now the warmth returned. He stayed there a long time, warming and grooming himself. Was he not at peace? Was his life not pleasant to him then?

I have seen the same peacefulness in a flock of wood ducks perched above the water in the branches of a fallen beech, preening and dozing in the sunlight of an autumn afternoon. Even while they dozed they had about them the exquisite alertness of wild things. If I had shown myself they would have been instantly in the air. But for the time there was no alarm among them, and no fear. The moment was whole in itself, satisfying to them and to me.

Or the sense of it may come with watching a flock of cedar waxwings eating wild grapes in the top of the woods on a November afternoon. Everything they do is leisurely. They pick the grapes with a curious deliberation, comb their feathers, converse in high windy whistles. Now and then one will fly out and back in a sort of dancing flight full of whimsical flutters and turns. They are like farmers loafing in their own fields on Sunday. Though they have no Sundays, their days are full of sabbaths.

*

One clear fine morning in early May, when the river was flooded, my friend and I came upon four rough-winged swallows circling over the water, which was still covered with frail wisps and threads of mist from the cool night. They were bathing, dipping down to the water until they touched the still surface with a little splash. They wound their flight over the water like the graceful falling loops of a fine cord. Later they perched on a dead willow, low to the water, to dry and groom themselves, the four together. We paddled the canoe almost within reach of them before they flew. They were neat, beautiful, gentle birds. Sitting there preening in the sun after their cold bath, they communicated a sense of domestic integrity, the serenity of living within order. We didn't belong within the order of the events and needs of their day, and so they didn't notice us until they had to.

*

But there is not only peacefulness, there is joy. And the joy, less deniable in its evidence than the peacefulness, is the confirmation of it. I sat one summer evening and watched a great blue heron make his descent from the top of the hill into the valley. He came down at a measured deliberate pace, stately as always, like a dignitary going down a stair. And then, at a point I judged to be midway over the river, without at all varying his wingbeat he did a backward turn in the air, a loop-the-loop. It could only have been a gesture of pure exuberance, of joy—a speaking of his sense of the evening, the day's fulfillment, his descent homeward. He made just the one slow turn, and then flew on out of sight in the direction of a slew farther down in the bottom. The movement was incredibly beautiful, at once exultant and stately, a benediction on the evening and on the river and on me. It seemed so perfectly to confirm the presence of a free nonhuman joy in the world—a joy I feel a great need to believe in—that I had the skeptic's impulse to doubt that I had seen it. If I had, I thought, it would be a sign of the presence of something heavenly in the earth. And then, one evening a year later, I saw it again.

*

Every man is followed by a shadow which is his death—dark, featureless, and mute. And for every man there is a place where his shadow is clarified and is made his reflection, where his face is mirrored in the ground. He sees his source and his destiny, and they are acceptable to him. He becomes the follower of what pursued him. What hounded his track becomes his companion.

That is the myth of my search and my return.

*

I have been walking in the woods, and have lain down on the ground to rest. It is the middle of October, and around me, all through the woods, the leaves are quietly sifting down. The newly fallen leaves make a dry, comfortable bed, and I lie easy, coming to rest within myself as I seem to do nowadays only when I am in the woods.

And now a leaf, spiraling down in wild flight, lands on my shirt at about the third button below the collar. At first I am bemused and mystified by the coincidence—that the leaf should have been so hung, weighted and shaped, so ready to fall, so nudged loose and slanted by the breeze, as to fall where I, by the same delicacy of circumstance, happened to be lying. The event, among all its ramifying causes and considerations, and finally its mysteries, begins to take on the magnitude of history. Portent begins to dwell in it.

And suddenly I apprehend in it the dark proposal of the ground. Under the fallen leaf my breastbone burns with imminent decay. Other leaves fall. My body begins its long shudder into humus. I feel my substance escape me, carried into the mold by beetles and worms. Days, winds, seasons pass over me as I sink under the leaves. For a time only sight is left me, a passive awareness of the sky overhead, birds crossing, the mazed interreaching of the treetops, the leaves falling—and then that, too, sinks away. It is acceptable to me, and I am at peace.

When I move to go, it is as though I rise up out of the world.

II

Nick and
Aunt Georgie

When I was three years old Nick Watkins, a black man, came to work for my Grandfather Berry. I don't remember when he came, which is to say that I don't remember not knowing him. When I was older and Nick and I would reminisce about the beginnings of our friendship, he used to laugh and tell me that when he first came I would follow him around calling him Tommy. Tommy was the hand who had lived there just before Nick. It was one of those conversations that are repeated ritually between friends. I would ask Nick to tell how it had been when he first came, and he would tell about me calling him Tommy, and he would laugh. At the age of eight or nine the story was very important to me because it meant that Nick and I had known each other since way back, and were old buddies.

I have no idea of Nick's age when I first knew him.

He must have been in his late fifties, and he worked for us until his death in, I believe, 1945 — a period of about eight years. During that time one of my two or three chief ambitions was to be with him. With my brother or by myself, I dogged his steps. So faithful a follower, and so young and self-important and venturesome as I was, I must have been a trial to him. But he never ran out of patience.

From something philosophical and serene in that patience, and from a few things he said to me, I know that Nick had worked hard ever since his childhood. He told me that when he was a small boy he had worked for a harsh white woman, a widow or a spinster. When he milked, the cow would often kick the bucket over, and he would have to carry it back to the house empty, and the white woman would whip him. He had worked for hard bosses. Like thousands of others of his race he had lived from childhood with the knowledge that his fate was to do the hardest of work for the smallest of wages, and that there was no hope of living any other way.

White people thought of Nick as "a good nigger," and within the terms of that designation he had lived his life. But in my memory of him, and I think in fact, he was possessed of a considerable dignity. I think this was because there was a very conscious peace and faithfulness that he had made between himself and his lot. When there was work to be done, he did it dependably and steadily and well, and thus escaped the indignity of being bossed. I do not remember seeing him servile or obsequious. My grandfather, within the bounds of the racial bias, thought highly of him. He admired him particularly, I remember, as a teamster, and was always pointing him out to me as an example: "Look a yonder how old Nick sets up to drive his mules. Look how he takes hold of the lines. Remember that, and you'll know something."

In the eight or so years that Nick lived on the place,

he and my grandfather spent hundreds and hundreds of work days together. When Nick first came there my grandfather was already in his seventies. Beyond puttering around and "seeing to things," which he did compulsively as long as he could stand up, he had come to the end of his working time. But despite the fact that my father had quietly begun to make many of the decisions in the running of the farm, and had assumed perhaps most of the real worries of running it, the old man still thought of himself as the sovereign ruler there, and it could be a costly mistake to attempt to deal with him on the assumption that he wasn't. He still got up at four o'clock as he always had, and when Nick and the other men on the place went to work he would be with them, on horseback, following the mule teams to the field. He rode a big bay mare named Rose; he would continue to ride her past the time when he could get into the saddle by himself. Through the long summer days he would stay with Nick, sitting and watching and talking, reminiscing, or riding behind him as he drove the rounds of a pasture on a mowing machine. When there was work that he could do, he would work until he tired out, and then he would invent an errand so he could get away with dignity.

Given Nick's steadiness at work, I don't think my grandfather stayed with him to boss him. I think he stayed so close because he couldn't stand not to be near what was going on, and because he needed the company of men of his own kind, working men. I have the clearest memory of the two of them passing again and again in the slowly shortening rounds of a big pasture, Nick driving a team of good black mules hitched to a mowing machine, my grandfather on the mare always only two or three steps behind the cutter bar. I don't know where I am in the memory, perhaps watching from the shade of some bush in a fencerow. In the bright hot sun of the summer day they pass out of sight and the whole landscape falls quiet. And then I hear the chuckling of the machine again, and then I see the mules' ears and my grandfather's hat appear over the top of the ridge, and they all come back into sight and pass around again. Within the steady monotonous racket of the machine, they keep a long silence, rich, it seems to me, with the deep camaraderie of men who have known hard work all their lives. Though their long labor in barns and fields had been spent in radically different states of mind, with radically different expectations, it was a common ground and a bond between them—never by men of their different colors, in that time and place, to be openly acknowledged or spoken of. Nick drives on and on into the day, deep in his silence, erect, alert and solemn faced with the patience that has kept with him through thousands of such days before, the elemental reassurance that dinnertime will come, and then quitting time, supper and rest. Behind him as the day lengthens, my grandfather dozes on the mare; when he sways in the saddle the mare steps under him, keeping him upright. Nick would claim that the mare did this out of a conscious sense of responsibility, and maybe she did.

On those days I know that Nick lived in constant fear that the mare too would doze and step over the cutter bar, and would be cut and would throw her rider before the mules could be stopped. Despite my grandfather's unshakable devotion to the idea that he was still in charge of things, it was clearly Nick who bore the great responsibility of those days. Because of childishness or whatever, the old man absolutely refused to accept the limits of age. He was fiercely headstrong in everything, and so was constantly on the verge of doing some damage to himself. I can see Nick working along, pretending not to watch him, but watching him all the same out the corner of his eye, and then hustling anxiously to the rescue: "Whoa, boss. Whoa. Wait, boss." When he had my brother and me, and maybe another boy or two, to look after as well, Nick must have been driven well nigh out of his mind, but he never showed it.

When they were in the mowing or other such work, Nick and my grandfather were hard to associate with. Of course we could get on horseback ourselves and ride along behind the old man's mare, but it was impossible to talk and was consequently boring. But there was other work, such as fencing or the handwork in the crops, that allowed the possibility of conversation, and whenever we could we got into that—in everybody's way, whether we played or tried to help, often getting scolded, often aware when we were not being scolded that we were being stoically put up with, but occasionally getting the delicious sense that we were being kindly indulged and catered to for all our sakes, or more rarely that we were being of use.

I remember one fine day we spent with Nick and our grandfather, cutting a young sassafras thicket that had grown up on the back of the place. Nick would fell the little trees with his ax, cutting them off about waist high, so that when they sprouted the cattle would browse off the foliage and so finally kill them. We would pile the trees high on the sled, my brother and I would lie on the mass of springy branches, in the spiced sweetness of that foliage, among the pretty leaves and berries, and Nick would drive us down the hill to unload the sled in a wash that our grandfather was trying to heal.

That was quiet slow work, good for talk. At such times the four of us would often go through a conversation about taking care of Nick when he got old. I don't remember how this conversation would start. Perhaps Nick would bring the subject up out of some anxiety he had about it. But our grandfather would say, "Don't you worry, Nick. These boys'll take care of you."

And one of us would say, "Yes sir, Nick, we sure will."

And our grandfather would shake his head in sober emphasis and say, "By God, they'll do it!"

Usually, then, there would follow an elaborately detailed fantasy in which Nick would live through a long carefree old age, with good foxhounds and time to hunt, looked after by my brother and me who by then would have grown up to be lawyers or farmers.

Another place we used to talk was in the barn. Usually this would be on a rainy day, or in the late evening after work. Nick and the old man would sit in the big doorway on upturned buckets, gazing out into the lot. They would talk about old times. Or we would all talk about horses, and our grandfather would go through his plan to buy six good colts for my brother and me to break and train. Or we would go through the plan for Nick's old age.

Or our grandfather would get into a recurrent plan all his own about buying a machine, which was his word for automobile. According to the plan, he would buy a good new machine, and Nick would drive it, and they would go to town and to "Louis-ville" and maybe other places. The intriguing thing about this plan was that it was based on the old man's reasoning that since Nick was a fine teamster he was therefore a fine automobile driver. Which Nick wasn't; he couldn't drive an automobile at all. But as long as Nick lived, our grandfather clung to that dream of buying a good machine. Under the spell of his own talk about it, he always believed that he was right on the verge of doing it.

We also talked about the war that was being fought "across the waters." The two men were deeply impressed with the magnitude of the war and with the ominous new weapons that were being used in it. I remember sitting there in the barn door one day and hearing our grandfather say to Nick: "They got cannons now that'll shoot clean across the water. Good God Amighty!" I suppose he meant the English Channel, but I thought then that he meant the ocean. It was one of the ways the war and modern times became immediate to my imagination.

A place I especially liked to be with Nick was at the woodpile. At his house and at my grandparents' the cooking was still done on wood ranges, and Nick had to keep both kitchens supplied with stove wood. The logs would be laid up in a sawbuck and sawed to the proper lengths with a crosscut saw, and then the sawed lengths would be split on the chopping block with an ax. It was a daily thing throughout the year, but more wood was needed of course in the winter than in the summer. When I was around I would often help Nick with the sawing, and then sit up on the sawbuck to watch while he did the splitting, and then I would help him carry the wood in to the woodbox in the kitchen. Those times I would carry on long conversations, mostly by myself; Nick, who needed his breath for the work, would reply in grunts and monosyllables.

Summer and winter he wore two pairs of pants, usually an old pair of dress pants with a belt under a pair of bib overalls, swearing they kept him cool in hot weather and warm in cold. Like my grandfather, he often wore an old pair of leather puttees, or he would have his pants legs tied snugly above his shoe tops with a piece of twine. This, he liked to tell us, was to keep the snakes and mice from running up his britches legs. He wore old felt hats that were stained and sweaty and shaped to his character. He had a sober open dignified face and gentle manners, was quick to smile and to laugh. His teeth were amber-stained from chewing tobacco. His hands were as hard as leather; one of my hopes was someday to have hands as hard as his. He seemed instinctively to be a capable handler of stock. He could talk untiringly of good saddle horses and good work teams that he had known. He was an incurable fox hunter and was never without a hound or two. I think he found it easy to be solitary and quiet.

I heard my grandfather say to him one day: "Nick, you're the first darkie I ever saw who didn't sing while he worked."

But there were times, *I* knew, when Nick did sing. It was only one little snatch of a song that he sang. When the two of us would go on horseback to the store or to see about some stock—Nick on my grandfather's mare, I on a pony—and we had finished our errand and started home, Nick would often sing: "Get along home, home, Cindy, get along home!" And he would laugh.

"Sing it again," I would say.

And he would sing it again.

But before I can tell any more about Nick, I will have to tell about Aunt Georgie. She came to live in the little two-room house with Nick in perhaps the third year he worked for us. Why did we call her Aunt when we never called Nick Uncle? I suppose it was because Nick was informal and she was formal. I remember my grandparents insisting that my brother and I should say Uncle Nick, but we would never do it. Our friendship was somehow too democratic for that. They might as well have insisted that we boys call each other mister. But we used the title Aunt Georgie from the first. She was a woman of a rather stiff dignity and a certain aloofness, and the term of respect was clearly in order.

She was short and squat, bowlegged, bent, her hands crooked with arthritis, her two or three snaggling front teeth stained with snuff. I suppose she was ugly— though I don't believe I ever made that judgment in those days. She looked like Aunt Georgie, who looked like nobody else.

Her arrival at Nick's house suddenly made that one of the most intriguing places that my brother and I had ever known. We began to spend a lot of our time there just sitting and talking. She would always greet us and make us at home with a most gracious display of pleasure in seeing us. Though she could cackle with delight like an old child, though she would periodically interrupt her conversation to spit ambeer into a coffee can she kept beside her chair, there was always a reserve about her, an almost haughty mannerliness that gave a peculiar sense of *occasion* to these visits. When she would invite us to eat supper, as she some-times did, her manner would impose a curious self-con-sciousness on us—not a *racial* self-consciousness, but the demanding self-consciousness of a child who has been made, in the fullest sense, the guest of an adult, and of whom therefore a certain dignity is expected. Her house was one of the few places I visited as a child where I am certain I always behaved well. There was something in her presence that kept you always conscious of how you were acting; in response to her you became capable of social del-icacy.

Thinking of her now, in spite of my rich experience of her, I realize how little I really *know* about her. The same is true of Nick. I knew them as a child knows people, as they revealed themselves to a child. What they were in themselves, as they spoke to each other, or thought in soli-tude, I can only surmise from that child's knowledge. I will never know.

Aunt Georgie had lived in a small rural community thirty or forty miles away. She had also lived in Louisville, where I believe she had relatives. She was a great reader of the Bible, and I assume of tracts of various sorts, and I don't know what else. The knowledge that came out in her talk—fantastical, superstitious, occult, theological, Bibli-cal, autobiographical, medical, historical—was amazing in extent and volume. She was one of the most intricate and powerful characters I have ever known. Perhaps not twenty-five per cent of her knowledge was subject to any kind of proof—a lot of it was the stuff of unwritten fairy tales and holy books, a lot I think she had made up herself—but all of it, every last occult or imaginary scrap of it, was caught up and held together in the force of her personality. As with artistic geniuses or witches or priestesses, nothing was odd to her, nothing she knew stood aside from her unassimilated into the restless wayward omnivorous force of her mind. I write of her with fear that I will misrepresent or underestimate her. I believe she had great intelligence, which had been forced to grow and form itself on the strange straggling wildly heterogeneous bits of information that sifted down to her through various leaks in the stratification of white society.

The character of Aunt Fanny in my book *A Place on Earth* is to some extent modeled on Aunt Georgie: "She is an accomplished seamstress, and the room is filled with her work: quilts, crocheted doilies, a linen wall-hanging with the Lord's Prayer embroidered on it in threads of many colors. In the house she is nearly always occupied with her needle, always complaining of her dim eyesight and arthritic hands. Her dark hands, though painfully crooked and drawn by the disease, are still . . . dexterous and capable. She is always anointing them with salves and ointments of her own making. The fingers wear rings made of copper wire, which she believes to have the power of prevention and healing. She is an excellent persistent canny gardener. The garden beside the house is her work. She makes of its small space an amplitude . . . rows of vegetables and flowers—and herbs, for which she knows the recipes and the uses." If that is her daylight aspect, there is also an aspect of darkness: ". . . the quilts on the bed or the quilting frame . . . always seem threatened, like earthquake country, by an ominous nearness of darkness in the character of their creator. Aunt Fanny has seen the Devil, not once but often, especially in her youth, and she calls him familiarly by his name: Red Sam. Her obsessions are Hell and Africa, and she has the darkest, most fire-lit notions of both. Her idea of Africa is a hair-raising blend of lore and hearsay and imagination. She thinks of it with nostalgia and longing — a kind of earthly Other Shore, Eden or Heaven — and yet she fears it because of its presumed darkness, its endless jungles, its stock of deliberately malevolent serpents and man-eating beasts. And by the thought of Hell she's held as endlessly fascinated as if her dearest ambition is to go there. She can talk at any length about it, cataloguing its tortures and labyrinths in almost loving detail . . . Stooped in the light of a coal-oil lamp at night, following her finger down some threatening page of the Bible, her glasses opaquely reflecting the yellow of the lamp, her pigtails sticking out like compass points around her head, she looks like a black Witch of Endor.

"She possesses a nearly inexhaustible lore of snakes and deaths, bottomless caves and pools, mysteries and ghosts and wonders."

But the purpose of Aunt Fanny in that book is not to represent Aunt Georgie, and she comes off as a much simpler character. Aunt Fanny had spent all her life in the country, but Aunt Georgie had lived for some time in the city, and her mind, in its way of rambling and sampling, had become curiously cosmopolitan. Like Aunt Fanny, she had an obsession with Africa, but I think it must have started with her under the influence of the Back to Africa movement. She must at some time or other have heard speakers involved in this movement, for I remember her quoting someone who said, "Don't let them tell you they won't know you when you go back. They know their own people, and they'll *welcome* you." There was much more of this talk, but I had no context in which to place it and understand it, and so I have lost the memory. She used to tell a lot of stories about Africa, and I remember only one of them: a story of a woman and her small child who some- how happened to be passing through the jungle alone. A lion was following them, and the woman was terrified. They ran on until they were exhausted and could go no farther. Not knowing what else to do, the woman resigned herself and sat down to wait for death. And the lion came up to them. But instead of attacking, he walked calmly up and laid his paw in the woman's lap. She saw that the paw had a thorn in it that had made a very sore wound. She re- moved the thorn and treated the wound, and the lion be- came her protector, driving away the other large animals that threatened them in the jungle, hunting and providing for them, and in all ways taking care of them. I suppose I remember that story among all the others she told because I visualized it very clearly as she told it; it has stayed in my mind all these years with the straightforwardness and in- nocence of a Rousseau painting, but darker, the foliage ranker and more blurred in detail. But also I have remem- bered it, I think, because of the sense that began then, and that remains poignant in the memory, that the lion had be- come the woman's husband.

It was from Aunt Georgie, sitting and listening to her by the hour when I was seven and eight and nine and ten years old, that I first heard talk of the question of civil rights for Negroes. Again, I could supply no context for what I heard, and so have forgotten most of it. But one phrase has stuck in my mind along with her manner of say- ing it. She said that many times the white people had prom- ised the Negro people "a right to the flag," and they never had given it to them. The old woman was capable of a mov- ing eloquence, and I was deeply disturbed by what she said. I remember that, and I remember the indignation of my white elders when I would try to check the point with them. After Aunt Georgie moved away it was probably ten years before I paid attention to any more talk about civil rights, and it was longer than that before I felt again anything like the same disturbed sense of personal responsibility that she made me feel.

She used to tell a story about the end of the First World War, of people dancing wildly through the streets, carrying the Kaiser's head impaled on the end of a fence rail. I keep a clear image of that scene, too. Was it some celebration she had seen in Louisville, at which the Kaiser had been mutilated in effigy? Was it something she had read or imagined? I don't know. I assumed then that it was really the Kaiser's head, that she had seen that barbaric celebration herself, and that it was one of the central events of the history of the world.

Germany was also a sort of obsession with her, I suppose because of the two world wars, and she had nothing good to say for it. If to her Africa was a darkish jungly place of marvels that enticed the deepest roots of her imagination, Germany was a medieval torture chamber, a place of dire purposes and devices, pieces of diabolical machinery. In her sense of it the guillotine had come to be its emblem. It was a sort of earthly hell where people were sent to be punished for such crimes as public drunkenness. According to her, if you were caught drunk once you were *warned,* if you were caught twice you were put in jail, but the *third* time you were put on the train and sent to Germany where the Kaiser would cut your head off. She told of a man and his son in the town of Finchville, Kentucky, who had been caught drunk for the third time. The people of the town went down to the railroad station to witness their departure for Germany. Through the coach windows the doomed father and son could be seen finding an empty seat and sitting down together to begin their awesome journey. Over the condemned men and over the watching crowd there hung a great heaviness of finality and fate and horror.

She told it as one who had been there and had seen it. And I remember it as if *I* had seen it; it is as vivid in my mind as anything that ever happened to *me*. The first time I heard her tell that story I believe I must have spent an hour or two cross-examining her, trying to find some small mitigation of the implacable finality of it, and she would not yield me the tiniest possibility of hope. Thinking about it now I feel the same contraction of despair that I felt then.

She told about awful sicknesses, and acts of violence, and terrible deaths. There was once a lion tamer who used to put his head in a lion's mouth, and one morning he nicked himself shaving and when he put his head into the lion's mouth that day, the lion tasted his blood and bit his head off. She talked about burials, bodies lying in the ground, dug-up bodies, ghosts.

And snakes. She believed that woman should bruise the head of the serpent with her heel. She would snick them up into little pieces with her sharp hoe. But they fascinated her, too, and they lived in her mind with the incandescence that her imagination gave to everything it touched. She was full of the lore of snakes—little and big snakes, deadly poisonous snakes, infernal snakes, *blue* snakes, snakes with yellow stripes and bright red heads, snakes that sucked cows, snakes that swallowed large animals such as people, hoop snakes. Once there was a woman who was walking in the woods, and her feet got tired and she sat down on a log to rest, and she took off her shoe and beat it on the log to dislodge a rock that was in it, and slowly that log began to *move. My* goodness gracious sakes alive!

The most formidable snake of all was the hoop snake. The hoop snake traveled by the law of gravity—a concept as staggering to the mind as atomic energy or perpetual motion. The hoop snake could travel on his belly like any other snake, but when he found himself on the top of a hill he was apt to whip himself up into the shape of a wheel, and go flying off down the slope at a dazzling speed. Once he had started his descent, of course, he had no sense of direction, and no way to stop or to turn aside and he had a deadly poisonous sharp point on the end of his tail that killed whatever it touched. Trees, horses and cattle, cats, dogs, men, women, and even *boys* were all brought down, like grass before the breath of the Lord, in the furious free-wheeling descent of the hoop snake, quicker than the eye. How could you know when he was coming? You couldn't. How could you get out of his way? You couldn't.

It has occurred to me to wonder if there wasn't a degree of conscious delight that Aunt Georgie took in scaring the wits out of two gullible little white boys. I expect there was. There was undoubtedly some impulse of racial vengeance in it; and it was bound to have given her a sense of power. But there was no cynicism in it; she believed what she said. I think, in fact, that she was motivated somewhat by a spirit of evangelism; she was instructing us, warning us against human evils, alerting us to the presence of ominous powers. Also she must have been lonely; we were company for her, and these things that she had on her mind were what she naturally talked to us about. And probably beyond any other reasons was that, like all naturally talkative people, she loved to listen to herself and to provide herself with occasions for eloquence.

But she was also a tireless loving gardener, a rambler in the fields, a gatherer of herbs and mushrooms, a raiser of chickens. And she talked well about all these things. She was a marvelous teller of what went on around the farm: How the mules ran the goat and the goat jumped up in the loading chute, safe, and looked back at the mules and wagged his head as if to say, "Ah ha!" How the hawk got after her chickens, and how she got her old self out of the house just in time and said, "Whoooeee! Hi! Get *out* of here, you *devil* you, and don't you come *back!*"

She knew about healing herbs and tonics and poul-
tices and ointments. In those years I was always worrying
about being skinny. I knew from the comic books that a
ninety-eight-pound weakling was one of the worst things
you could grow up to be; I foresaw my fate, and dreaded it.
I confided my worry to Aunt Georgie, as I did to nearly
everybody who seemed willing to listen, and she instantly
prescribed a concoction known as Dr. Bell's Pine Tar
Honey. By propounding the cure she ratified the ill; no one
would ever persuade me again that I was not disastrously
skinny. But Dr. Bell's Pine Tar Honey was nowhere to be
found. No drugstore had it. The more I failed to find it,
the more I believed in its power. It could turn a skinny boy
into a *normal* boy. It was the elusive philosopher's stone
of my childhood. And Aunt Georgie stood by her truth.
She never quit recommending it. She would recommend no
substitute.

She and Nick never married, though I believe she
never abandoned the hope that they would. She always referred to Nick, flirtatiously and a little wistfully, as Nickum-Nackum. But Nick, with what I believe to have been
a very pointed discretion, always called her *Miss* Georgie.

*

If Aunt Georgie was formal and austere, Nick was
casual and familiar. If the bent of her mind was often
otherworldly, Nick's belonged incorrigibly to this world;
he was a man of the fields and the barns and the long night-
time courses of fox hunts. When he spoke of the Lord he
called him, as my grandfather did, the Old Marster, by
which they meant a god of mystery, the maker of weather
and seasons, of abundance and dearth, of growth and
death—a god far more remote, and far less talkative, than
the god of the churches.

A lot of nights after I had finished supper in my

grandmother's kitchen I would walk down across the field to where Nick's house sat at the corner of the woods. He would come out, lighting his pipe, and we would sit down on the stones of the doorstep, and Nick would smoke and we would talk while it got dark and the stars came out. Up the hill we could see the lighted windows of my grandparents' house. In front of us the sloping pasture joined the woods. The woods would become deep and softly massive in its darkness. At dusk a toad frog who lived under the doorstep would come out, and always we would notice him and Nick would comment that he lived there and that he came out every night. Often as we sat there, comfortable with all the outdoors and the night before us, Aunt Georgie would be sitting by the lamp in the house behind us, reading aloud from the Bible, or trying to lecture to Nick on the imminence of eternity, urging him to think of the salvation of his soul. Nick's reluctance to get disturbed over such matters was always a worry to her. Occasionally she would call out the door: "Nickum-Nackum? Are you listening to me?" And Nick would serenely interrupt whatever he was telling me—"Yessum, Miss Georgie"—and go on as before.

What we would often be talking about was a fine fox hound named Waxy that Nick had owned a long time ago. He would tell of the old fox hunts, saying who the hunters had been and what kind of dogs they'd had. He would tell over the whole course of some hunt. By the time the race was over his Waxy would always have far outdistanced all the other dogs, and everybody would have exclaimed over what a great, fleet, wise hound she was, and perhaps somebody would have tried to buy her from Nick at a high price, which Nick never would take. Thinking about it since, I have had the feeling that those dogs so far outhunted and outrun by Nick's Waxy were white men's dogs. But I don't know for sure. In addition to telling how well Waxy had performed in some fox race or other, Nick would always tell how she looked, how she was marked and made. And he would frequently comment that Waxy was a fine name for a foxhound. He had thought a lot about how things ought to be named. In his mind he had lists of the best names for milk cows and horses and dogs. Blanche, I remember, he thought to be the prettiest name for a certain kind of light-coated Jersey cow. As long as he was with us I don't think he ever had the luck to give that name to a cow. Among others whose names I have forgotten, I remember that he milked one he called Mrs. Williams.

There were certain worldly ideals that always accompanied him, as hauntingly, I think, as Aunt Georgie was accompanied by devils and angels and snakes and ghosts. There was the ideal foxhound and the ideal team of mules and the ideal saddle horse, and he could always name some animal he had known that had not been quite perfect but had come close. Someday he would like to own a foxhound like Waxy but just a little better. Someday he would like to work a team of gray mare mules each just a little better than the one named Fanny that my grandfather owned.

We talked a great deal about the ideal saddle horse, because I persistently believed that I was going to pick out and buy one of my own. In the absence of any particular horse that I intended to buy, the conversational possibilities of this subject were nearly without limit. Listing points of color, conformation, breeding, disposition, size, and gait, we would arrive within a glimpse of the elusive outlines of the ideal. And then, supposing some divergence from one of the characteristics we had named, we might prefigure a horse of another kind. We were like those experts who from a track or a single bone can reconstruct an extinct animal: give us a color or a trait of conformation or character, and we could produce a horse to go with it. And once we had the horse, we had to settle on a name and on the way it should be broke and fed and kept.

But our *great* plan, the epic of our conversation, was to go camping and hunting in the mountains. I don't think that either Nick or my brother and I knew very much about the mountains. None of us had been there. My own idea seems to have blended what I had read of the virgin Kentucky woods of Boone's time with Aunt Georgie's version of Africa. My brother and I believed there was a great tract of wilderness in the mountains, thickly populated with deer and bears and black panthers and mountain lions. We thought we would go up there and kill some of those beasts and eat their flesh and dress in their skins and make ornaments and weapons out of their long teeth, and live in the untouched maidenhood of history.

I don't know what idea Nick may have had of the mountains; he always seemed more or less to go along with our idea of them; whether or not he contributed to the notions we had, I don't remember. Though he was an ignorant man, he was knowing and skilled in the realities that had been available to him, and so he was bound to have known that we would never make any such trip. But he elaborated this plan with us year after year; it was, in fact, in many ways more his creature than ours. It was generous—one of the most generous things anybody ever did for us. And yet it was more than generous, for I think Nick believed in that trip as a novelist believes in his novel: his imagination was touched by it; he couldn't resist it.

We were going to get new red tassels to hang on the mules' harness, and polish the brass knobs on their hames. And then one night we were going to load the wagon—we had told over many times what all we were going to put in it. And the next morning early, way before daylight so my grandfather wouldn't catch us, we would slip off and go to the mountains. We had a highly evolved sense of the grandeur of the spectacle we would make as we went through New Castle, where everybody who saw us, of course, would know where we were going and what a fine adventure it was. Here we would come through the town just as everybody was getting up and out into the street. Nick would be driving, my brother and I sitting on either side of him, his ready henchmen. We would have the mules in a spanking trot, the harness jangling, the red tassels swinging, and everything fine—right on through town past the last house. From there to the tall wilderness where we would make our camp we had no plans. The trip didn't interest us after people we knew quit watching.

When we got to the mountains we were going to build a log cabin, and we talked a lot about the proper design and construction of that. And there were any number of other matters, such as cooking, and sewing the clothes we would make out of the skins of animals. Sometimes, talking of the more domestic aspects of our trip, we would get into a bind and have to plan to take Aunt Georgie. She never could work up much enthusiasm for the project; it was too mundane for her.

There were several times when we actually named the day of our departure, and my brother and I went to bed expecting to leave in the morning. We had agreed that to wake us up Nick would rattle a few tin cans in the milk bucket. But we never woke up until too late. I remember going out one morning and finding the very tin cans that Nick had rattled floating in the rain barrel. Later I realized that of course Nick had never rattled those cans or any others. But in the years since I have often imagined him taking the time to put those cans there for me to see, and then slipping off to his day's work—conspiring with himself like Santa Claus to deceive and please me.

In the present time, when the working man in the old sense of the phrase is so rapidly disappearing from the scene, his conversation smothered in the noise of machinery, it may be necessary to point out that such talk as we carried on with Nick was by no means uncommon among the farming people of that place, and I assume of other places as well. It was one of the natural products and pleasures of the life there. With the hands occupied in the work, the mind was set free; and since there was often considerable misery in the work, the mind turned naturally to what would be desirable or pleasant. When one was at work with people with whom one had worked many days or years before, one naturally spoke of the good things that were on one's mind. And once the conversation was started, it began to be a source of pleasure in itself, producing and requiring an energy that propelled it beyond the bounds of reality or practicality. As long as one was talking about what would be good, why not go ahead and talk about what would be *really* good? My childhood was surrounded by a communal daydreaming, the richest sort of imaginative talk, that began in this way—in work, in the misery of work, to make the work bearable and even pleasant. Such talk ranged all the way from a kind of sensuous realism to utter fantasy, but because the bounds of possibility were almost always ignored I would say that the impetus was always that of fantasy. I have heard crews of men, weary and hungry and hot near the end of a day's work, construct long elaborate conversations on the subject of what would be good to eat and drink, dwelling at length and with subtlety on the taste and the hotness or the coldness of various dishes and beverages, and on combinations of dishes and beverages, the menu lengthening far beyond the capacity of any living stomach. I knew one man who every year got himself through the ordeal of the tobacco harvest by elaborating from one day to the next the fantasy of an epical picnic and celebration which was always to occur as soon as the work was done—and which never did occur except in the minds of his listeners. Such talk could be about anything: where you would like to go, what you would like to do when you got there, what you would like to be able to buy, what would be a good kind of a farm, what science was likely to do, and so on.

Nick often had fox hunting on his mind, and he always knew where there was a fox, and he was always going to hunt as soon as he had time. Occasionally he *would* have time—a wet afternoon or a night when he didn't feel too tired—and he would go, and would sometimes take one of us. I like the thought of Nick, alone as he often was, out in the woods and the fields at night with his dogs. I think he transcended his lot then, and was free in the countryside and in himself—beyond anybody's knowledge of where he was and anybody's notion of what he ought to do and anybody's claim on his time, his dogs mouthing out there in the dark, and all his senses with them, discovering the way the fox had gone. I don't remember much about any hunt I ever made with him, but I do remember the sense of accompanying him outside the boundaries of his life as a servant, into that part of his life that clearly belonged to him, in which he was competent and knowing. And I remember how it felt to be riding sleepily along on the pony late at night, the country all dark around us, not talking, not sure where we were going. Nick would be ahead of me on old Rose, and I could hear her footsteps soft on the grass, or hard on the rocks when we crossed a creek. I knew that Nick knew where we were, and I felt comfortable and familiar with the dark because of that.

When Joe Louis fought we would eat supper and then walk across the fields to the house of the man who was raising my grandfather's tobacco; we would have been planning for days to go there to hear the fight on the radio. My grandparents had a radio, too, but Nick would never have thought of going there. That he felt comfortable in

going to another household of white people and sitting
down by the radio with them was always a little embarras-
sing to me, and it made me a little jealous. And yet I understood it, and never questioned it. It was one of those complex operations of race consciousness that a small child
will comprehend with his feelings, and yet perhaps never
live long enough to unravel with his mind. The prowess of
Joe Louis, anyhow, was something Nick liked to talk
about; it meant a great deal to him. And so the champion-
ship matches of those days were occasions when I felt
called on to manifest my allegiance to Nick. Though I
could have listened to the fight in my grandparents' living
room, I would go with Nick, and the more my grandmother declared she didn't know why I had to do that the
more fierce and clear my loyalty to Nick became.

The people of that house had a boy a little older
than I was, and so I also had my own reasons for going
there. We boys would listen to the fight and then, while the
grownups talked, go out to play, or climb the sugar pear
trees and sit up in the branches, eating. And then holding
Nick's hand, I would walk with him back home across the
dark fields.

One winter there suddenly appeared in the neighborhood a gaunt possessed-looking white man who was, as
people said, "crazy on religion" or "religious crazy." He
was, I believe, working on a nearby farm. Somehow he discovered Aunt Georgie, and found that she could quote the
Bible and talk on religion as long as he could. He called
Nick Mix, and so in derision and reprisal Nick and my
brother and I called *him* Mix, and that was the only name
we ever knew him by. We would see him coming over the
hill, his ragged clothes flapping in the cold wind, and see
him go into the little house. And then after a while we
would go down, too, and listen. The tone of their conversations was very pious and oratorical; they more or less

preached at each other, and the sessions would go on for hours.

Of it all, I remember only a little fragment: Mix, sitting in a chair facing Aunt Georgie, sticks his right hand out into the air between them, dramatically, and asks her to put hers out there beside it. She does, and then he raises his left hand like a Roman orator and, glaring into her eyes, says: "There they are, Auntie! *There* they are! Look at 'em! One of 'em's white, and one of 'em's black! But *inside,* they both white!"

What impresses me now, as I remember those times, is that while Mix was never anything but crazy and absurd, ranting mad, Aunt Georgie always seemed perfectly dignified and sane. It seems to me that this testifies very convincingly to the strength of her intelligence: she had *comprehended* the outlandishness of her own mind, and so she could keep a sort of grace before the unbridled extravagance of his. In her way she had faced the worst. The raging of Lear himself would not have perturbed her; she would have told him stories worse than his, and referred him to the appropriate Scripture. To Nick, who took a very detached and secular view of most things, these sessions were a source of ironic amusement. He liked to look over at us through the thick of the uproar and wink.

*

There is an inescapable tentativeness in writing of one's own formative experiences: as long as the memory of them stays alive they *remain* formative; the power of growth and change remains in them, and they never become quite predictable in their influence. If memory is in a way the ancestor of consciousness, it yet remains dynamic within consciousness. And so, though I can write about Nick and Aunt Georgie as two of the significant ancestors of my mind, I must also deal with their memory as a live resource, a *power* that will live and change in me as long as I live. To fictionalize them, as I did Aunt Georgie to some extent in *A Place on Earth,* would be to give them an imaginative stability at the cost of oversimplifying them. To attempt to tell the "truth" about them as they really were is to resign oneself to enacting a small fragment of an endless process. Their truth is inexhaustible both in their lives as they were, and in my life as I think they were.

The peculiar power of my memory of them comes, I think, from the fact that all my association with them occurred within a tension between the candor and openness of a child's view of things, and the racial contrivances of the society we lived in. As I have already suggested, there were times when I was inescapably aware of the conflict between what I felt about them, in response to what I knew of them, and the feelings that were prescribed to me by the society's general prejudice against their race. Being with them, it was hard to escape for very long from the sense of racial difference prepared both in their minds and in my own.

The word *nigger* might be thought of as rattling around, with devastating noise and impact, within a silence, a black-man-shaped hollow, inside our language. When the word was spoken abstractly, I believe that it seemed as innocuous and casual to me as any other word. I used it that way myself, in the *absence* of black people, without any consciousness that I was participating in a judgment and a condemnation; certainly I used it without any feeling that my use of it manifested anything that was wrong with *me.* But when it was used with particular reference to a person one cared for, as a child cares, it took on a tremendous force; its power reached ominously over one's sense of things. I remember the shock and confusion I felt one night when, saying good-bye to Nick, I impulsively kissed his hand, which I had held as we brought the milk to the house, and then came into the kitchen to hear: "Lord, child, how can you kiss that old nigger's hand?"

And I remember sitting down at Nick's house one day when he and Aunt Georgie had company. There was a little boy, four or five years old, who was rambunctious and continually on the verge of mischief. To keep him in hand Nick would lean over and rattle his old leather leggings that he had taken off and put behind the drum stove, and he would say to the boy: "John's going to get you. If you don't quit that, John's going to get you." All this—the rattling of the leggings, the threat, the emphatic result—impressed me a good deal, and I wondered about it. Was this John-the-Leggings somebody Nick had thought up on the spur of the moment? Was he one of the many associates of Red Sam? And then it hit me. That John that my friend Nick was speaking of in so formidable a tone was my father! The force of a realization like that is hardly to be measured; it's the sort of thing that can initiate a whole epoch of the development of a mind, and yet remain on as a force. It gave me the strongest sort of a hint of the existence of something large and implacable and rigid that I had been born into, and lived in—something I have been trying to get out of ever since. In justice to my father, I must say that I don't believe his name was used in this way because of anything he had *done,* but because of his place in the system. In spite of my grandfather's insistences to the contrary, Nick knew as I did that my father had become the man really in charge of things. Thus he had entered the formidable role of "boss man": whoever he was, whatever he did, he had the power and the austerity of that role; the society assigned it to him, as it assigned to Nick the role of "nigger."

That sense of difference, given the candor and the affection and the high spirits of children, could only beget in us its opposite: a strong sense of allegiance. Whenever there was a conflict of interest between Nick and Aunt Georgie and our family, neither my brother nor I ever hesitated to take the side of Nick and Aunt Georgie. We had an uncle who would make a game of insulting Nick in our presence because it tickled him the way we would come to the rescue; we would attack him and fight him as readily as if he had been another child. And there were winter Saturdays that we spent with our goat hitched to a little sled we had made, hauling coal from our grandfather's pile down to Nick's. That was stealing, and we knew it; it had the moral flair and the dangerous loyalty of the adventures of Robin Hood.

But the clearest of all my own acts of taking sides happened at a birthday party my grandmother gave for me when I must have been nine or ten years old. As I remember, she invited all the family and perhaps some of the neighbors. I issued one invitation of my own, to Nick. I believe that in my eagerness to have him come, assuming that as my friend he ought to be there, I foresaw none of the social awkwardness that I caused. But I had, in fact, surrounded us all with the worst sort of discomfort. Nick, trying to compromise between his wish to be kind to me and his embarrassment at my social misconception, quit work at the time of the party and came and sat on the cellar wall behind the house. By that time even I had begun to feel the uneasiness. I had done a thing more powerful than I could have imagined at the time; I had scratched the wound of racism, and all of us, our heads beclouded in the social dream that all was well, were feeling the pain. It was suddenly evident to me that Nick neither would nor could come into the house and be a member of the party. My grandmother, to her credit, allowed me to follow my instincts in dealing with the situation, and I did. I went out and spent the time of the party sitting on the cellar wall with Nick.

It was obviously the only decent thing I could have done; if I had thought of it in moral terms I would have had to see it as my duty. But I didn't. I didn't think of it in moral terms at all. I did simply what I *preferred* to do. If Nick had no place at my party, then I would have no place there either; my place would be where he was. The cellar wall became the place of the enactment of friendship, in which by the grace of a child's honesty and a man's simple-hearted generosity, we transcended our appointed roles. I like the thought of the two of us sitting out there in the sunny afternoon, eating ice cream and cake, with all my family and my presents in there in the house without me. I was full of a sense of loyalty and love that clarified me to myself as nothing ever had before. It was a time I would like to live again.

*

One day when we were all sitting in the barn door, resting and talking, my grandfather sat gazing out a while in silence, and then he pointed to a far corner of the lot and said: "When I'm dead, Nick, I want you to bury me there."

And Nick laughed and said, "Boss, you got to go farther away from here than that."

My grandfather's words bore the forlorn longing to remain in the place, in the midst of the work and the stirring, that had interested him all his life. It was also a characteristic piece of contrariness: if he didn't want to go, then by God he *wouldn't*. Nick's rejoinder admitted how tough it would be on everybody to have such a stubborn old boss staying on there forever, and it told a plain truth: there wasn't to be any staying; good as it might be to be there, we were all going to have to leave.

Those words stand in my memory in high relief;

strangely powerful then (it was an exchange that we younger ones quoted over and over in other conversations) they have assumed a power in retrospect that is even greater. That whole scene—the two old men, two or three younger ones, two boys, all looking out that big doorway at the world, and beyond the world—seems to me now not to belong to my childhood at all, but to stand like an illuminated capital at the head of the next chapter. It presages a series of deaths and departures and historical changes that would put an end both to my childhood and to the time and the way of life I knew as a child. Within two or three years of my tenth summer both Nick and my grandfather died, and after Nick's death Aunt Georgie moved away. Also the war ended, and our part of the country moved rapidly into the era of mechanized farming. People, especially those who had worked as hired hands in the fields, began to move to the cities, and the machines moved from the cities out into the fields. Soon nearly everybody had a tractor; the few horses and mules still left in the country were being kept only for old times' sake.

It was a school day in the winter and I was at home in New Castle eating breakfast, when my grandmother telephoned from the farm to tell us that Nick had had a stroke. He had eaten breakfast and was starting to go up to the barn when he fell down in the doorway. He had opened the door before he fell and Aunt Georgie was unable to move him, and so he had lain in the cold for some time before help came. Until he died a few days later he never moved or spoke. I wasn't allowed to go to see him, but afterward my grandmother told me how he had been. He lay there on his back, she said, unable to move, looking up at the ceiling. When she would come in he would recognize her; she could tell that by his eyes. And I am left with that image of him: lying there still as death, his life only showing in his eyes. As if I had been there, I am aware of the intelligence and the gentleness and the sorrow of his eyes. He had fallen completely into the silence that had so nearly surrounded him all his life. It was not the silence of death, which men may speak of with words, and so know each other. It was the racial silence in the speech of white men, the wound of their history, formed three hundred years before my birth to stand between him and me, so that when I think of him now, as important as his memory is to me, it must be partly to wonder if I knew him.

One night not long after Nick's death I went with my father down to the little house to see Aunt Georgie. She had a single lamp lighted in the bedroom, and we went in and sat down. For a time, while they talked, I sat there without hearing, saddened and bewildered by the heavy immanence of change I felt in the room and by Nick's absence from it. And then I began to listen to what was being said. Aunt Georgie's voice was without the readiness of laughter I had always known in her. She spoke quietly and deliberately, avoiding betrayal of her grief. My father was talking, I remember, very gently and generously to her, helping her to get her affairs in order, discussing an insurance policy that Nick had, determining what her needs were. And all at once I realized that Aunt Georgie was going to leave. I hadn't expected it; she was deeply involved in my history and my affections; she had been there what seemed to me a long long time. Perhaps because of those conversations we used to have about taking care of Nick when he got old, I had supposed that such permanent arrangements were made as a matter of course. I interrupted and said something to the effect that I thought Aunt Georgie ought to stay, I didn't want her to go. And they turned to me and explained that it was not possible. She had relatives in Louisville; she would go to live with them. Their few words made it clear to me that there were great and demanding realities that I had never considered: realities of allegiance, realities of economics. I waited in silence then until their talk was finished, and we went out into the winter night and walked back up the hill.

I don't know if I saw Aunt Georgie again before she left. That is the last memory I have of her: strangely detached and remote from the house as though she already no longer lived there, an old woman standing in the yellow lamplight among the shadowy furnishings of the room, stooped and slow as if newly aware of the heaviness of her body.

And so it ended.

from

A Continuous Harmony

III

Discipline
and Hope

1

INTRODUCTORY NOTE

I begin with what I believe is a safe premise, at least
in the sense that most of the various sides of the current
public argument would agree, though for different reasons:
that we have been for some time in a state of general cultural disorder, and that this disorder has now become critical. My interest here has been to examine to what extent
this disorder is a failure of discipline—specifically, a failure
of those disciplines, both private and public, by which desired ends might be reached, or by which the proper means
to a desired end might be determined, or by which it might
be perceived that one apparently desirable end may contradict or forestall another more desirable. Thus we have
not asked how the "quality of life," as we phrase it, may be
fostered by social and technological means that are sensi-

Reprinted by permission of Harcourt Brace Jovanovich, Inc. from *A Continuous Harmony*, © 1972, by Wendell Berry.

tive only to quantitative measures; we have not really questioned the universal premise of power politics that peace (among the living) is the natural result of war; we have hardly begun to deal with the fact that an economy of waste is not compatible with a healthy environment.

I realize that I have been rather severely critical of several, perhaps all, sides of the present disagreement, having in effect made this a refusal to be a partisan of *any* side. If critical intelligence has a use it is to prevent the coagulation of opinion in social or political cliques. My purpose has been to invoke the use of principle, rather than partisanship, as a standard of behavior, and to clear the rhetoric of the various sides from what ought to be the ground of personal experience and common sense.

It appears to me that the governing middle, or the government, which supposedly represents the middle, has allowed the extremes of left and right to force it into an extremism of its own. These three extremes of left, right, and middle, egged on by and helplessly subservient to each other's rhetoric, have now become so self-righteous and self-defensive as to have no social use. So large a ground of sanity and good sense and decency has been abandoned by these extremes that it becomes possible now to think of a New Middle made up of people conscious and knowledgeable enough to despise the blandishments and oversimplifications of the extremes—and roomy and diverse enough to permit a renewal of intelligent cultural dialogue. That is what I hope for: a chance to live and speak as a person, not as a function of some political bunch.

2

THE POLITICS OF KINGDOM COME

Times of great social stress and change, when realities become difficult to face and to cope with, give occasion to forms of absolutism, demanding perfection. We are in such a time now, and it is producing the characteristic symptoms. It has suddenly become clear to us that practices and ambitions that we have been taught from the cradle to respect have made us the heirs apparent of a variety of dooms; some of the promised solutions, on which we have been taught to depend, are not working, are probably not going to work. As a result the country is burdened with political or cultural perfectionists of several sorts, demanding that the government or the people create *right now* one or another version of the ideal state. The air is full of dire prophecies, warnings, and threats of what will happen if the Kingdom of Heaven is not precipitately landed at the nearest airport.

It is important that we recognize the childishness of this. Its ancestor is the kicking fit of childhood, a sort of behavioral false rhetoric that offers the world two absolute alternatives: "If I can't have it, I'll tear it up." Its cultural model is the fundamentalist preacher, for whom there are no degrees of behavior, who cannot tell the difference between a shot glass and a barrel. The public *demand* for perfection, as opposed to private striving for it, is almost always productive of violence, and is itself a form of violence. It is totalitarian in impulse, and often in result.

The extremes of public conviction are always based upon rhetorical extremes, which is to say that their words —and their actions—have departed from facts, causes, and arguments, and have begun to follow the false logic of a feud in which nobody remembers the cause but only what was last said or done by the other side. Language and behavior become purely negative in function. The opponents no longer speak in support of their vision or their arguments or their purposes, but only in opposition to each other. Language ceases to bind head to heart, action to principle, and becomes a weapon in a contention deadly as war, shallow as a game.

But it would be an oversimplification to suggest that

the present contention of political extremes involves only the left and the right. These contend not so much against each other as against the middle—the administration in power—which each accuses of *being* the other. In defending itself, the middle characteristically adopts the tactics of the extremes, corrupting its language by a self-congratulatory rhetoric bearing no more kinship to the truth and to honest argument than expediency demands, and thus it becomes an extreme middle. Whereas the extreme left and right see in each other the imminence of Universal Wrong, the extreme middle appears to sense in itself the imminence of the Best of All Possible Worlds, and therefore looks upon all critics as traitors. The rhetoric of the extreme middle equates the government with the country, loyalty to the government with patriotism, the will of the Chief Executive with the will of the people. It props itself with the tone of divine good will and infallibility, demanding an automatic unquestioning faith in its actions, upholding its falsehoods and errors with the same unblinking piety with which it obscures its truths and its accomplishments.

Because the extreme middle is characteristically in power, its characteristic medium is the one that is most popular—television. How earnestly and how well this middle has molded itself to the demands of television is apparent when one considers how much of its attention is given to image making, or remaking, and to public relations. It has given up almost altogether the disciplines of political discourse (considerations of fact and of principle and of human and historical limits and possibilities), and has taken up the cynical showmanship of those who have cheap goods for sale. Its catch phrases do not rise from any viable political tradition; their next of kin are the TV jingles of soup and soap. It is a politics of illusion, and its characteristic medium is pre-eminently suited—as it is almost exclusively limited—to the propagation of illusion.

Of all the illusions of television, that of its much-touted "educational value" is probably the first. Because of its utter transience as a medium and the complete passivity of its audience, television is doomed to have its effect within the limits of the most narrow and shallow definition of entertainment—that is, entertainment as diversion. The watcher sees the program at the expense of no effort at all; he is inert. All the live connections are broken. More important, a TV program can be seen only once; it cannot be re-examined or judged upon the basis of study, as even a movie can be; a momentous event or a serious drama slips away from us among the ordinary furniture of our lives, as transient and fading as the most commonplace happenings of every day. For these reasons a political speech on television has to be first and last a show, simply because it has no chance to become anything else. The great sin of the medium is not that it presents fiction as truth, as undoubtedly it sometimes does, but that it cannot help presenting the truth as fiction, and that of the most negligible sort—a way to keep awake until bedtime.

In depending so much upon a medium that will not permit scrutiny, the extreme middle has perhaps naturally come to speak a language that will not *bear* scrutiny. It has thus abased its own part in the so-called political dialogue to about the level of the slogans and chants and the over-simplified invective of the extreme left and right—a fact that in itself might sufficiently explain the obsession with image making. Hearing the televised pronouncements of the political leaders of our time upon the great questions of human liberty, community obligation, war and peace, poverty and wealth, one might easily forget that such as John Adams and Thomas Jefferson once spoke here upon those questions. Indeed, our contemporary men of power have produced in their wake an industry of journalistic commentary and interpretation, because it is so difficult to determine *what* they have said and whether or not they meant it. Thus one sees the essential contradiction in the expedient doctrine that the end may justify the means. Corrupt or false means must inevitably corrupt or falsify the end. There is an important sense in which the end *is* the means.

What is disturbing, then, about these three "sides" of our present political life is not their differences but their similarities. They have all abandoned discourse as a means of clarifying and explaining and defending and implementing their ideas. They have taken almost exclusively to the use of the rhetoric of ad-writers: catch phrases, slogans, clichés, euphemisms, flatteries, falsehoods, and various forms of cheap wit. This has led them—as such rhetoric must—to the use of power and the use of violence against each other. But however their ideological differences might be graphed, they are, in effect, all on the same side. They are on the side of their quarrel, and are against all other, and all better, possibilities. There is a political and social despair in this that is the greatest peril a country can come to, short of the inevitable results of such despair should it continue very long. "We are fatalists," Edward Dahlberg wrote, "only when we cease telling the truth, but, so long as we communicate the truth, we move ourselves, life, history, men. There is no other way."

Our present political rhetoric is the desperation of argument. It is like a weapon in its inflexibility, in its insensitivity to circumstance, and in its natural inclination toward violence. It is by this recourse to loose talk—this willingness to say whatever will be easiest to say and most willingly heard—that the left permits its methods to contradict its avowed aims, as when it contemplates violence as a means of peace or permits arguments to shrink into slogans. By this process the right turns from its supposed aim of conserving the best of the past and undertakes the defense of economic privilege and the deification of symbols. And by this process the middle abandons its obligation to lead and enlighten the majority it claims as its constituency, and takes to the devices of a sterile showmanship, by which it hopes to elude criticism and obscure its failures.

The political condition in this country now is one in which the means or the disciplines necessary to the achievement of professed ends have been devalued or corrupted or abandoned altogether. We are offered peace without forbearance or tolerance or love, security without effort and without standards, freedom without risk or responsibility, abundance without thrift. We are asked repeatedly by our elected officials to console ourselves with that most degenerate of political arguments: though we are not doing as well as we might, we could do worse, and we are doing better than some.

3

THE KINGDOM OF EFFICIENCY
AND SPECIALIZATION

But this political indiscipline is exemplary of a condition that is widespread and deeply rooted in almost all aspects of our life. Nearly all the old standards, which implied and required rigorous disciplines, have now been replaced by a new standard of efficiency, which requires not discipline, not a mastery of means, but rather a carelessness of means, a relentless subjection of means to immediate ends. The standard of efficiency displaces and destroys the standards of quality because, by definition, it cannot even consider them. Instead of asking a man what he can do well, it asks him what he can do fast and cheap. Instead of asking the farmer to practice the best husbandry, to be a good steward and trustee of his land and his art, it puts irresistible pressures on him to produce more and more food and fiber more and more cheaply, thereby destroying the health of the land, the best traditions of husbandry, and the farm population itself. And so when we examine the principle of efficiency as we now practice it, we see that it is not really efficient at all. As we use the word, efficiency means no such thing, or it means short-term or temporary efficiency; which is a contradiction in terms. It means cheapness at any price. It means hurrying to nowhere. It means the profligate waste of humanity and of nature. It means the greatest profit to the greatest liar. What we have called efficiency has produced among us, and to our incalculable cost, such unprecedented monuments of destructiveness and waste as the strip-mining industry, the Pentagon, the federal bureaucracy, and the family car.

Real efficiency is something entirely different. It is neither cheap (in terms of skill and labor) nor fast. Real efficiency is long-term efficiency. It is to be found in means that are in keeping with and preserving of their ends, in methods of production that preserve the sources of production, in workmanship that is durable and of high quality. In this age of planned obsolescence, frivolous horsepower and surplus manpower, those salesmen and politicians who talk about efficiency are talking, in reality, about spiritual and biological death.

Specialization, a result of our nearly exclusive concern with the form of exploitation that we call efficiency, has in its turn become a destructive force. Carried to the extent to which we have carried it, it is both socially and ecologically destructive. That specialization has vastly increased our knowledge, as its defenders claim, cannot be disputed. But I think that one might reasonably dispute the underlying assumption that knowledge per se, undisciplined knowledge, is good. For while specialization has increased knowledge, it has fragmented it. And this fragmen-

tation of knowledge has been accompanied by a fragmentation of discipline. That is, specialization has tended to
draw the specialist toward the discipline that will lead to
the discovery of new facts or processes within a narrowly
defined area, and it has tended to lead him away from or
distract him from those disciplines by which he might consider the *effects* of his discovery upon human society or
upon the world.

Nowhere are these tendencies more apparent than
in agriculture. For years now the agricultural specialists
have tended to think and work in terms of piecemeal solutions and in terms of annual production, rather than in
terms of a whole and coherent system that would maintain
the fertility and the ecological health of the land over a period of centuries. Focused nearly exclusively upon so-called
efficiency with respect to production, as if the only discipline pertinent to agriculture were that of economics, they
have eagerly abetted a rapid industrialization of agriculture
that is potentially catastrophic, both in the ecological deterioration of farm areas and in the dispossession and displacement of the rural population.

Ignoring the ample evidence that a healthy, ecologically sound agriculture is highly diversified, using the
greatest possible variety of animals and plants, and that it
returns all organic wastes to the soil, the specialists of the
laboratories have promoted the specialization of the farms,
encouraging one-crop agriculture and the replacement of
humus by chemicals. And as the pressures of urban populations upon the land have grown, the specialists have turned
more and more, not to the land, but to the laboratory.

Ignoring the considerable historical evidence that to
have a productive agriculture over a long time it is necessary to have a stable, prosperous rural population closely
bound in sympathy and association to the land, the specialists have either connived in the dispossession of small

farmers by machinery and technology, or have actively encouraged their migration into the cities.

The result of the short-term vision of these experts
is a whole series of difficulties that together amount to a
rapidly building ecological and social disaster, which there
is little disposition at present to regret, much less to correct.
The organic wastes of our society, for which our land is
starved and which in a sound agricultural economy would
be returned to the land, are flushed out through the sewers
to pollute the streams and rivers and, finally, the oceans; or
they are burned and the smoke pollutes the air; or they are
wasted in other ways. Similarly, the small farmers who in a
healthy society ought to be the mainstay of the country—
whose allegiance to their land, continuing and deepening in
association from one generation to another, would be the
motive and guarantee of good care—are forced out by the
homicidal economics of efficiency, to become emigrants
and dependents in the already overcrowded cities. In both
instances, by the abuse of knowledge in the name of efficiency, assets have been converted into staggering problems.

The metaphor governing these horrendous distor-
tions has been that of the laboratory. The working assumption has been that nature and society, like laboratory ex-
periments, can be manipulated by processes that are for the
most part comprehensible toward ends that are for the
most part foreseeable. But the analogy, as any farmer
knows, is too simple, for both nature and humanity are
unpredictable and ultimately mysterious. Sir Albert Howard was speaking to this problem in *An Agricultural Tes-
tament:* "Instead of breaking up the subject into fragments
and studying agriculture in piecemeal fashion by the ana-
lytical methods of science, appropriate only to the discovery of new facts, we must adopt a synthetic approach and
look at the wheel of life as one great subject and not as if it

were a patchwork of unrelated things." A much more appropriate model for the agriculturist, scientist, or farmer is the forest, for the forest, as Howard pointed out, "manures itself" and is therefore self-renewing; it has achieved that "correct relation between the processes of growth and the processes of decay that is the first principle of successful agriculture." A healthy agriculture can take place only within nature, and in co-operation with its processes, not in spite of it and not by "conquering" it. Nature, Howard points out, in elaboration of his metaphor, "never attempts to farm without livestock; she always raises mixed crops; great pains are taken to preserve the soil and to prevent erosion; the mixed vegetable and animal wastes are converted into humus; *there is no waste* [my emphasis]; the processes of growth and the processes of decay balance one another; ample provision is made to maintain large reserves of fertility; the greatest care is taken to store the rainfall; both plants and animals are left to protect themselves against disease."

The fact is that farming is not a laboratory science, but a science of practice. It would be, I think, a good deal more accurate to call it an art, for it grows not only out of factual knowledge but out of cultural tradition; it is learned not only by precept but by example, by apprenticeship; and it requires not merely a competent knowledge of its facts and processes, but also a complex set of attitudes, a certain culturally evolved stance, in the face of the unexpected and the unknown. That is to say, it requires *style* in the highest and richest sense of that term.

One of the most often repeated tenets of contemporary optimism asserts that "a nation that can put men on the moon certainly should be able to solve the problem of hunger." This proposition seems to me to have three important flaws, which I think may be taken as typical of our official view of ourselves:

1—It construes the flight to the moon as an historical event of a complete and coherent significance, when in fact it is a fragmentary event of very uncertain significance. Americans have gone to the moon as they came to the frontiers of the New World: with their minds very much upon getting there, very little upon what might be involved in *staying* there. I mean that because of our history of waste and destruction here, we have no assurance that we can survive in America, much less on the moon. And until we can bring into balance the processes of growth and decay, the white man's settlement of this continent will remain an incomplete event. When a Japanese peasant went to the fields of his tiny farm in the preindustrial age, he worked in the governance of an agricultural tradition that had sustained the land in prime fertility for thousands of years, in spite of the pressures of a population that in 1907 had reached a density, according to F. H. King's *Farmers of Forty Centuries,* of "more than three people to each acre." Such a farmer might look upon his crop year as a complete and coherent historical event, suffused and illuminated with a meaning and mystery that were both its own and the world's, because in his mind and work agricultural process had come into an enduring and preserving harmony with natural process. To him the past confidently promised a future. What are we to say, by contrast, of a society that places no value at all upon such a tradition or such a man, that instead works the destruction of such imperfect agricultural tradition as it has, that replaces the farm people with machines, that values the techniques of production far above the techniques of land maintenance, and that has espoused as an ideal a depopulated countryside farmed by a few technicians for the supposedly greater benefit of hundreds of millions crowded into cities and helpless to produce food or any other essential for themselves?

2—The agricultural optimism that bases itself upon the moon-landings assumes that there is an equation between agriculture and technology, or that agriculture is a kind of technology. This grows out of the much-popularized false assumptions of the agricultural specialists, who have gone about their work as if agriculture was answerable only to the demands of economics, not to those of ecology or human culture, just as most urban consumers conceive eating to be an activity associated with economics but not with agriculture. The ground of agricultural thinking is so narrowly circumscribed, one imagines, to fit the demands of laboratory science, as well as the popular prejudice that prefers false certainties to honest doubts. The discipline proper to eating, of course, is not economics but agriculture. The discipline proper to agriculture, which survives not just by production but also by the return of wastes to the ground, is not economics but ecology. And ecology may well find its proper disciplines in the arts, whose function is to refine and enliven *perception,* for ecological principle, however publicly approved, can be enacted only upon the basis of each man's perception of his relation to the world.

Under the governance of the laboratory analogy, the *device,* which is simple and apparently simplifying, becomes the focal point and the standard rather than the human need, which is complex. Thus an agricultural specialist, prescribing the best conditions for the use of a harvesting machine, thinks only of the machine, not its cultural or ecological effects. And because of the fixation on optimum conditions, big-farm technology has come to be highly developed, whereas the technology of the family farm, which must still involve methods and economies that are "old-fashioned," has been neglected. For this reason, and others perhaps more pressing, small-farm technology is rapidly passing from sight, along with the small farmers.

As a result we have an increasing acreage of supposedly "marginal" but potentially productive land for the use of which we have neither methods nor people—an alarming condition in view of the likelihood that someday we will desperately need to farm these lands again.

The drastic and incalculably dangerous assumption is that farming can be considered apart from farmers, that the land may be conceptually divided in its use from human need and human care. The assumption is that moving a farmer into a factory is as simple a cultural act as moving a worker from one factory to another. It is inconceivably more complicated, and more final. American agricultural tradition has been for the most part inadequate from the beginning, and we have an abundance of diminished land to show for it. But American farmers are nevertheless an agricultural population of long standing. Most settlers who farmed in America farmed in Europe. The farm population in this country therefore embodies a knowledge and a set of attitudes and interests that have been thousands of years in the making. This mentality is, or was, a great resource upon which we might have built a truly indigenous agriculture, fully adequate to the needs and demands of American regions. Ancient as it is, it is destroyed in a generation in every family that is forced off the farm into the city—or in less than a generation, for the farm mentality can survive only in sustained vital contact with the land.

A truer agricultural vision would look upon farming not as a function of the economy or even of the society, but as a function of the land; and it would look upon the farm population as an indispensable and inalienable part of the ecological system. Among the Incas, according to John Collier *(Indians of the Americas),* the basic social and economic unit was the tribe, or *ayllu,* but "the *ayllu* was not merely its people, and not merely the land, but people and land wedded through a mystical bond." The union of the land and the people was indissoluble, like marriage or grace. Chief Rekayi of the Tangwena tribe of Rhodesia, in refusing to leave his ancestral home, which had been claimed by the whites, is reported in recent newspaper accounts to have said: "I am married to this land. I was put here by God . . . and if I am to leave, I must be removed by God who put me here." This altogether natural and noble sentiment was said by the Internal Affairs Minister to have been "Communist inspired."

3 — The notion that the moon voyages provide us assurance of enough to eat exposes the shallowness of our intellectual confidence, for it is based upon our growing inability to distinguish between training and education. The fact is that a man can be made an astronaut much more quickly than he can be made a good farmer, for the astronaut is produced by training and the farmer by education. Training is a process of conditioning, an orderly and highly efficient procedure by which a man learns a prescribed pattern of facts and functions. Education, on the other hand, is an obscure process by which a person's experience is brought into contact with his place and his history. A college can train a person in four years; it can barely begin his education in that time. A person's education begins before his birth in the making of the disciplines, traditions, and attitudes of mind that he will inherit, and it continues until his death under the slow, expensive, uneasy tutelage of his experience. The process that produces astronauts may produce soldiers and factory workers and clerks; it will never produce good farmers or good artists or good citizens or good parents.

White American tradition, so far as I know, contains only one coherent social vision that takes such matters into consideration, and that is Thomas Jefferson's. Jefferson's public reputation seems to have dwindled to that of Founding Father and advocate of liberty, author of several documents and actions that have been enshrined and forgotten. But in his thinking, democracy was not an ideal that stood alone. He saw that it would have to be secured by vigorous disciplines or its public offices would become merely the hunting grounds of mediocrity and venality. And so those who associate his name only with his political utterances miss both the breadth and depth of his wisdom. As Jefferson saw it, two disciplines were indispensable to democracy: on the one hand, education, which was to produce a class of qualified leaders, an aristocracy of "virtue and talents" drawn from all economic classes; and on the other hand, widespread land ownership, which would assure stable communities, a tangible connection to the country, and a permanent interest in its welfare. In language that recalls Collier's description of the *ayllu* of the Incas, and the language of Chief Rekayi of the Tangwenans, Jefferson wrote that farmers "are tied to their country, and wedded to its liberty and interests, by the most lasting bonds." And: ". . . legislators cannot invent too many devices for subdividing property. . . ." And: ". . . it is not too soon to provide by every possible means that as few as possible shall be without a little portion of land. The small landholders are the most precious part of a state." For the discipline of education of the broad and humane sort that Jefferson had in mind, to produce a "natural aristocracy . . . for the instruction, the trusts, and government of society," we have tended more and more to substitute the specialized training that will most readily secure the careerist in his career. For the ownership of "a little portion of land" we have, and we apparently wish, to substitute the barbarous abstraction of nationalism, which puts our minds within the control of whatever demagogue can soonest rouse us to self-righteousness.

On September 10, 1814, Jefferson wrote to Dr. Thomas Cooper of the "condition of society" as he saw it at that time: ". . . we have no paupers, the old and crippled among us, who possess nothing and have no families to take care of them, being too few to merit notice as a separate section of society. . . . The great mass of our population is of laborers; our rich . . . being few, and of moderate wealth. Most of the laboring class possess property, cultivate their own lands . . . and from the demand for their labor are enabled . . . to be fed abundantly, clothed above mere decency, to labor moderately. . . . The wealthy . . . know nothing of what the Europeans call luxury." This has an obvious kinship with the Confucian formula: ". . . that the producers be many and that the mere consumers be few; that the artisan mass be energetic and the consumers temperate . . ."

In the loss of that vision, or of such a vision, and in the abandonment of that possibility, we have created a society characterized by degrading urban poverty and an equally degrading affluence—a society of undisciplined abundance, which is to say a society of waste.

4

THE KINGDOM OF CONSUMPTION

The results have become too drastic to be concealed by our politicians' assurances that we have built a "great society" or that we are doing better than India. Official pretense has begun to break down under the weight of the obvious. In the last decade we have become unable to condition our children's minds to approve or accept our errors. Our history has created in the minds of our young people a bitter division between official pretense and social fact, and we have aggravated this division by asking many of them to fight and die in support of official pretense. In this way we have produced a generation whose dissidence and alienation are without precedent in our national experience.

The first thing to be said about this rebelliousness is that it is understandable, and that it deserves considerate attention. Many of this generation have rejected values and practices that they believe to be destructive, and they should do so. Many of them have begun to search for better values and forms of life, and they should do so. But the second thing to be said is that this generation is as subject as any other to intelligent scrutiny and judgment, and as deserving of honest criticism. It has received much approbation and condemnation, very little criticism.

One of its problems is that it has been isolated in its youthfulness, cut off from the experience and the counsel of older people, as probably no other generation has ever been. It is true that the dissident young have had their champions among the older people, but it is also true, I think, that these older people have been remarkably uncritical of the young, and so have abdicated their major responsibility to them. Some appear to have *joined* the younger generation, buying their way in by conniving in the notion that idealistic youth can do no wrong—or that one may reasonably hope to live without difficulty or effort or tragedy, or that surfing is "a life." The uncritical approval of a band of senior youth freaks is every bit as isolating and every bit as destructive as the uncritical condemnation of those who have made hair length the foremost social issue of the time.

And so a number of the problems of the young people now are problems that have always attended youthfulness, but which isolation has tended to aggravate in the present generation: impetuousness, a haste to undertake work that one is not yet prepared for; a tendency to underestimate difficulty and overestimate possibility, which is apt, through disillusionment, to lead to the overestimation of difficulty and the underestimation of possibility; oversimplification, as when rejection takes the place of evaluation; and, finally, naïve prejudice, as when people who rightly condemn the use of such terms as "nigger" or "greaser" readily use such terms as "pig" and "redneck."

Another of its problems, and a much larger one, is that the propaganda both of the "youth culture" and of those opposed to it has inculcated in many minds, both young and old, the illusion that this is a wholly new generation, a generation free of history. The proposition is dangerously silly. The present younger generation is, as much as any other, a product of the past; it would not be as it is if earlier generations had not been as they were. Like every other young generation, this one bears the precious human burden of new possibility and new hope, the opportunity to put its inheritance to better use. And like every other, it also bears the germ of historical error and failure and weakness—which it rarely forgives in its predecessors, and seldom recognizes in itself. In the minds of those who do not know it well, and who have not mastered the disciplines of self-criticism, historical error is a subtle virus indeed. It is of the greatest importance that we recognize in the youth culture the persistence in new forms of the mentality of waste, certain old forms of which many of the young have rightly repudiated.

Though it has forsworn many of the fashions and ostentations of the "affluent society," the youth culture still supports its own forms of consumerism, the venerable American doctrine which holds that if enough is good too much is better. As an example, consider the present role of such drugs as marijuana and the various hallucinogens. To deal sensibly with this subject, it is necessary to say at the outset that the very concept of drug abuse implies the possibility of drug use that is *not* abusive. And it is, in fact, possible to produce examples of civilizations that have employed drugs in disciplines and ceremonies that have made them culturally useful and prevented their abuse.

Tobacco, for instance, is a drug that we have used so massively and thoughtlessly that we have, in typical fashion, come to be endangered by it. This is the pattern of the consumer economy and it applies not just to drugs, but to such commodities as the automobile and electrical power. But American Indians attached to tobacco a significance that made it more valuable to them than it has ever been to us, and at the same time kept them from misusing it as we have. In the Winnebago Origin Myth tobacco had a ceremonial and theological role. According to this myth, Paul Radin wrote in his Introduction to *The Road of Life and Death,* man "is not to save himself or receive the wherewithal of life through the accidental benefactions of culture-heroes. On the contrary, he is to be in dire straits and saved. Earthmaker is represented as withholding tobacco from the spirits in order to present it to man and as endowing these same spirits with an overpowering craving for it. In short, it is to be the mechanism for an exchange between man and the deities. He will give them tobacco; they will give him powers to meet life and overcome obstacles."

The use of alcohol has had, I believe, a similar history: a decline and expansion from ceremonial use to use as a commodity and extravagance, from cultural usefulness to cultural liability.

The hallucinogenic drugs have now also run this course of cultural diminishment, and at the hands not of the salesmen of the corporations and the advertising agencies, but of the self-proclaimed enemies of those salesmen. Most of these drugs have been used by various cultures in association with appropriate disciplines and ceremonies. Anyone who reads an account of the Peyote Meeting of the Native American Church will see that it resembles very much the high ritual and art of other cultures but very little indeed the usual account of the contemporary "dope scene."

A very detailed and well-understood account of the disciplined use of such drugs is in Carlos Castenada's *The Teachings of Don Juan: A Yaqui Way of Knowledge*. Don Juan, a medicine man and sorcerer, a Yaqui Indian from Sonora, Mexico, undertakes to teach Castenada the uses of jimson weed, peyote, and the psilocybe mushrooms. The book contains some remarkable accounts of the author's visions under the influence of these drugs, but equally remarkable is the rigor of the disciplines and rituals by which his mentor prepared him for their use. At one point early in their association the old Indian said to him: "A man goes to knowledge as he goes to war, wide awake, with fear, with respect, and with absolute assurance. Going to knowledge or going to war in any other manner is a mistake, and whoever makes it will live to regret his steps."

The cultural role of both hallucinogens and intoxicants, in societies that have effectively disciplined their use, has been strictly limited. They have been used either for the apprehension of religious or visionary truth or, a related function, to induce in conditions prescribed by ceremony and festivity a state of self-abandon in which one may go free for a limited time of the obscuring and distorting preoccupation with one's own being. Other cultures have used other means—music or dance or poetry, for examples—to produce these same ends, and although the substance of Don Juan's teaching may be somewhat alien to the mainstream of our tradition, the terms of its discipline are not.

By contrast, the youth culture tends to use drugs in a way very similar to the way its parent culture uses alcohol: at random, as a social symbol and crutch, and with the emphasis upon the fact and quantity of use rather than the quality and the content of the experience. It would be false to say that these drugs have come into contemporary use without any of their earlier cultural associations. Indeed, a good deal of importance has been assigned to the "religious" aspect of the drug experience. But too often, it seems to me, the tendency has been to make a commodity of religion, as if in emulation of some churches. Don Juan looked upon drugs as a way to knowledge, difficult and fearful as other wise men have conceived other ways to knowledge, and therefore to be rigorously prepared for and faithfully followed; the youth culture, on the other hand, has tended to look upon drugs as a sort of instant Holy Truth, of which one need not become worthy. When they are inadequately prepared for the use of drugs, that is to say, people "consume" and waste them.

The way out of this wastefulness obviously cannot lie simply in a shift from one fashionable commodity to another commodity equally fashionable. The way out lies only in a change of mind by which we will learn not to think of ourselves as "consumers" in any sense. A consumer is one who uses things up, a concept that is alien to the creation, as are the concepts of waste and disposability. A more realistic and accurate vision of ourselves would teach us that our ecological obligations are to use, not use up; to use by the standard of real need, not of fashion or whim; and then to relinquish what we have used in a way that returns it to the common ecological fund from which it came.

The key to such a change of mind is the realization that the first and final order of creation is not such an order as men can impose on it, but an order in the creation itself by which its various parts and processes sustain each other, and which is only to some extent understandable. It is, moreover, an order in which things find their places and their values not according to their inert quantities or substances but according to their energies, their powers, by which they co-operate or affect and influence each other. The order of the creation, that is to say, is closer to that of drama than to that of a market.

This relation of power and order is another of the major concerns of the Winnebago Creation Myth. "Having created order within himself and established it for the stage on which man is to play," Paul Radin says, "Earthmaker proceeds to create the first beings who are to people the Universe, the spirits and deities. To each one he assigns a fixed and specific amount of power, to some more, to some less. . . . This principle of gradation and subordination is part of the order that Earthmaker is represented as introducing into the Universe. . . . The instant it is changed there is danger and the threat of disruption." The principle is dramatized, according to Radin, in the legend of Morning Star: ". . . one of the eight great Winnebago deities, Morning Star, has been decapitated by his enemy, a waterspirit. The body of the hero still remains alive and is being taken care of by his sister. The waterspirit, by keeping the head of Morning Star, has added the latter's power to his own. So formidable is this combination of powers that none of the deities [is] a match for him now. In fact only Earthmaker is his equal. Here is a threat of the first magnitude to the order ordained by Earthmaker and it must be met lest destruction overtake the world."

The point is obvious: to take and keep, to consume, the power of another creature is an act profoundly disordering, contrary to the nature of the creation. And equally obvious is its applicability to our own society, which sees its chief function in such accumulations of power. A man grows rich by strip mining, adding the power of a mountain to himself in such a way that he cannot give it back. As a nation, we have so far grown rich by adding the power of the continent to ourselves in such a way that we cannot give it back. "Here is a threat of the first magnitude to the order ordained by Earthmaker and it must be met lest destruction overtake the world."

Though we generally concede that a man may have

more of the world's goods than he deserves, I think that we
have never felt that a man may have more light than he deserves. But an interesting implication of the Winnebago
doctrine of power and order is that a man must not only
become worthy of enlightenment, but has also an ethical
obligation to make himself worthy of the world's goods.
He can make himself worthy of them only by using them
carefully, preserving them, relinquishing them in good
order when he has had their use. That a man shall find his
life by losing it is an ethical concept that applies to the
body as well as the spirit.

An aspect of the consumer mentality that has
cropped up with particular virulence in the youth culture is
an obsessive fashionableness. The uniformity of dress, hair
style, mannerism, and speech is plain enough. But more serious, because less conscious and more pretentious, is an
intellectual fashionableness pinned up on such shibboleths
as "the people" (the most procrustean of categories), "rel-
evance" (the most reactionary and totalitarian of educational doctrines), and "life style."

This last phrase furnishes a particularly clear example of the way poor language can obscure both a problem and the possibility of a solution. Compounded as "alternate life style," the phrase becomes a part of the very
problem it aspires to solve. There are, to begin with, two
radically different, even opposed meanings of style: style as
fashion, an imposed appearance, a gloss upon superficiality; and style as the signature of mastery, the efflorescence
of long discipline. It is obvious that the style of mastery can
never become the style of fashion, simply because every
master of a discipline is different from every other; his mastery is suffused with his own character and his own materials. Cézanne's paintings could not have been produced by a
fad, for the simple reason that they could not have been
produced by any other person. As a popular phrase, "life

style" necessarily has to do only with what is imitable in another person's life, its superficial appearances and trappings; it cannot touch its substances, disciplines, or devotions. More important is the likelihood that a person who has identified his interest in another person as an interest in his "life style" will be *aware* of nothing but appearances. The phrase "alternate life style" attempts to recognize our great need to change to a kind of life that is not wasteful and destructive, but stifles the attempt, in the same breath, by infecting it with that superficial concept of style. An essential recognition is thus obscured at birth by the old lie of advertising and public relations: that you can alter substance by altering appearance. "Alternate life style" suggests, much in the manner of the fashion magazines, that one can change one's life by changing one's clothes.

Another trait of consumption that thrives in the youth culture is that antipathy to so-called "drudgery" that has made us, with the help of salesmen and advertisers, a nation of suckers. This is the pseudoaristocratic notion, early popularized in America, that one is too good for the fundamental and recurring tasks of domestic order and biological necessity; to dirty one's hands in the soil or to submerge them for very long in soapy water is degrading and brutalizing. With one's hands thus occupied, the theory goes, one is unlikely to reach those elusive havens of "self-discovery" and "self-fulfillment"; but if one can escape such drudgery, one then has a fair chance of showing the world that one is *really* better than all previous evidence would have indicated. In every drudge there is an artist or a tycoon yearning to breathe free.

The entire social vision, as I understand it, goes something like this: man is born into a fallen world, doomed to eat bread in the sweat of his face. But there is an economic redemption. He should go to college and get an education—that is, he should acquire the "right" certifi-

cates and meet the "right" people. An education of this sort should enable him to get a "good" job—that is, short hours of work that is either easy or prestigious for a lot of money. Thus he is saved from the damnation of drudgery, and is presumably well on the way to proving the accuracy of his early suspicion that he is *really* a superior person.

Or, in a different version of the same story, the farmer at his plow or the housewife at her stove dreams of the neat outlines and the carefree boundaries of a factory worker's eight-hour day and forty-hour week, and his fat, unworried paycheck. They will leave their present drudgery to take the bait, in this case, of leisure, time, and money to enjoy the "good things of life."

In reality, this despised drudgery is one of the constants of life, like water only changing its form in response to changes of atmosphere. Our aversion to the necessary work that we call drudgery and our strenuous efforts to avoid it have not diminished it at all, but only degraded its forms. The so-called drudgery has to be done. If one is "too good" to do it for oneself, then it must be done by a servant, or by a machine manufactured by servants. If it is not done at home, then it must be done in a factory, which degrades both the conditions of work and the quality of the product. If it is not done well by the hands of one person, then it must be done poorly by the hands of many. But somewhere the hands of someone must be soiled with the work. Our aversion to this was once satisfied by slavery, or by the abuse of a laboring class; now it is satisfied by the assembly line, or by similar redundancy in bureaus and offices. For decades now our people have streamed into the cities to escape the drudgery of farm and household. Where do they go to escape the drudgery of the city? Only home at night, I am afraid, to the spiritual drudgery of factory-made suppers and TV. On weekends many of them continue these forms of urban drudgery in the country.

The youth culture has accepted, for the most part uncritically, the conviction that all recurring and necessary work is drudgery, even adding to it a uniquely gullible acquiescence in the promoters' myth that the purpose of technology is to free mankind for spiritual and cultural pursuits. But to the older idea of economic redemption from drudgery, the affluent young have added the even more simple-minded idea of redemption by spontaneity. Do what you feel like, they say—as if every day one could "feel like" doing what is necessary. Any farmer or mother knows the absurdity of this. Human nature is such that if we waited to do anything until we felt like it, we would do very little at the start, even of those things that give us pleasure, and would do less and less as time went on. One of the common experiences of people who regularly do hard work that they enjoy is to find that they begin to "feel like it" only after the task is begun. And one of the chief uses of discipline is to assure that the necessary work gets done even when the worker *doesn't* feel like it.

Because of the prevalence of the economics and the philosophy of laborsaving, it has become almost a heresy to speak of hard work, especially manual work, as an inescapable human necessity. To speak of such work as good and ennobling, a source of pleasure and joy, is almost to declare oneself a pervert. Such work, and any aptitude or taste for it, are supposedly mere relics of our rural and primitive past—a past from which it is the business of modern science and technology to save us.

Before one can hope to use any intelligence in this matter, it is necessary to resurrect a distinction that was probably not necessary before the modern era, and that has so far been made only by a few eccentrics and renegades. It is a distinction not made in business and government, and very little made in the universities. I am talking about the distinction between work that is necessary and therefore meaningful, and work that is unnecessary or devoid of meaning. There is no intelligent defense of what Thoreau called "the police of meaningless labor." The unnecessary work of producing notions or trinkets or machines intended to be soon worn out, or necessary work the meaning of which has been destroyed by mechanical process, is as degrading as slavery. And the purpose of such slavery, according to the laborsaving philosophy, is to set men free from work. Freed from work, men will presumably take to more "worthy" pursuits such as "culture." Noting that there have always been some people who, when they had leisure, studied literature and painting and music, the prophets of the technological paradise have always assured us that once we have turned all our work over to machines we will become a nation of artists or, at worst, a nation of art critics. This notion seems to me highly questionable on grounds both of fact and of principle.

In fact, we already know by experience what the "leisure" of most factory and office workers usually is, and we may reasonably predict that what it is it is likely to continue to be. Their leisure is a frantic involvement with salesmen, illusions, and machines. It is an expensive imitation of their work—anxious, hurried, unsatisfying. As their work offers no satisfactions in terms of work but must always be holding before itself the will-o'-the-wisp of freedom from work, so their leisure has no leisurely goals but must always be seeking its satisfaction outside itself, in some activity or some thing typically to be provided by a salesman. A man doing wholesome and meaningful work that he is pleased to do well is three times more at rest than the average factory or office worker on vacation. A man who does meaningless work does not have his meaning at hand. He must go anxiously in search of it—and thus fail to find it. The farmer's Sunday afternoon of sitting at home in the shade of a tree has been replaced by the "long weekend" of a thousand miles. The difference is that the farmer was where he wanted to be, understood the value of being there, and therefore when he had no work to do could sit still. How much have we spent to obscure so simple and obvious a possibility? The point is that there is an indissoluble connection and dependence between work and leisure. The freedom from work must produce not leisure, but an ever more frantic search for something to do.

The principle was stated by Thoreau in his *Journal:* "Hard and steady and engrossing labor with the hands, especially out of doors, is invaluable to the literary man and serves him directly. Here I have been for six days surveying in the woods, and yet when I get home at evening, somewhat weary at last . . . I find myself more susceptible than usual to the finest influences, as music and poetry." That is, certainly, the testimony of an exceptional man, a man of the rarest genius, and it will be asked if such work could produce such satisfaction in an ordinary man. My answer is that we do not have to look far or long for evidence that all the fundamental tasks of feeding and clothing and housing—farming, gardening, cooking, spinning, weaving, sewing, shoemaking, carpentry, cabinetwork, stonemasonry—were once done with consummate skill by ordinary people, and as that skill indisputably involved a high measure of pride, it can confidently be said to have produced a high measure of satisfaction.

We are being saved from work, then, for what? The answer can only be that we are being saved from work that is meaningful and ennobling and comely in order to be put to work that is unmeaning and degrading and ugly. In 1930, the Twelve Southerners of *I'll Take My Stand* issued as an Introduction to their book "A Statement of Principles" in which they declared for the agrarian way of life as opposed to the industrial. The book, I believe, was never popular. At the time, and during the three decades that followed, it might have been almost routinely dismissed by the dominant cultural factions as an act of sentimental allegiance to a lost cause. But now it has begun to be possible to say that the cause for which the Twelve Southerners spoke in their Introduction was not a lost but a threatened cause: the cause of human culture. "The regular act of applied science," they said, "is to introduce into labor a labor-saving device or a machine. Whether this is a benefit depends on how far it is advisable to save the labor. The philosophy of applied science is generally quite sure that the saving of labor is a pure gain, and that the more of it the better. This is to assume that labor is an evil, that only the end of labor or the material product is good. On this assumption labor becomes mercenary and servile. . . . The act of labor as one of the happy functions of human life has been in effect abandoned. . . .

"Turning to consumption, as the grand end which justifies the evil of modern labor, we find that we have been deceived. We have more time in which to consume, and many more products to be consumed. But the tempo of our labors communicates itself to our satisfactions, and these also become brutal and hurried. The constitution of the natural man probably does not permit him to shorten his labor-time and enlarge his consuming-time indefinitely. He has to pay the penalty in satiety and aimlessness."

The outcry in the face of such obvious truths is always that if they were implemented they would ruin the economy. The peculiarity of our condition would appear to be that the implementation of *any* truth would ruin the economy. If the Golden Rule were generally observed among us, the economy would not last a week. We have made our false economy a false god, and it has made blasphemy of the truth. So I have met the economy in the road, and am expected to yield it right of way. But I will not get over. My reason is that I am a man, and have a better right to the ground than the economy. The economy is no god for me, for I have had too close a look at its wheels. I have seen it at work in the strip mines and coal camps of Kentucky, and I know that it has no moral limits. It has emptied the country of the independent and the proud, and has crowded the cities with the dependent and the abject. It has always sacrificed the small to the large, the personal to the impersonal, the good to the cheap. It has ridden to its questionable triumphs over the bodies of small farmers and tradesmen and craftsmen. I see it, still, driving my neighbors off their farms into the factories. I see it teaching my students to give themselves a price before they can give themselves a value. Its principle is to waste and destroy the living substance of the world and the birthright of posterity for a monetary profit that is the most flimsy and useless of human artifacts.

Though I can see no way to defend the economy, I recognize the need to be concerned for the suffering that would be produced by its failure. But I ask if it is necessary for it to fail in order to change; I am assuming that if it does not change it must sooner or later fail, and that a great deal that is more valuable will fail with it. As a deity the economy is a sort of egotistical French monarch, for it apparently can see no alternative to itself except chaos, and perhaps that is its chief weakness. For, of course, chaos is not the only alternative to it. A better alternative is a better economy. But we will not conceive the possibility of a better economy, and therefore will not begin to change, until we quit deifying the present one.

A better economy, to my way of thinking, would be one that would place its emphasis not upon the *quantity* of notions and luxuries but upon the *quality* of necessities. Such an economy would, for example, produce an automobile that would last at least as long, and be at least as easy to maintain, as a horse.* It would encourage workmanship to be as durable as its materials; thus a piece of furniture would have the durability not of glue but of wood. It would substitute for the pleasure of frivolity a pleasure in the high quality of essential work, in the use of good tools, in a healthful and productive countryside. It would encourage a migration from the cities back to the farms, to assure a work force that would be sufficient not only to the production of the necessary quantities of food, but to the production of food of the best *quality* and to the maintenance of the land at the highest fertility—work that would require a great deal more personal attention and care and hand labor than the present technological agriculture that is focused so exclusively upon production. Such a change in the economy would not involve large-scale unemployment, but rather large-scale changes and shifts of employment.

"You are tilting at windmills," I will be told. "It is a hard world, hostile to the values that you stand for. You will never enlist enough people to bring about such a change." People who talk that way are eager to despair, knowing how easy despair is. The change I am talking about appeals to me precisely because it need not wait upon "other people." Anybody who wants to do so can begin it in himself and in his household as soon as he is ready—by becoming answerable to at least some of his own needs, by acquiring skills and tools, by learning what his real needs are, by refusing the glamorous and the frivolous. When a person learns to *act* on his best hopes he enfranchises and validates them as no government or public

---

*If automobiles are not more durable and economic than horses, then obviously a better economy would replace them with horses. It would be progressive to do so.

policy ever will. And by his action the possibility that other people will do the same is made a likelihood.

But I must concede that there is also a sense in which I *am* tilting at windmills. While we have been preoccupied by various ideological menaces, we have been invaded and nearly overrun by windmills. They are drawing the nourishment from our soil and the lifeblood out of our veins. Let us tilt against the windmills. Though we have not conquered them, if we do not keep going at them they will surely conquer us.

5

THE KINGDOM OF ABSTRACTION
AND ORGANIZATION

I do not wish to discount the usefulness of either abstraction or organization, but rather to point out that we have given them such an extravagant emphasis and such prodigal subsidies that their *functioning* has come to overbear and obscure and even nullify their usefulness. Their ascendancy no doubt comes naturally enough out of the need to deal with the massive populations of an urban society. But their disproportionate, their almost exclusive, importance among us can only be explained as a disease of the specialist mentality that has found a haven in the government bureaus and the universities.

The bureaucrat who has formulated a plan, the specialist who has discovered a new fact or process, and the student who has espoused a social vision or ideal, all are of a kind in the sense that they all tend to think that they are at the end of a complete disciplinary process when in fact they have little more than reached the beginning of one. And this is their weakness: that they conceive abstractions to be complete in themselves, and therefore have only the

simplest and most mechanical notions of the larger processes within which the abstractions will have their effect—processes that are apt, ultimately, to be obscure or
mysterious in their workings and are therefore alien to the
specialist mentality in the first place.

Having produced or espoused an abstraction, they
next seek to put it to use by means of another abstraction
—that is, an organization. But there is a sense in which organization is not a means of implementation, but rather a
way of clinging to the clear premises and the neat logic of
abstraction. The specialist mentality, unable by the terms
of its narrow discipline to relinquish the secure order of abstraction, is prevented by a sort of Zeno's law from ever
reaching the real ground of proof in the human community
or in the world; it never *meets* the need it purports to answer. Demanding that each step toward the world be a
predictable one, the specialist is by that very token not
moving in the direction of the world at all, but on a course
parallel to it. He can reach the world, not by any organizational process, but only by a reverse leap of faith from the
ideal realm of the laboratory or theoretical argument onto
the obscure and clumsifying ground of experience, where
other and larger disciplines are required.

The man who must actually put the specialist's abstraction to use and live with its effects is never a part of
the specialist organization. The organization can only de-
liver the abstraction to him and, of necessity, largely turn
him loose with it. The farmer is not a part of the college of
agriculture and the extension service; he is, rather, their object. The impoverished family is not a part of the welfare
structure, but its object. The abstraction handed to these
object-people is either true only in theory or it has been
tried only under ideal (laboratory) conditions. For the bureaucrat, social planning replaces social behavior; for the
agricultural scientist, chemistry and economics replace cul-

ture and ecology; for the political specialist (student or politician), theory replaces life, or tries to. Thus we institutionalize an impasse between the theoretical or ideal and the real, between the abstract and the particular; the specialist maintains a sort of esthetic distance between himself and the ground of proof and responsibility; and we delude ourselves that precept can have life and useful force without example.

Abstractions move toward completion only in the particularity of enactment or of use. Their completion is only in that mysterious whole that Sir Albert Howard and others have called the wheel of life. A vision or a principle or a discovery or a plan is therefore only *half* a discipline, and, practically speaking, it is the least important half. Black Elk, the holy man of the Sioux, said in his autobiography, *Black Elk Speaks:* "I think I have told you, but if I have not, you must have understood, that a man who has a vision is not able to use the power of it until after he has performed the vision on earth for the people to see." And only a few years later another American, William Carlos Williams, said much the same: "No ideas but in things." The difference of which both men spoke is that between knowledge and the *use* of knowledge. Similarly, one may speak of the difference between the production of an idea or a thing and its use. The disciplines of production are always small and specialized. The disciplines of use and continuity are both different and large. A man who produces a fact or an idea has not completed his responsibility to it until he sees that it is well used in the world. A man may grow potatoes as a specialist of sorts, but he falsifies himself and his potatoes too if he eats them and fails to live as a man.

If the culture fails to provide highly articulate connections between the abstract and the particular, the organizational and the personal, knowledge and behavior, pro-

duction and use, the ideal and the world—that is, if it fails
to bring the small disciplines of each man's work within the
purview of those larger disciplines implied by the conditions of our life in the world—then the result is a profound
disorder in which men release into their community and
dwelling place powerful forces the consequences of which
are unconsidered or unknown. New knowledge, political
ideas, technological innovations, all are injected into society merely on the ground that to the specialists who produce them they appear to be good in themselves. A "labor-
saving" device that does the work it was intended to do is
thought by its developers to be a success: in terms of their
discipline and point of view it *works*. That, in working, it
considerably lowers the quality of a product and makes ob-
solete a considerable number of human beings is, to the
specialists, merely an opportunity for other specialists.

If this attitude were restricted to the elite of government and university it would be bad enough; but it has
been so popularized by their propaganda and example that
the general public is willing to attribute to declarations,
promises, mere words, the force of behavior. We have allowed and even encouraged a radical disconnection between our words and our deeds. Our speech has drifted out
of the world into a realm of fantasy in which whatever we
say is true. The President of the republic* openly admits
that there is no connection between what he says and what
he does—this in spite of his evident wish to be re-elected on
the strength of what he says. We find it not extraordinary
that lovers of America are strip mining in Appalachia, that
lovers of peace are bombing villages in Southeast Asia, that
lovers of freedom are underwriting dictatorships. If we *say*
we are lovers of America and peace and freedom, then this
must be what lovers of America and peace and freedom *do*.
Having no need to account for anything they have done,

*Nixon.

187 Discipline and Hope

our politicians do not find it necessary to trouble us with either evidence or argument, or to confess their errors, or to subtract their losses from their gains; they speak like the gods of Olympus, assured that if they *say* they are our servants anything they do in their own interest is right. Our public discourse has been reduced to the manipulation of uprooted symbols: good words, bad words, the names of gods and devils, emblems, slogans, flags. For some the flag no longer stands for the country, it *is* the country; they plant their crops and bury their dead in it.

There is no better example of this deterioration of language than in the current use of the word "freedom." Across the whole range of current politics this word is now being mouthed as if its devotees cannot decide whether it should be kissed or eaten, and this adoration has nothing to do with its meaning. The government is protecting the freedom of people by killing them or hiding microphones in their houses. The government's opponents, left and right, wish to set people free by telling them exactly what to do. All this is for the sake of the political power the word has come to have. The up-to-date politician no longer pumps the hand of a prospective constituent; he offers to set him—or her—free. And yet it seems to me that the word has no political meaning at all; the government cannot serve freedom except negatively—"by the alacrity," in Thoreau's phrase, "with which it [gets] out of its way."*

The going assumption seems to be that freedom can be granted only by an institution, that it is the gift of the government to its people. I think it is the other way around. Free men are not set free by their government; they have set their government free of themselves; they have made it unnecessary. Freedom is not accomplished by a declaration. A declaration of freedom is either a futile and

*And—still negatively—by keeping the selfish or vicious intentions of people out of its way.

empty gesture, or it is the statement of a finished fact. Freedom is a personal matter; though we may be enslaved as a group, we can be free only as persons. We can set each other free only as persons. It is a matter of discipline. A person can free himself of a bondage that has been imposed on him only by accepting another bondage that he has chosen. A man who would not be the slave of other men must be the master of himself—that is the real meaning of self-government. If we all behaved as honorably and honestly and as industriously as we expect our representatives to behave, we would soon put the government out of work.

A person dependent on somebody else for everything from potatoes to opinions may declare that he is a free man, and his government may issue a certificate granting him his freedom, but he will not be free. He is that variety of specialist known as a consumer, which means that he is the abject dependent of producers. How can he be free if he can do nothing for himself? What is the First Amendment to him whose mouth is stuck to the tit of the "affluent society"? Men are free precisely to the extent that they are equal to their own needs. The most able are the most free.

6

DISCIPLINE AND HOPE, MEANS AS ENDS

The various problems that I have so far discussed can best be understood, I think, as failures of discipline caused by a profound confusion as to the functions and the relative values of means and ends. I do not suggest simply that we fall with the ease of familiarity into the moral expedient of justifying means by ends, but that we have also come to attribute to ends a moral importance that far outweighs that which we attribute to means. We expect ends not only to justify means, but to rectify them as well. Once we have reached the desired end, we think, we will turn back to purify and consecrate the means. Once the war that we are fighting for the sake of peace is won, then the generals will become saints, the burned children will proclaim in heaven that their suffering is well repaid, the poisoned forests and fields will turn green again. Once we have peace, we say, or abundance or justice or truth or comfort, everything will be all right. It is an old dream.

It is a vicious illusion. For the discipline of ends is no discipline at all. The end is preserved in the means; a desirable end may perish forever in the wrong means. Hope lives in the means, not the end. Art does not survive in its revelations, or agriculture in its products, or craftsmanship in its artifacts, or civilization in its monuments, or faith in its relics.

That good ends are destroyed by bad means is one of the dominant themes of human wisdom. The *I Ching* says: "If evil is branded it thinks of weapons, and if we do it the favor of fighting against it blow for blow, we lose in the end because thus we ourselves get entangled in hatred and passion. Therefore it is important to begin at home, to be on guard in our own persons against the faults we have branded. . . . For the same reasons we should not combat our own faults directly. . . . As long as we wrestle with them, they continue victorious. Finally, the best way to fight evil is to make energetic progress in the good." Confucius said of riches that "if not obtained in the right way, they do not last." In the Sermon on the Mount, Jesus said: "Ye have heard that it hath been said, An eye for an eye, and a tooth for a tooth: But I say unto you, That ye resist not evil. . . ." And for that text Ken Kesey supplies the modern exegesis: "As soon as you resist evil, as soon as it's gone, you fold, because it's what you're based on." In 1931, Judge Lusk of the Chattanooga criminal court handed down a decision in which he wrote: "The best way, in my judgment, to combat Communism, or any other movement inimical to our institutions, is to show, if we can, that the injustices which they charge against us are, in fact, non-existent." And a friend of mine, a graduate of the University of Emily's Run, was once faced with the argument that he could "make money" by marketing some inferior lambs; he refused, saying that his purpose was the production of *good* lambs, and he would sell no other kind. He meant that his disciplines had to be those of a farmer, and that he would be diminished as a farmer by adopting the disciplines of a money-changer. It is a tragedy of our society that it neither pays nor honors a man for this sort of integrity—though it depends on him for it.

It is by now a truism that the great emphasis of our present culture is upon things, things as things, things in quantity without respect to quality; and that our predominant techniques and attitudes have to do with production and acquisition. We persist in the belief—against our religious tradition, and in the face of much evidence to the contrary—that if we leave our children wealthy we will assure their happiness. A corollary of this is the notion, rising out of the work of the geneticists, that we can assure a brighter future for the world by *breeding* a more intelligent race of humans—even though the present problems of the world are the result, not of human stupidity, but of human intelligence without adequate cultural controls. Both ideas are typical of the materialist assumption that human destiny can be improved by being constantly tinkered at, as if it were a sort of balky engine. But we can do nothing for the human future that we will not do for the human present. For the amelioration of the future condition of our kind we must look, not to the wealth or the genius of the coming generations, but to the quality of the disciplines and attitudes that we are preparing now for their use.

We are being virtually buried by the evidence that

those disciplines by which we manipulate *things* are inadequate disciplines. Our cities have become almost unlivable because they have been built to be factories and vending machines rather than communities. They are conceptions of the desires for wealth, excitement, and ease—all illegitimate motives from the standpoint of community, as is proved by the fact that without the community disciplines that make for a stable, neighborly population, the cities have become scenes of poverty, boredom, and dis-ease.

The rural community—that is, the land and the people—is being degraded in complementary fashion by the specialists' tendency to regard the land as a factory and the people as spare parts. Or, to put it another way, the rural community is being degraded by the fashionable premise that the exclusive function of the farmer is production and that his major discipline is economics. On the contrary, both the function and the discipline of the farmer have to do with provision: he must provide, he must look ahead. He must look ahead, however, not in the economic-mechanistic sense of anticipating a need and fulfilling it, but the sense of using methods that preserve the source. In his work sound economics becomes identical with sound ecology. The farmer is not a factory worker, he is the trustee of the life of the topsoil, the keeper of the rural community. In precisely the same way, the dweller in a healthy city is not an office or a factory worker, but part and preserver of the urban community. It is in thinking of the whole citizenry as factory workers—as readily interchangeable parts of an entirely mechanistic and economic order—that we have reduced our people to the most abject and aimless of nomads, and displaced and fragmented our communities.

An index of the health of a rural community—and, of course, of the urban community, its blood kin—might be found in the relative acreages of field crops and tree crops. By tree crops I mean not just those orchard trees of comparatively early bearing and short life, but also the fruit and nut and timber trees that bear late and live long. It is characteristic of an unsettled and anxious farm population—a population that feels itself, because of economic threat or the degradation of cultural value, to be ephemeral—that it farms almost exclusively with field crops, within economic and biological cycles that are complete in one year. This has been the dominant pattern of American agriculture. Stable, settled populations, assured both of an economic sufficiency in return for their work and of the cultural value of their work, tend to have methods and attitudes of a much longer range. Though they have generally also farmed with field crops, established farm populations have always been planters of trees. In parts of Europe, according to J. Russell Smith's important book, *Tree Crops,* steep hillsides were covered with orchards of chestnut trees, which were kept and maintained with great care by the farmers. Many of the trees were ancient, and when one began to show signs of dying, a seedling would be planted beside it to replace it. Here is an agricultural discipline that could develop only among farmers who felt secure—as individuals and also as families and communities—in their connection to their land. Such a discipline depends not just on the younger men in the prime of their workdays but also on the old men, the keepers of tradition. The model figure of this agriculture is an old man planting a young tree that will live longer than a man, that he himself may not live to see in its first bearing. And he is planting, moreover, a tree whose worth lies beyond any conceivable market prediction. He is planting it because the good sense of doing so has been clear to men of his place and kind for generations. The practice has been continued because it is ecologically and agriculturally sound; the economic soundness of it must be assumed. While the planting of a field crop, then, may be looked upon as a "short-term investment," the planting of a chestnut tree is a covenant of faith.

An urban discipline that in good health is closely analogous to healthy agriculture is teaching. Like a good farmer, a good teacher is the trustee of a vital and delicate organism: the life of the mind in his community. The standard of his discipline is his community's health and intelligence and coherence and endurance. This is a high calling, deserving of a life's work. We have allowed it to degenerate into careerism and specialization. In education as in agriculture we have discarded the large and enlarging disciplines of community and place, and taken up in their stead the narrow and shallow discipline of economics. Good teaching is an investment in the minds of the young, as obscure in result, as remote from immediate proof as planting a chestnut seedling. But we have come to prefer ends that are entirely foreseeable, even though that requires us to shorten our vision. Education is coming to be, not a long-term investment in young minds and in the life of the community, but a short-term investment in the economy. We want to be able to tell how many dollars an education is worth and how soon it will begin to pay.

To accommodate these frivolous desires, education becomes training and specialization, which is to say, it institutionalizes and justifies ignorance and intellectual irresponsibility. It produces a race of learned mincers, whose propriety and pride it is to keep their minds inside their "fields," as if human thoughts were a kind of livestock to be kept out of the woods and off the roads. Because of the obsession with short-term results that may be contained within the terms and demands of a single life, the interest of community is displaced by the interest of career. The careerist teacher judges himself, and is judged by his colleagues, not by the influence he is having upon his students or the community, but by the number of his publications, the size of his salary and the status of the place to which his career has taken him thus far. And in ambition he is where he is only temporarily; he is on his way to a more lucrative and prestigious place. Because so few stay to be aware of the *effects* of their work, teachers are not judged by their teaching, but by the short-term incidentals of publication and "service." That teaching is a long-term service, that a teacher's best work may be published in the children or grandchildren of his students, cannot be considered, for the modern educator, like his "practical" brethren in business and industry, will honor nothing that he cannot see. That is not to say that books do not have their progeny in the community, or that a legitimate product of a teacher's life may not be a book. It *is* to say that if *good* books are to be written, they will be written out of the same resources of talent and discipline and character and delight as always, and not by institutional coercion.

It is not from the standpoint of the university itself that we will see its faults, but from the standpoint of the whole community. Looking only at the university, one might perhaps believe that its first obligation is to become a better exemplar of its species: a *bigger* university, with more prestigious professors publishing more books and articles. But look at the state of Kentucky—whose land is being vandalized and whose people are being impoverished by the absentee owners of coal; whose dispossessed are refugees in the industrial cities to the north; whose farm population and economy are under the heaviest threat of their history; whose environment is generally deteriorating; whose public schools have become legendary for their poor quality; whose public offices are routinely filled by the morally incompetent. Look at the *state* of Kentucky, and it is clear that, more than any publication of books and articles, or any research, we need an annual increment of several hundred competently literate *graduates* who have some critical awareness of their inheritance and a sense of their obligation to it, and who know the use of books.

That, and that only, is the disciplining idea of education, and the methods must be derived accordingly. It has nothing to do with number or size. It would be impossible to value economically; it is the antithesis of that false economy which thrives upon the exploitation of stupidity. It stands forever opposed to the assumption that you can produce a good citizen by subjecting a moral simpleton to specialized training or expert advice.

It is the obsession with immediate ends that is degrading, that destroys our disciplines, and that drives us to our inflexible concentration upon number and price and size. I believe that the closer we come to correct discipline, the less concerned we are with ends, and with questions of futurity in general. Correct discipline brings us into alignment with natural process, which has no explicit or deliberate concern for the future. We do not eat, for instance, because we want to live until tomorrow, but because we are hungry today and it *satisfies* us to eat. Similarly, a good farmer plants, not because of the abstractions of demand or market or his financial condition, but because it is planting time and the ground is ready—that is, he plants in response to his discipline and to his place. And the real teacher does not teach with reference to the prospective job market or some program or plan for the society's future; he teaches because he has something to teach and because he has students. A poet could not write a poem in order to earn a place in literary history. His place in literary history is another subject, and as such a distraction. He writes because he has a poem to write, he knows how, the work pleases him, and he has forgotten all else. "Take therefore no thought for the morrow: for the morrow shall take thought for the things of itself." This passage rests, of course, on the fact that we do not know what tomorrow will be, and are therefore strictly limited in our ability to take thought for it. But it also rests upon the assumption of correct disciplines. The man who works and behaves well today *need* take no thought for the morrow; he has discharged today's only obligation to the morrow.

7

THE ROAD AND THE WHEEL

There are, I believe, two fundamentally opposed views of the nature of human life and experience in the world: one holds that though natural processes may be cyclic, there is within nature a human domain the processes of which are linear; the other, much older, holds that human life is subject to the same cyclic patterns as all other life. If the two are contradictory that is not so much because one is wrong and the other right as because one is partial and the other complete. The linear idea, of course, is the doctrine of progress, which represents man as having moved across the oceans and the continents and into space on a course that is ultimately logical and that will finally bring him to a man-made paradise. It also sees him as moving through time in this way, discarding old experience as he encounters new. The cyclic vision, on the other hand, sees our life ultimately not as a cross-country journey or a voyage of discovery, but as a circular dance in which certain basic *and necessary* patterns are repeated endlessly. This is the religious and ethical basis of the narrative of Black Elk: "Everything the Power of the World does is done in a circle. The sky is round, and I have heard that the earth is round like a ball, and so are all the stars. The wind, in its greatest power, whirls. Birds make their nests in circles, for theirs is the same religion as ours. The sun comes forth and goes down again in a circle. The moon does the same, and both are round. Even the seasons form a great circle in their changing, and always come back again to where they were. The life of a man is a circle from child-hood to childhood, and so it is in everything where power moves. Our tepees were round like the nests of birds, and these were always set in a circle, the nation's hoop, a nest of many nests, where the Great Spirit meant for us to hatch our children." The doctrine of progress suggests that the fluctuations of human fortune are a series of ups and downs in a road tending generally upward toward the earthly paradise. To Black Elk earthly blessedness did not lie ahead or behind; it was the result of harmony within the circle of the people and between the people and the world. A man was happy or sad, he thought, in proportion as he moved toward or away from "the sacred hoop of [his] peo-ple [which] was one of many hoops that made one circle, wide as daylight and as starlight. . . ."

Characteristic of the linear vision is the idea that anything is justifiable only insofar as it is immediately and obviously good for something else. The linear vision tends to look upon everything as a cause, and to require that it proceed directly and immediately and obviously to its ef-fect. What is it good for? we ask. And only if it proves im-mediately to be good *for* something are we ready to raise the question of value: How much is it worth? But we mean how much money, for if it can only be good for something else then obviously it can only be *worth* something else. Education becomes training as soon as we demand, in this spirit, that it serve some immediate purpose and that it be worth a predetermined amount. Once we accept so specific a notion of utility, all life becomes subservient to its use; its value is drained into its use. That is one reason why these are such hard times for students and old people: they are living either before or after the time of their social utility. It is also the reason why so many non-human species are threatened with extinction. Any organism that is not contributing obviously and directly to the workings of the economy is now endangered—which means, as the ecologists are showing, that human society is to the same extent endangered. The cyclic vision is more accepting of mystery and more humble. Black Elk *assumes* that all things have a use—that is the condition of his respect for all things—but he does not know what all their uses are. Because he does not value them for their uses, he is free to value them for their own sake: "The Six Grandfathers have placed in this world many things, all of which should be happy. Every little thing is sent for something, and in that thing there should be happiness and the power to make happy." It should be emphasized that this is ecologically sound. The ecologists recognize that the creation is a great union of interlocking lives and processes and substances, all dependent on each other; and because they cannot discover the whole pattern of interdependency, they recognize the need for the greatest possible care in the use of the world. Black Elk and his people, however, were further advanced, for they possessed the cultural means for the enactment of a ceremonious respect for and delight in the lives with which they shared the world, and that respect and delight afforded those other lives an effective protection.

The linear vision looks fixedly straight ahead. It never looks back, for its premise is that there is no return. The doctrine of possession is complemented by no doctrine of relinquishment. Our shallow concept of use does not imply good use or preservation; thus quantity depresses quality, and we arrive at the concepts of waste and disposability. Similarly, life is lived without regard or respect for death. Death thus becomes accidental, the chance interruption of a process that might otherwise go on forever—therefore, always a surprise and always feared. Dr. Leon R. Kass, of the National Academy of Sciences, recently said that "medicine seems to be sharpening its tools to do battle

with death as though death were just one more disease."
The cyclic vision, at once more realistic and more generous,
recognizes in the creation the essential principle of return:
what is here will leave to come again; if there is to be having there must also be giving up. And it sees death as an
integral and indispensable part of life. In one of the medicine rites of the Winnebago, according to Paul Radin, an
old woman says: "Our father has ordained that my body
shall fall to pieces. I am the earth. Our father ordained that
there should be death, lest otherwise there be too many
people and not enough food for them." Because death is
inescapable, a biological and ecological necessity, its acceptance becomes a spiritual obligation, the only means of
making life whole: "Whosoever shall seek to save his life
shall lose it; and whosoever shall lose his life shall preserve
it."

The opposing characteristics of the linear and cyclic
visions might, then, be graphed something like this:

Linear	*Cyclic*
Progress. The conquest of nature.	Atonement with the creation.
The Promised Land motif in the Westward Movement.	Black Elk's sacred hoop, the community of creation.
Heavenly aspiration without earthly reconciliation or stewardship. The creation as commodity.	Reconciliation of heaven and earth in aspiration toward responsible life. The creation as source *and end.*
Training. Programming.	Education. Cultural process.
Possession.	Usufruct, relinquishment.
Quantity.	Quality.
Newness. The unique and "original."	Renewal. The recurring.
Life.	Life and death.

The linear vision flourishes in ignorance or contempt of the processes on which it depends. In the face of these processes our concepts and mechanisms are so unrealistic, so *impractical,* as to have the nature of fantasy. The processes are invariably cyclic, rising and falling, taking and giving back, living and dying. But the linear vision places its emphasis entirely on the rising phase of the cycle—on production, possession, life. It provides for no returns. Waste, for instance, is a concept that could have been derived only from the linear vision. According to the scheme of our present thinking, every human activity produces waste. This implies a profound contempt for correct discipline; it proposes, in the giddy faith of prodigals, that there can be production without fertility, abundance without thrift. We take and do not give back, and this causes waste. It is a hideous concept, and it is making the world hideous. It is consumption, a wasting disease. And this disease of our material economy becomes also the disease of our spiritual economy, and we have made a shoddy merchandise of our souls. We want the truth to be easy and spectacular, and so we waste our verities; we are always hastening from the essential to the novel. We want to have love without a return of devotion or fidelity; to us, Aphrodite is a peeping statistician, the seismographer of orgasms. We want a faith that demands no return of good work. And art—we want it to be instantaneous and effortless; we want it to involve no apprenticeship to a tradition or a discipline or a master, no devotion to an ideal of workmanship. We want our art to support the illusion that high achievement is within easy reach, for we want to believe that, though we are demeaned by our work and driven half crazy by our pleasures, we are all mute inglorious Miltons.

To take up again my theme of agriculture, it is obvious that the modern practice concentrates almost exclusively on the productive phase of the natural cycle. The means of production become more elaborate all the time, but the means of return—the building of health and fertility in the soil—are reduced more and more to the shorthand of chemicals. According to the industrial vision of it, the life of the farm does not rise and fall in the turning cycle of the year; it goes on in a straight line from one harvest to another. This, in the long run, may well be more productive of waste than of anything else. It wastes the soil. It wastes the animal manures and other organic residues that industrialized agriculture frequently fails to return to the soil. And what may be our largest agricultural waste is not usually recognized as such, but is thought to be both an urban product and an urban problem: the tons of garbage and sewage that are burned or buried or flushed into the rivers. This, like all waste, is the abuse of a resource. It was ecological stupidity of exactly this kind that destroyed Rome. The chemist Justus von Liebig wrote that "the sewers of the immense metropolis engulfed in the course of centuries the prosperity of Roman peasants. The Roman Campagna would no longer yield the means of feeding her population; these same sewers devoured the wealth of Sicily, Sardinia and the fertile lands of the coast of Africa."

To recognize the magnitude and the destructiveness of our "urban waste" is to recognize the shallowness of the notion that agriculture is only another form of technology to be turned over to a few specialists. The sewage and garbage problem of our cities suggests, rather, that a healthy agriculture is a cultural organism, not merely a universal necessity but a universal obligation as well. It suggests that, just as the cities exist within the environment, they also exist within agriculture. It suggests that, like farmers, city-dwellers have agricultural responsibilities: to use no more than necessary, to waste nothing, to return organic residues to the soil.

Our ecological or agricultural responsibilities, then,

call for a corresponding set of disciplines that would be a part of the cultural common ground, and that each person would have an obligation to preserve in his behavior. Seeking his own ends by the correct means, he transcends selfishness and makes a just return to the ecological source; by his correct behavior, both the source and the means for its proper use are preserved. This is equally true of other cultural areas: it is the discipline, not the desire, that is the common ground. In politics, for example, it is only the personal career that can be advanced by "image making." *Politics* cannot be advanced except by honest, informed, open discourse—by determining and telling and implementing the truth, by assuming the truth's heavy responsibilities and great risks. The political careerist, by serving his "image" rather than the truth, becomes a consumer of the political disciplines. Similarly, in art, the common ground is workmanship, the artistic means, the technical possibility of art—not the insights or visions of particular artists. A person who practices an art without mastering its disciplines becomes his art's consumer; he obscures the means, and encumbers his successors. The art lives *for* its insights and visions, but it cannot live *upon* them. An art is inherited and handed down in its workmanly aspects. Workmanship is one of the means by which the artist prepares for—becomes worthy of, earns—his vision and his insights. "Art," A. R. Ammons says, "is the conscious preparation for the unconscious event. . . ."

Learning the correct and complete disciplines—the disciplines that take account of death as well as life, decay as well as growth, return as well as production—is an indispensable form of cultural generosity. It is the one effective way a person has of acknowledging and acting upon the fact of mortality: he will die, others will live after him.

One reason, then, for the disciplinary weakness of the linear vision is that it is incomplete. Another is that it sees history as always leading not to renewal but to the new: the road may climb hills and descend into valleys, but it is always going ahead; it never turns back on itself. "We have constructed a fate . . . that never turns aside," Thoreau said of the railroad; "its orbit does not look like a returning curve. . . ." But when the new is assumed to be a constant, discipline fails, for discipline is preparation, and the new cannot be prepared for; it cannot, in any very meaningful way, be expected. Here again we come upon one of the reasons for the generational disconnections that afflict us: all times, we assume, are different; we therefore have nothing to learn from our elders, nothing to teach our children. Civilization is thus reduced to a sequence of last-minute improvisations, desperately building today out of the wreckage of yesterday. There are two genres of writing that seem to me to be characteristic (or symptomatic) of the linear vision. The first is, not prophecy, though it is sometimes called that, but the most mundane and inquisitive taking of thought for the morrow. What will tomorrow be like? (We mean, what new machines or ideas will be invented by then?) What will the world be like in ten or fifty or a hundred years? Our preoccupation with these questions, besides being useless, is morbid and scared; mistaking appearance for substance, it assumes a condition of *absolute* change: the future will be *entirely* different from the past and the present, we think, because our vision of history and experience has not taught us to imagine persistence or recurrence or renewal. We disregard the necessary persistence of ancient needs and obligations, patterns and cycles, and assume that the human condition is entirely determined by human *devices*.

The other genre—complementary, obviously—is that of the death sentence. Because we see the human situation as perpetually changing, the new bearing down with annihilating force, we appear to ourselves to be living always at the end of possibilities. For the new to happen, the old must be destroyed. Our own lives, which are pleasant to us at least insofar as they represent a *kind* of life that we recognize, seem always on the verge of being replaced by a kind of life that is unrecognizable, or by a death that is equally so. Thus a common theme for the writers of feature articles and critical essays is the death or the impending death of something: of the fashions of dress and appearance, of the novel, of printing, of freedom, of Christianity, of Western civilization, of the human race, of the world, of God.

This genre is difficult to criticize, because there is always a certain justice, or likelihood of justice, in it. There is no denying that we fear the end of things because our way of life has brought so many things to an end. The sunlit road of progress never escapes a subterranean dread that threatens to undermine the pavement. Thoreau knew that the railroad was built upon the bodies of Irishmen, and not one of us but secretly wonders when *he* will be called upon to lie down and become a sleeper beneath the roadbed of progress. And so some of this death-sentence literature is faithfully reporting the destructiveness of the linear vision; it is the chorus of accusation and dread and mourning that accompanies Creon's defiance of the gods.

But at times it is no more than one of the sillier manifestations of the linear vision itself: the failure to see any pattern in experience, the failure to transform experience into useful memory. There is a sort of journalistic greenness in us that is continuously surprised by the seasons and the weather, as if these were no more than the inventions (or mistakes) of the meteorologists. History, likewise, is always a surprise to us; we read its recurring disasters as if they were the result merely of miscalculations of our intelligence—as if they could not have been foreseen in the flaws of our character. And the heralds of the push-button

Eden of the future would be much put off to consider that
those button-pushers will still have to deal with problems
of food and sewage, with the picking up of scraps and the
disposal of garbage, with building and maintenance and
reclamation—with, that is, the fundamental work, much
of it handwork, that is necessary to life; they would be even
more put off to consider that the "quality of life" will not
depend nearly so much on the distribution of pushbuttons
as on the manner and the quality of that fundamental and
endlessly necessary work.

Some cycles revolve frequently enough to be well
known in a man's lifetime. Some are complete only in the
memory of several generations. And others are so vast that
their motion can only be assumed: like our galaxy, they
appear to us to be remote and exalted, a Milky Way, when
in fact they are near at hand, and we and all the humble
motions of our days are their belongings. We are kept in
touch with these cycles, not by technology or politics or
any other strictly human device, but by our necessary biological relation to the world. It is only in the processes of
the natural world, and in analogous and related processes
of human culture, that the new may grow usefully old, and
the old be made new.

The ameliorations of technology are largely illusory.
They are always accompanied by penalties that are equal
and opposite. Like the weather reports, they suggest the
possibility of better solutions than they can provide; and
by this suggestiveness—this glib and shallow optimism of
gimcrackery—they have too often replaced older skills that
were more serviceable to life in a mysterious universe. The
farmer whose weather eye has been usurped by the radio
has become less observant, has lost his old judicious fatal-
ism with respect to the elements—and he is no more certain of the weather. It is by now obvious that these so-
called blessings have not made us better or wiser. And their

expense is growing rapidly out of proportion to their use. How many plastic innards can the human race afford? How many mountains can the world afford to the strip miners, to light the whole outdoors and overheat our rooms? The limits, as Thoreau knew, have been in sight from the first: "To make a railroad round the world available to all mankind," he said in *Walden*, "is equivalent to grading the whole surface of the planet. Men have an indistinct notion that if they keep up this activity of joint stocks and spades long enough all will at length ride . . . but though a crowd rushes to the depot . . . when the smoke is blown away and the vapor condensed, it will be perceived that a few are riding, but the rest are run over. . . ."

We cannot look for happiness to any technological paradise or to any New Earth of outer space, but only to the world as it is, and as we have made it. The only life we may hope to live is here. It seems likely that if we are to reach the earthly paradise at all, we will reach it only when we have ceased to strive and hurry so to get there. There is no "there." We can only wait here, where we are, in the world, obedient to its processes, patient in its taking away, faithful to its returns. And as much as we may know, and all that we deserve, of earthly paradise will come to us.

8

KINDS OF DISCIPLINE

The disciplines we most readily think of are technical; they are the means by which we define and enact our relationship to the creation, and destroy or preserve the commonwealth of the living. There is no disputing the importance of these, and I have already said a good deal in their support. But alone, without the larger disciplines of community and faith, they fail of their meaning and their aim; they cannot even continue for very long. People who practice the disciplines of workmanship for their own sake—that is, as specializations—begin a process of degeneracy in those disciplines, for they remove from them the ultimate sense of use or effect by which their vitality and integrity are preserved. Without a proper sense of use a discipline declines from community responsibility to personal eccentricity; cut off from the common ground of experience and need, vision escapes into wishful or self-justifying fantasy, or into greed. Artists lose the awareness of an audience, craftsmen and merchants lose the awareness of customers and users.

Community disciplines, which can rise only out of the cyclic vision, are of two kinds. First there is the discipline of principle, the essence of the experience of the historical community. And second there is the discipline of fidelity to the living community, the community of family and neighbors and friends. As our society has become increasingly rootless and nomadic, it has become increasingly fashionable among the rhetoricians of dissatisfaction to advocate, or to seem to advocate, a strict and solitary adherence to principle in simple defiance of other people. "I don't care what they think" has become public currency with us; saying it, we always mean to imply that we are persons solemnly devoted to high principle—"rugged individuals" in the somewhat fictional sense Americans usually give to that term. In fact, this ready defiance of the opinions of others is a rhetorical fossil from our frontier experience. Once it meant that if our neighbors' opinions were repugnant to us, we were prepared either to kill our neighbors or to move west. Now it doesn't mean anything; it is adolescent bluster. For when there is no frontier to retreat to, the demands of one's community will be felt, and ways must be found to deal with them. The great moral labor of any age is probably not in the conflict of opposing principles, but in the tension between a living community and those principles that are the distillation of its experience. Thus the present anxiety and anguish in this country have very little to do with the much-heralded struggle between capitalism and communism, or left and right, and very much indeed to do with the rapidly building discord and tension between American principles and American behavior.

This sort of discord is the subject of tragedy. It is tragic because—outside the possibility of a renewal of harmony, which may depend upon the catharsis of tragedy—there are no possible resolutions that are not damaging. To choose community over principle is to accept in consequence a diminishment of the community's moral inheritance; it is to accept the great dangers and damages of life without principle. To choose principle over community is even worse, it seems to me, for that is to accept as the condition of being "right" a loneliness in which the right is ultimately meaningless; it is to destroy the only ground upon which principle can be enacted, and renewed; it is to raise an ephemeral hope upon the ground of final despair.

Facing exactly this choice between principle and community, on April 20, 1861, Robert E. Lee resigned his commission in the army of the United States. Lee had clearly understood the evil of slavery. He disapproved and dreaded secession; almost alone among the Virginians, he foresaw the horrors that would follow. And yet he chose to go with his people. Having sent in his resignation, he wrote his sister: ". . . though I recognize no necessity for this state of things, and would have forborne and pleaded to the end for a redress of grievances, real or supposed, yet in my own person I had to meet the question whether I should take part against my native state. With all my devotion to the Union and the feeling of loyalty and duty of an American citizen, I have not been able to make up my mind to raise my hand against my relatives, my children, my home."

He was right. As a highly principled man, he could not bring himself to renounce the very ground of his principles. And devoted to that ground as he was, he held in himself much of his region's hope of the renewal of principle. His seems to me to have been an exemplary American choice, one that placed the precise Jeffersonian vision of a rooted devotion to community and homeland above the abstract "feeling of loyalty and duty of an American citizen." It was a tragic choice on the theme of Williams' maxim: "No ideas but in things."

If the profession of warfare has so declined in respectability since 1861 as to obscure my point, then change the terms. Say that a leader of our own time, in spite of his patriotism and his dependence on "the economy," nevertheless held his people and his place among them in such devotion that he would not lie to them or sell them shoddy merchandise or corrupt their language or degrade their environment. Say, in other words, that he would refuse to turn his abilities against his people. That is what Lee did, and there have been few public acts of as much integrity since.*

It is the intent of community disciplines, of course, to prevent such radical conflicts. If these disciplines are practiced at large among the members of the community, then the community holds together upon a basis of principle that is immediately clarified in feeling and behavior; and then destructive divisions, and the moral agonies of exceptional men, are averted.

In the Sermon on the Mount a major concern is with the community disciplines. The objective of this concern is a social ideal: ". . . all things whatsoever that men should do to you, do ye even so to them. . . ." But that ev-

---

*If loyalty to home and community allied one with a manifest evil, then it would be necessary to stand alone on principle. But it would be foolish to expect a choice so clean-cut.

eryone would do as he would be done by is hardly a realistic hope, and Jesus was speaking out of a moral tradition that was eminently realistic and tough-minded. It was a tradition that, in spite of its spiritual aspirations, was very worldly in its expectations: it would have spared Sodom for the sake of ten righteous men. And so the focus of the Sermon is not on the utopian social ideal of the Golden Rule, but on the *personal* ideal of nonresistance to evil: ". . . whosoever shall smite thee on thy right cheek, turn to him the other also. . . . Love your enemies, bless them that curse you, do good to them that hate you, and pray for them which despitefully use you, and persecute you. . . ." The point, I think, is that the anger of one man need not destroy the community, if it is contained by the peaceableness and long-suffering of another, but in the anger of *two* men, in anger repaid—"An eye for an eye, and a tooth for a tooth"—it is destroyed altogether.

Community, as a discipline, extends and enlarges the technical disciplines by looking at them within the perspective of their uses or effects. Community discipline imposes upon our personal behavior an ecological question: What is the effect, on our neighbors and on our place in the world, of what we do? It is aware that *all* behavior is social. It is aware, as the ecologists are aware, that there is a unity in the creation, and that the behavior and the fate of one creature must therefore affect the whole, though the exact relationships may not be known.

But essential as are the disciplines of technique and community, they are not sufficient in themselves. All such disciplines reach their limit of comprehensibility and at that point enter mystery. Thus an essential part of a discipline is that relinquishment or abandonment by which we acknowledge and accept its limits. We do not finally know what will be the result of our actions, however correct and excellent they may be. The good work we do today may be undone by some mere accident tomorrow. Our neighborly acts may be misunderstood and repaid with anger. With respect to what is to come, our real condition is that of abandonment; one of the primary functions of religion is to provide the ceremonial means of acknowledging this: we are in the hands of powers that we do not know.

The ultimate discipline, then, is faith: faith, if in nothing else, in the propriety of one's disciplines. We have obscured the question of faith by pretending that it is synonymous with the question of "belief," which is personal and not subject to scrutiny. But if one's faith is to have any public validity or force, then obviously it must meet some visible test. The test of faith is consistency—not the fanatic consistency by which one repudiates the influence of knowledge, but rather a consistency between principle and behavior. A man's behavior should be the creature of his principles, not the creature of his circumstances. The point has great practical bearing, because belief and the principles believed in, and whatever hope and promise are implied in them, are destroyed in contradictory behavior; hypocrisy salvages nothing but the hypocrite. If we put our faith in the truth, then we risk everything—the truth included—by telling lies. If we put our faith in peace, then we must see that violence makes us infidels. When we institute repressions to protect democracy from enemies abroad, we have already damaged it at home. The demands of faith are absolute: we must put all our eggs in one basket; we must burn our bridges.

An exemplary man of faith was Gideon, who reduced his army from thirty-two thousand to three hundred in earnest of his trust, and marched that remnant against the host of the Midianites, armed, not with weapons, but with "a trumpet in every man's hand, with empty pitchers, and lamps within the pitchers."

Beside this figure of Gideon, the hero as man of

faith, let us place our own "defender," the Pentagon, which has faith in nothing except its own power. That, as the story of Gideon makes clear, is a dangerous faith for mere men; it places them in the most dangerous moral circumstance, that of *hubris,* in which one boasts that "mine own hand hath saved me." To be sure, the Pentagon is supposedly founded upon the best intentions and the highest principles, and there is a plea that justifies it in the names of Christianity, peace, liberty, and democracy. But the Pentagon is an institution, not a person; and unless constrained by the moral vision of persons in them, institutions move in the direction of power and self-preservation, not high principle. Established, allegedly, in defense of "the free world," the Pentagon subsists complacently upon the involuntary servitude of millions of young men whose birthright, allegedly, is freedom. To wall our enemies out, it is walling us in.

Because its faith rests entirely in its own power, its mode of dealing with the rest of the world is not faith but suspicion. It recognizes no friends, for it knows that the face of friendship is the best disguise of an enemy. It has only enemies, or prospective enemies. It must therefore be prepared for *every possible* eventuality. It sees the future as a dark woods with a gunman behind every tree. It is passing through the valley of the shadow of death without a shepherd, and thus is never still. But as long as it can keep the public infected with its own state of mind, this spiritual dis-ease, it can survive without justification, and grow huge. Whereas the man of faith may go armed with only a trumpet and an empty pitcher and a lamp, the institution of suspicion arms with the death of the world; trusting nobody, it must stand ready to kill everybody.

The moral is that those who have no faith are apt to be much encumbered by their equipment, and overborne by their precautions. For the institution of suspicion there is no end of toiling and spinning. The Pentagon exists continually, not only on the brink of war, but on the brink of the exhaustion of its moral and material means. But the man of faith, even in the night, in the camp of his enemies, is at rest in the assurance of his trust and the correctness of his ways.* He has become the lily of the field.

9

THE LIKENESSES OF ATONEMENT (AT-ONE-MENT)

Living in our speech, though no longer in our consciousness, is an ancient system of analogies that clarifies a series of mutually defining and sustaining unities: of farmer and field, of husband and wife, of the world and God. The language both of our literature and of our everyday speech is full of references and allusions to this expansive metaphor of farming and marriage and worship. A man planting a crop is like a man making love to his wife, and vice versa: he is a husband or a husbandman. A man praying is like a lover, or he is like a plant in a field waiting for rain. As husbandman, a man is both the steward and the likeness of God, the greater husbandman. God is the lover of the world and its faithful husband. Jesus is a bridegroom. And he is a planter; his words are seeds. God is a shepherd and we are his sheep. And so on.

All the essential relationships are comprehended in this metaphor. A farmer's relation to his land is the basic and central connection in the relation of humanity to the creation; the agricultural relation *stands for* the larger relation. Similarly, marriage is the basic and central community tie; it begins and stands for the relation we have to family and to the larger circles of human association. And these relationships to the creation and to the human community

---

*That is not to suggest that faith may not be extremely dangerous, especially to the faithful.

are in turn basic to, and may stand for, our relationship to God—or to the sustaining mysteries and powers of the creation.

(These three relationships are dependent—and even intent—upon renewals of various sorts: of season, of fertility, of sexual energy, of love, of faith. And these concepts of renewal are always accompanied by concepts of loss or death; in order for the renewal to take place, the old must be not forgotten but relinquished; in order to become what we may be, we must cease to be as we are; in order to have life we must lose it. Our language bears abundant testimony to these deaths; the year's death that precedes spring; the burial of the seed before germination; sexual death, as in the Elizabethan metaphor; death as the definitive term of marriage; the spiritual death that must precede rebirth; the death of the body that must precede resurrection.)

As the metaphor comprehends all the essential relationships, so too it comprehends all the essential moralities. The moralities are ultimately emulative. For the metaphor does not merely perceive the likeness of these relationships. It perceives also that they are understandable only in terms of each other. They are the closed system of our experience; no instructions come from outside. A man finally cannot act upon the basis of absolute law, for the law is more fragmentary than his own experience; finally, he must emulate in one relationship what he knows of another. Thus, if the metaphor of atonement is alive in his consciousness, he will see that he should love and care for his land as for his wife, that his relation to his place in the world is as solemn and demanding, and as blessed, as marriage; and he will see that he should respect his marriage as he respects the mysteries and transcendent powers—that is, as a sacrament. Or—to move in the opposite direction through the changes of the metaphor—in order to care properly for his land he will see that he must emulate the

Creator: to learn to use and preserve the open fields, as Sir Albert Howard said, he must look into the woods; he must study and follow natural process; he must understand the *husbanding* that, in nature, always accompanies providing.

Like any interlinking system, this one fails in the failure of any one of its parts. When we obscure or corrupt our understanding of any one of the basic unities, we begin to misunderstand all of them. The vital knowledge dies out of our consciousness and becomes fossilized in our speech and our culture. This is our condition now. We have severed the vital links of the atonement metaphor, and we did this initially, I think, by degrading and obscuring our connection to the land, by looking upon the land as merchandise and ourselves as its traveling salesmen.

I do not know how exact a case might be made, but it seems to me that there is an historical parallel, in white American history, between the treatment of the land and the treatment of women. The frontier, for instance, was notoriously exploitive of both, and I believe for largely the same reasons. Many of the early farmers seem to have worn out farms and wives with equal regardlessness, interested in both mainly for what they would produce, crops and dollars, labor and sons; they clambered upon their fields and upon their wives, struggling for an economic foothold, the having and holding that cannot come until both fields and wives are properly cherished. And today there seems to me a distinct connection between our nomadism (our "social mobility") and the nearly universal disintegration of marriages and families.

The prevalent assumption appears to be that marriage problems are problems strictly of "human relations": if the husband and wife will only assent to a number of truisms about "respect for the other person," "giving and taking," et cetera, and if they will only "understand" each other, then it is believed that their problems will be solved.

The difficulty is that marriage is only partly a matter of "human relations," and only partly a circumstance of the emotions. It is also, and as much as anything, a practical circumstance. It is very much under the influence of things and people outside itself; that is, it must make a household, it must make a place for itself in the world and in the community. But with us, getting someplace always involves going somewhere. Every professional advance leads to a new place, a new house, a new neighborhood. Our marriages are always being cut off from what they have made; their substance is always disappearing into the thin air of human relations.

I think there is a limit to the portability of human relationships. Tribal nomads, when they moved, moved as a tribe; their personal and cultural identity—their household and community—accompanied them as they went. But our modern urban nomads are always moving away from the particulars by which they know themselves, and moving into abstraction (*a* house, *a* neighborhood, *a* job) in which they can only feel threatened by new particulars. The marriage becomes a sort of assembly-line product, made partly here and partly there, the whole of it never quite coming into view. Provided they stay married (which is unlikely) until the children leave (which is usually soon), the nomadic husband and wife who look to see what their marriage has been—that is to say, what it *is*—are apt to see only the lines in each other's face.

The carelessness of place that must accompany our sort of nomadism makes a vagueness in marriage that is its antithesis. And vagueness in marriage, the most sacred human bond and perhaps the basic metaphor of our moral and religious tradition, cannot help but produce a diminishment of reverence, and of the care for the earth that must accompany reverence.

When the metaphor of atonement ceases to live in

our consciousness, we lose the means of relationship. We become isolated in ourselves, and our behavior becomes the erratic behavior of people who have no bonds and no limits.

10

THE PRACTICALITY OF MORALS

What I have been preparing at such length to say is that there is only one value: the life and health of the world. If there is only one value, it follows that conflicts of value are illusory, based upon perceptual error. Moral, practical, spiritual, esthetic, economic, and ecological values are all concerned ultimately with the same question of life and health. To the virtuous man, for example, practical and spiritual values are identical; it is only corruption that can see a difference. Esthetic value is always associated with sound values of other kinds. "Beauty is truth, truth beauty," Keats said, and I think we may take him at his word.* Or to say the same thing in a different way: beauty is wholeness; it is health in the ecological sense of amplitude and balance. And ecology is long-term economics. If these identities are not apparent immediately, they are apparent *in time.* Time is the merciless, infallible critic of the specialized disciplines. In the ledgers that justify waste the ink is turning red.

Moral value, as should be obvious, is not separable from other values. An adequate morality would be ecologically sound; it would be esthetically pleasing. But the point I want to stress here is that it would be *practical.* Morality is long-term practicality.

Of all specialists the moralists are the worst, and the

*I now consider this reference to Keats to be misleading. The ideal beauty of the "Ode on a Grecian Urn" is very different from the common, earthly, mortal beauty I had in mind.

processes of disintegration and specialization that have characterized us for generations have made moralists of us all. We have obscured and weakened morality, first, by advocating it for its own sake—that is, by deifying it, as esthetes have deified art—and then, as our capacity for reverence has diminished, by allowing it to become merely decorative, a matter of etiquette.

What we have forgotten is the origin of morality in fact and circumstance; we have forgotten that the nature of morality is essentially practical. Moderation and restraint, for example, are necessary, not because of any religious commandment or any creed or code, but because they are among the assurances of good health and a sufficiency of goods. Likewise, discipline is necessary if the necessary work is to be done; also if we are to know transport, transcendence, joy. Loyalty, devotion, faith, self-denial are not ethereal virtues, but the concrete terms upon which the possibility of love is kept alive in this world. Morality is neither ethereal nor arbitrary; it is the definition of what is humanly possible, and it is the definition of the penalties for violating human possibility. A person who violates human limits is punished or he prepares a punishment for his successors, not necessarily because of any divine or human law, but because he has transgressed the order of things.* A live and adequate morality is an accurate perception of the order of things, and of humanity's place in it. By clarifying the human limits, morality tells us what we risk when we forsake the human to behave like false gods or like animals.

One would not wish to say—indeed, it is precisely my point that one *should* not say—that social *forms* will not change with changing conditions. They probably *will* do so, wholly regardless of whether or not they *should*. But I believe that it is erroneous to assume that a change of

*The order of things, of course, *is* a law—and not a human one.

form implies a change of discipline. Under the influence of the rapid changes of modern life, it is persistently assumed that we are moving toward a justifiable relaxation of disciplines. This is wishful thinking, and it invites calamity, for the human place in the order of things, the human limits, the human tragedy remain the same. It seems altogether possible, as a final example, that for various reasons the forms of marriage will change.* But this does not promise a new age of benefit without obligation—which, I am afraid, is what many people mean by freedom. Though the forms of marriage may change, if it continues to exist in any form it will continue to rest upon the same sustaining disciplines, and to incorporate the same tragic awareness: that it is made "for better for worse, for richer for poorer, in sickness and in health, to love and to cherish, till death. . . ."

11

THE SPRING OF HOPE

The most destructive of ideas is that extraordinary times justify extraordinary measures. This is the ultimate relativism, and we are hearing it from all sides. The young, the poor, the minority races, the Constitution, the nation, traditional values, sexual morality, religious faith, Western civilization, the economy, the environment, the world are all now threatened with destruction—so the arguments run—therefore let us deal with our enemies by whatever means are handiest and most direct; in view of our high aims history will justify and forgive. Thus the violent have always rationalized their violence.

But as wiser men have always known, all times are extraordinary in precisely this sense. In the condition of mortality all things are always threatened with destruction.

---

*But to change them quickly is simply to destroy them. It is, I think, foolish to think that ancient community forms can be satisfactorily altered or safely discarded by the intention of individuals.

The invention of atomic holocaust and the other man-made dooms renews for us the immediacy of the worldly circumstance as the religions have always defined it: we know "neither the day nor the hour. . . ."

Our bewilderment is not the time but our character. We have come to expect too much from outside ourselves. If we are in despair or unhappy or uncomfortable, our first impulse is to assume that this cannot be our fault; our second is to assume that some institution is not doing its duty. We are in the curious position of expecting from others what we can only supply ourselves. One of the Confucian ideals is that the "archer, when he misses the bullseye, turns and seeks the cause of the error in himself."

Goodness, wisdom, happiness, even physical comfort, are not institutional conditions. The real sources of hope are personal and spiritual, not public and political. A man is not happy by the dispensation of his government or by the fortune of his age. He is happy only in doing well what is in his power, and in being reconciled to what is not in his power. Thoreau, who knew such happiness, wrote in "Life Without Principle": "Of what consequence, though our planet explode, if there is no character involved in the explosion? In health we have not the least curiosity about such events. We do not live for idle amusement. I would not run round a corner to see the world blow up."

Asked why the Shakers, who expected the end of the world at any moment, were nevertheless consummate farmers and craftsmen, Thomas Merton replied: "When you expect the world to end at any moment, you know there is no need to hurry. You take your time, you do your work well."

from

The Unforeseen Wilderness

IV

A Country
of Edges

It is a country of overtowering edges. Again and again, walking down from the wooded ridge tops above the Red River Gorge one comes into the sound of water falling—the steady pouring and spattering of a tiny stream that has reached its grand occasion. And then one arrives at a great shady scoop in the cliff where the trail bends and steps and skids down to the foot of the fall. One looks up twenty or thirty or fifty or more feet to where the water leaps off the rock lip, catching the sunlight as it falls. Maybe there will be a rainbow in the spray. The trail may have passed through little shelves or terraces covered with wild iris in bloom. Or along the streamsides below the falls there may be pink lady's slippers. The slopes will be thickly shrubbed with rhododendron, darkened by the heavy green shade of hemlocks. And always on the wet faces of the rock there will be liverwort and meadow rue and mosses and ferns.

These places are as fresh, and they stay as fresh in the memory, as a clear, cold drink of water. They have a way of making me thirsty, whether I need a drink or not, and I like to hunt out a pool among the rocks and drink. The water is clean and cold. It is what water ought to be, for here one gets it "high and original," uncorrupted by any scientific miracle. There will be a clean gravelly bottom to the pool and its edges will bear the delicate garden-growth of the wet woods. There are the enclosing sounds of the water falling, and the voices of the phoebes and the Carolina wrens that nest in the sheltered places of the cliffs. Looking and listening are as important as tasting. One drinks in the sense of being in a good place.

The critical fact about water, wherever you find it in the Red River Gorge, is motion. Moving, it is gathering. All the little seeps and trickles of the slopes, the tiny streams heading up near the ridgetops and leaping and tumbling down the steep ravines—all are moving toward their union in the river.

And in the movement of its waters the place also is in motion; not to the human eye, nor to the collective vision of human history, but within the long gaze of geologic time the Gorge is moving within itself, deepening, changing the outline of its slopes; the river is growing into it like a great tree, steadily incising its branches into the land. For however gentle it may appear at certain seasons, this network of water known in sum as the Red River moves in its rocky notches as abrasive as a file.

How the river works as maker of the landscape, sculptor, arm of creation will always remain to some degree unknown, for it works with immeasurable leisure and patience, and often it works in turmoil. Although its processes may be hypothesized very convincingly, every vantage point of the country is also a point of speculation, a point of departure from the present surface into the shadowy questions of origin and of process.

By what complex interaction of flowing water, of weather, of growth and decay was that cliff given its shape? Where did this house-sized boulder fall from, what manner of sledging and breaking did it do coming down, what effect has it had on the course of the stream? What is happening now in all the swirling rapids and falls and eddies and pools of the river in flood? We know the results. But because we have not a thousand years to sit and watch, because our perspective is not that of birds or fish or of the lichens on the cliff face but only of men, because the life of the Gorge has larger boundaries than the life of a man, we know little of the processes.

To come to any understanding of the Red River one must consider how minute and manifold are its workings, how far beyond count its lives and aspects and manifestations. But one must also sense its great power and its vastness. One must see in it the motive force of a landscape, the formal energy of all the country that drains into it. And one must stand on its banks aware that its life and meaning are not merely local but are intricately involved in all life and all meaning. It belongs to a family of rivers whose gathering will finally bring its water to mingle with the waters of the Yellowstone and the Kanahwa and the ocean. Its life belongs within—is dependent upon and to some extent necessary to—the life of the planet.

And so in the aspect of the river, in any of its moods, there is always a residual mystery. In its being it is too small and too large, too complex and too simple, too powerful and too delicate, too transient and too ancient and durable ever to be comprehended within the limits of a human life.

On the last Saturday in March we set out from Fletcher Ridge to walk down Mariba Fork, Laurel Fork, and Gladie Creek to the river. Last weekend there was deep snow. This morning it is sunny and warm. We walk past an old house site on the ridge—the clearing now grown up in thicket, the ground still covered with the dooryard periwinkles—and then down a steep path through the cliffs. As we approach the stream at the foot of the slope we begin to find hepaticas in bloom. They are everywhere, standing up in bright jaunty clumps like Sunday bouquets beneath the big poplars and beeches and hemlocks, and on the tops of boulders.

The path fades out. We follow the rocky edges of the stream, descending with the water gradually deeper into the land. As along all the streams of the Gorge, the country is divided by stones or cliffs or trees into distinct enclosures, a series of rooms, each one different in light and look and feeling from all the rest.

We find other flowers in bloom: trout lilies, rue anemones, trailing arbutus with its delicately scented blossoms almost hidden among the dead leaves. But running through all that day like an insistent, endlessly varied theme in a piece of music are the little gardens of hepaticas. Climbing onto a streamside terrace or entering the mouth of a ravine, we find the ground suddenly rich with them, the flowers a deep blue or lavender or pink or white. They are like Easter gone wild and hiding in the woods.

Downstream from where we camp that night we can see the rocky point of a cliff, high up, with a dead tree standing alone on it. And at twilight a pair of pileated woodpeckers cast off from that tree and make a long steep descent into the woods below, their flight powerful and somehow abandoned, joyous, accepting of the night.

Our walk ends the next day in the midst of a violent

downpour. We know that, behind us, the country we have passed through is changing. Its maker has returned to it yet again to do new work.

Flowing muddy and full, frothing over its rapids, its great sound filling the valley to the brim, the river is inscrutable and forbidding. The mind turns away from it, craving dry land like a frightened swimmer. The river will not stay still to be regarded or thought about. Its events are too much part of the flow, melting rapidly into one another, drawn on by the singular demand of the current.

Other times when the river is low, idling in its pools, its mysteries become inviting. One's thoughts eagerly leave solid ground then and take to the water. The current has ceased to be a threat and become an invitation. The thought of a boat comes to mind unasked and makes itself at home.

At such a time, a bright morning in early June, a canoe seems as satisfying and liberating as a pair of wings. One is empowered to pass beyond the shore, to follow the current that, other times, standing on the shore, one has merely wished to follow.

We wake at dawn, camped high on one of the ridges. Below us the hollows are drifted deep in white mist. While we eat breakfast and pack up we watch the mist shift with the stirrings of the air, rising, thickening and then thinning out, opening here and there so that we can see through to the treetops below, and closing again. It is as if the whole landscape is moving with a gentle dreaming motion. And then we drive down the windings of Highway 715, through the rapidly thinning mist, to the river. And now our canoe lies on the water in the shade-dappled weak light of the early morning. We have the day and the river before us.

Through the morning we paddle or drift through the long pools, idling with the river, stopping to look wherever our curiosity is tempted. We see a kingfisher, a water thrush, a Kentucky warbler, a muskrat, a snake asleep on an old tire caught on a snag, a lot of big, fat tadpoles three or four inches long, dragonflies with brilliant green bodies and black wings. In the clear shoals we see fish, and at intervals we pass the camps of fishermen, places their minds will turn back to, homesick, out of the confinement of winter and city and job. These are usually quiet and deserted; we have already passed the fishermen, fishing from the top of a boulder upstream, or we will find them in a boat a little way below.

On the bar at the mouth of Wolfpen Creek, where we stop for lunch, we watch several black and yellow swallowtail butterflies drinking together on a spot of damp sand. They are like a bouquet of flowers that occasionally fly away and return again.

Where the swift clear water of Wolfpen enters the river a school of minnows is feeding. They work up the current over a little shoal of rippled sand, and then release themselves into the flow, drifting down through the quick water shadows to start again.

And all along the stream are boulders as big as houses that have broken from the cliffs and tumbled down. They are splotched with gray lichens and with mosses and liverworts; where enough dirt has collected in cracks and depressions in the stone there will be clumps of ferns or meadow rue or little patches of bluets. Above the high water line, where the current cannot sweep them, the long drama of soil-building has taken place on the tops of some of these rocks, so that they are now covered with plants and trees, and their surfaces look much like the surrounding forest floor. Those within reach of the floods are cleaner and more stony looking. They are not to be imperceptibly eaten away by the acids of the decay of vegetation and by the prizing of root and frost; they are being hewed out like sculptures by the direct violence of the river. Those that stand in the stream have been undercut by the steady abrasion of the current so that they rise out of the water like mushrooms. Going by them, one thinks of the thousands of miles of water that have flowed past them, and of the generations of boatmen, Indians and white men, that have paddled around them or stopped to fish in their shadows — and one feels their great weight and their silence and endurance. In the slanting light of the early morning the reflections off the water waver and flicker along their sides, the light moving over them with the movement of water.

There is no river more intimate with its banks. Everywhere the shore rises up steeply from the water like a page offered to be read. Water-borne, one seems always within arm's reach of the land. One has a walker's intimacy with the animals and plants of the shore as well as a boatman's intimacy with the life of the water. Without rising from one's seat in the canoe one looks into the mossy cup of a phoebe's nest fastened to the rock and sees the five white eggs.

At intervals through the day we tense and focus ourselves as the river does, and move down into the head of a rapid. We pass through carefully, no longer paddling as we wish but as we must, following the main current as it bends through the rocks and the grassy shoals. And then we enter the quiet water of the pool below. Ahead of us a leaf falls from high up in a long gentle fall. In the water its reflection rises perfectly to meet it.

An Entrance
to the Woods

On a fine sunny afternoon at the end of September I leave my work in Lexington and drive east on I-64 and the Mountain Parkway. When I leave the Parkway at the little town of Pine Ridge I am in the watershed of the Red River in the Daniel Boone National Forest. From Pine Ridge I take Highway 715 out along the narrow ridgetops, a winding tunnel through the trees. And then I turn off on a Forest Service Road and follow it to the head of a foot trail that goes down the steep valley wall of one of the tributary creeks. I pull my car off the road and lock it, and lift on my pack.

It is nearly five o'clock when I start walking. The afternoon is brilliant and warm, absolutely still, not enough air stirring to move a leaf. There is only the steady somnolent trilling of insects, and now and again in the woods below me the cry of a pileated woodpecker. Those, and my footsteps on the path, are the only sounds.

From the dry oak woods of the ridge I pass down into the rock. The foot trails of the Red River Gorge all seek these stony notches that little streams have cut back through the cliffs. I pass a ledge overhanging a sheer drop of the rock, where in a wetter time there would be a waterfall. The ledge is dry and mute now, but on the face of the rock below are the characteristic mosses, ferns, liverwort, meadow rue. And here where the ravine suddenly steepens and narrows, where the shadows are long-lived and the dampness stays, the trees are different. Here are beech and hemlock and poplar, straight and tall, reaching way up into the light. Under them are evergreen thickets of rhododendron. And wherever the dampness is there are mosses and ferns. The faces of the rock are intricately scalloped with veins of ironstone, scooped and carved by the wind.

Finally from the crease of the ravine I am following there begins to come the trickling and splashing of water. There is a great restfulness in the sounds these small streams make; they are going down as fast as they can, but their sounds seem leisurely and idle, as if produced like gemstones with the greatest patience and care.

A little later, stopping, I hear not far away the more voluble flowing of the creek. I go on down to where the trail crosses and begin to look for a camping place. The little bottoms along the creek here are thickety and weedy, probably having been kept clear and cropped or pastured not so long ago. In the more open places are little lavender asters, and the even smaller-flowered white ones that some people call beeweed or farewell-summer. And in low wet places are the richly flowered spikes of great lobelia, the blooms an intense startling blue, exquisitely shaped. I choose a place in an open thicket near the stream, and make camp.

It is a simple matter to make camp. I string up a shelter and put my air mattress and sleeping bag in it, and I am ready for the night. And supper is even simpler, for I have brought sandwiches for this first meal. In less than an hour all my chores are done. It will still be light for a good while, and I go over and sit down on a rock at the edge of the stream.

And then a heavy feeling of melancholy and lonesomeness comes over me. This does not surprise me, for I have felt it before when I have been alone at evening in wilderness places that I am not familiar with. But here it has a quality that I recognize as peculiar to the narrow hollows of the Red River Gorge. These are deeply shaded by the trees and by the valley walls, the sun rising on them late and setting early; they are more dark than light. And there will often be little rapids in the stream that will sound, at a certain distance, exactly like people talking. As I sit on my rock by the stream now, I could swear that there is a party of campers coming up the trail toward me, and for several minutes I stay alert, listening for them, their voices seeming to rise and fall, fade out and lift again, in happy conversation. When I finally realize that it is only a sound the creek is making, though I have not come here for company and do not want any, I am inexplicably sad.

These are haunted places, or at least it is easy to feel haunted in them, alone at nightfall. As the air darkens and the cool of the night rises, one feels the immanence of the wraiths of the ancient tribesmen who used to inhabit the rock houses of the cliffs; of the white hunters from east of the mountains; of the farmers who accepted the isolation of these nearly inaccessible valleys to crop the narrow bottoms and ridges and pasture their cattle and hogs in the woods; of the seekers of quick wealth in timber and ore. For though this is a wilderness place, it bears its part of the burden of human history. If one spends much time here and feels much liking for the place, it is hard to escape the sense of one's predecessors. If one has read of the prehistoric Indians whose flint arrowpoints and pottery and hominy

holes and petroglyphs have been found here, then every
rock shelter and clifty spring will suggest the presence of
those dim people who have disappeared into the earth.
Walking along the ridges and the stream bottoms, one will
come upon the heaped stones of a chimney, or the slowly
filling depression of an old cellar, or will find in the spring
a japonica bush or periwinkles or a few jonquils blooming
in a thicket that used to be a dooryard. Wherever the land
is level enough there are abandoned fields and pastures.
And nearly always there is the evidence that one follows in
the steps of the loggers.

That sense of the past is probably one reason for
the melancholy that I feel. But I know that there are other
reasons.

One is that, though I am here in body, my mind
and my nerves too are not yet altogether here. We seem to
grant to our high-speed roads and our airlines the rather
thoughtless assumption that people can change places as
rapidly as their bodies can be transported. That, as my own
experience keeps proving to me, is not true. In the middle
of the afternoon I left off being busy at work, and drove
through traffic to the freeway, and then for a solid hour or
more I drove sixty or seventy miles an hour, hardly aware
of the country I was passing through, because on the freeway one does not have to be. The landscape has been subdued so that one may drive over it at seventy miles per hour
without any concession whatsoever to one's whereabouts.
One might as well be flying. Though one is in Kentucky one
is not experiencing Kentucky; one is experiencing the
highway, which might be in nearly any hill country east of
the Mississippi.

Once off the freeway, my pace gradually slowed, as
the roads became progressively more primitive, from seventy miles an hour to a walk. And now, here at my camping
place, I have stopped altogether. But my mind is still keyed

to seventy miles an hour. And having come here so fast, it is still busy with the work I am usually doing. Having come here by the freeway, my mind is not so fully here as it would have been if I had come by the crookeder, slower state roads; it is incalculably farther away than it would have been if I had come all the way on foot, as my earliest predecessors came. When the Indians and the first white hunters entered this country they were altogether here as soon as they arrived, for they had seen and experienced fully everything between here and their starting place, and so the transition was gradual and articulate in their consciousness. Our senses, after all, were developed to function at foot speeds; and the transition from foot travel to motor travel, in terms of evolutionary time, has been abrupt. The faster one goes, the more strain there is on the senses, the more they fail to take in, the more confusion they must tolerate or gloss over—and the longer it takes to bring the mind to a stop in the presence of anything. Though the freeway passes through the very heart of this forest, the motorist remains several hours' journey by foot from what is living at the edge of the right-of-way.

But I have not only come to this strangely haunted place in a short time and too fast. I have in that move made an enormous change: I have departed from my life as I am used to living it, and have come into the wilderness. It is not fear that I feel; I have learned to fear the everyday events of human history much more than I fear the everyday occurrences of the woods; in general, I would rather trust myself to the woods than to any government that I know of. I feel, instead, an uneasy awareness of severed connections, of being cut off from all familiar places and of being a stranger where I am. What is happening at home? I wonder, and I know I can't find out very easily or very soon.

Even more discomforting is a pervasive sense of unfamiliarity. In the places I am most familiar with—my house, or my garden, or even the woods near home that I have walked in for years—I am surrounded by associations; everywhere I look I am reminded of my history and my hopes; even unconsciously I am comforted by any number of proofs that my life on the earth is an established and a going thing. But I am in this hollow for the first time in my life. I see nothing that I recognize. Everything looks as it did before I came, as it will when I am gone. When I look over at my little camp I see how tentative and insignificant it is. Lying there in my bed in the dark tonight, I will be absorbed in the being of this place, invisible as a squirrel in his nest.

Uneasy as this feeling is, I know it will pass. Its passing will produce a deep pleasure in being here. And I have felt it often enough before that I have begun to understand something of what it means:

Nobody knows where I am. I don't know what is happening to anybody else in the world. While I am here I will not speak, and will have no reason or need for speech. It is only beyond this lonesomeness for the places I have come from that I can reach the vital reality of a place such as this. Turning toward this place, I confront a presence that none of my schooling and none of my usual assumptions have prepared me for: the wilderness, mostly unknowable and mostly alien, that is the universe. Perhaps the most difficult labor for my species is to accept its limits, its weakness and ignorance. But here I am. This wild place where I have camped lies within an enormous cone widening from the center of the earth out across the universe, nearly all of it a mysterious wilderness in which the power and the knowledge of men count for nothing. As long as its instruments are correct and its engines run, the airplane now flying through this great cone is safely within the human freehold; its behavior is as familiar and predictable to those concerned as the inside of a man's living room. But let its instruments or its engines fail, and at once it enters the wilderness where nothing is foreseeable. And these steep narrow hollows, these cliffs and forested ridges that lie below, are the antithesis of flight.

Wilderness is the element in which we live encased in civilization, as a mollusk lives in his shell in the sea. It is a wilderness that is beautiful, dangerous, abundant, oblivious of us, mysterious, never to be conquered or controlled or second-guessed, or known more than a little. It is a wilderness that for most of us most of the time is kept out of sight, camouflaged, by the edifices and the busyness and the bothers of human society.

And so, coming here, what I have done is strip away the human facade that usually stands between me and the universe, and I see more clearly where I am. What I am able to ignore much of the time, but find undeniable here, is that all wildernesses are one: there is a profound joining between this wild stream deep in one of the folds of my native country and the tropical jungles, the tundras of the north, the oceans and the deserts. Alone here, among the rocks and the trees, I see that I am alone also among the stars. A stranger here, unfamiliar with my surroundings, I am aware also that I know only in the most relative terms my whereabouts within the black reaches of the universe. And because the natural processes are here so little qualified by anything human, this fragment of the wilderness is also joined to other times; there flows over it a nonhuman time to be told by the growth and death of the forest and the wearing of the stream. I feel drawing out beyond my comprehension perspectives from which the growth and the death of a large poplar would seem as continuous and sudden as the raising and the lowering of a man's hand, from which men's history in the world, their brief clearing of the ground, will seem no more than the opening and shutting of an eye.

And so I have come here to enact—not because I want to but because, once here, I cannot help it—the loneliness and the humbleness of my kind. I must see in my flimsy shelter, pitched here for two nights, the transience of capitols and cathedrals. In growing used to being in this place, I will have to accept a humbler and a truer view of myself than I usually have.

A man enters and leaves the world naked. And it is only naked—or nearly so—that he can enter and leave the wilderness. If he walks, that is; and if he doesn't walk it can hardly be said that he has entered. He can bring only what he can carry—the little that it takes to replace for a few hours or a few days an animal's fur and teeth and claws and functioning instincts. In comparison to the usual traveler with his dependence on machines and highways and restaurants and motels—on the economy and the government, in short—the man who walks into the wilderness is naked indeed. He leaves behind his work, his household, his duties, his comforts—even, if he comes alone, his words. He immerses himself in what he is not. It is a kind of death.

The dawn comes slow and cold. Only occasionally, somewhere along the creek or on the slopes above, a bird sings. I have not slept well, and I waken without much interest in the day. I set the camp to rights, and fix breakfast, and eat. The day is clear, and high up on the points and ridges to the west of my camp I can see the sun shining on the woods. And suddenly I am full of an ambition: I want to get up where the sun is; I want to sit still in the sun up there among the high rocks until I can feel its warmth in my bones.

I put some lunch into a little canvas bag, and start

out, leaving my jacket so as not to have to carry it after the day gets warm. Without my jacket, even climbing, it is cold in the shadow of the hollow, and I have a long way to go to get to the sun. I climb the steep path up the valley wall, walking rapidly, thinking only of the sunlight above me. It is as though I have entered into a deep sympathy with those tulip poplars that grow so straight and tall out of the shady ravines, not growing a branch worth the name until their heads are in the sun. I am so concentrated on the sun that when some grouse flush from the undergrowth ahead of me, I am thunderstruck; they are already planing down into the underbrush again before I can get my wits together and realize what they are.

The path zigzags up the last steepness of the bluff and then slowly levels out. For some distance it follows the backbone of a ridge, and then where the ridge is narrowest there is a great slab of bare rock lying full in the sun. This is what I have been looking for. I walk out into the center of the rock and sit, the clear warm light falling unobstructed all around. As the sun warms me I begin to grow comfortable not only in my clothes, but in the place and the day. And like those light-seeking poplars of the ravines, my mind begins to branch out.

Southward, I can hear the traffic on the Mountain Parkway, a steady continuous roar—the corporate voice of twentieth-century humanity, sustained above the transient voices of its members. Last night, except for an occasional airplane passing over, I camped out of reach of the sounds of engines. For long stretches of time I heard no sounds but the sounds of the woods.

Near where I am sitting there is an inscription cut into the rock:

A · J · SARGENT
fEB · 24 · 1903

Those letters were carved there more than sixty-six years ago. As I look around me I realize that I can see no evidence of the lapse of so much time. In every direction I can see only narrow ridges and narrow deep hollows, all covered with trees. For all that can be told from this height by looking, it might still be 1903—or, for that matter, 1803 or 1703, or 1003. Indians no doubt sat here and looked over the country as I am doing now; the visual impression is so pure and strong that I can almost imagine myself one of them. But the insistent, the overwhelming, evidence of the time of my own arrival is in what I can hear—that roar of the highway off there in the distance. In 1903 the continent was still covered by a great ocean of silence, in which the sounds of machinery were scattered at wide intervals of time and space. Here, in 1903, there were only the natural sounds of the place. On a day like this, at the end of September, there would have been only the sounds of a few faint crickets, a woodpecker now and then, now and then the wind. But today, two-thirds of a century later, the continent is covered by an ocean of engine noise, in which silences occur only sporadically and at wide intervals.

From where I am sitting in the midst of this island of wilderness, it is as though I am listening to the machine of human history—a huge flywheel building speed until finally the force of its whirling will break it in pieces, and the world with it. That is not an attractive thought, and yet I find it impossible to escape, for it has seemed to me for years now that the doings of men no longer occur within nature, but that the natural places which the human economy has so far spared now survive almost accidentally within the doings of men. This wilderness of the Red River now carries on its ancient processes *within* the human climate of war and waste and confusion. And I know that the distant roar of engines, though it may *seem* only to be passing through this wilderness, is really bearing down upon it.

The machine is running now with a speed that produces blindness—as to the driver of a speeding automobile the only thing stable, the only thing not a mere blur on the edge of the retina, is the automobile itself—and the blindness of a thing with power promises the destruction of what cannot be seen. That roar of the highway is the voice of the American economy; it is sounding also wherever strip mines are being cut in the steep slopes of Appalachia, and wherever cropland is being destroyed to make roads and suburbs, and wherever rivers and marshes and bays and forests are being destroyed for the sake of industry or commerce.

No. Even here where the economy of life is really an economy—where the creation is yet fully alive and continuous and self-enriching, where whatever dies enters directly into the life of the living—even here one cannot fully escape the sense of an impending human catastrophe. One cannot come here without the awareness that this is an island surrounded by the machinery and the workings of an insane greed, hungering for the world's end—that ours is a "civilization" of which the work of no builder or artist is symbol, nor the life of any good man, but rather the bulldozer, the poison spray, the hugging fire of napalm, the cloud of Hiroshima.

Though from the high vantage point of this stony ridge I see little hope that I will ever live a day as an optimist, still I am not desperate. In fact, with the sun warming me now, and with the whole day before me to wander in this beautiful country, I am happy. A man cannot despair if he can imagine a better life, and if he can enact something of its possibility. It is only when I am ensnarled in the meaningless ordeals and the ordeals of meaninglessness, of which our public and political life is now so productive, that I lose the awareness of something better, and feel the despair of having come to the dead end of possibility.

Today, as always when I am afoot in the woods, I feel the possibility, the reasonableness, the practicability of living in the world in a way that would enlarge rather than diminish the hope of life. I feel the possibility of a frugal and protective love for the creation that would be unimaginably more meaningful and joyful than our present destructive and wasteful economy. The absence of human society, that made me so uneasy last night, now begins to be a comfort to me. I am afoot in the woods. I am alive in the world, this moment, without the help or the interference of any machine. I can move without reference to anything except the lay of the land and the capabilities of my own body. The necessities of foot travel in this steep country have stripped away all superfluities. I simply could not enter into this place and assume its quiet with all the belongings of a family man, property holder, etc. For the time, I am reduced to my irreducible self. I feel the lightness of body that a man must feel who has just lost fifty pounds of fat. As I leave the bare expanse of the rock and go in under the trees again, I am aware that I move in the landscape as one of its details.

Walking through the woods, you can never see far, either ahead or behind, so you move without much of a sense of getting anywhere or of moving at any certain speed. You burrow through the foliage in the air much as a mole burrows through the roots in the ground. The views that open out occasionally from the ridges afford a relief, a recovery of orientation, that they could never give as mere "scenery," looked at from a turnout at the edge of a highway.

The trail leaves the ridge and goes down a ravine into the valley of a creek where the night chill has stayed. I pause only long enough to drink the cold clean water. The trail climbs up onto the next ridge.

It is the ebb of the year. Though the slopes have not

yet taken on the bright colors of the autumn maples and oaks, some of the duller trees are already shedding. The foliage has begun to flow down the cliff faces and the slopes like a tide pulling back. The woods is mostly quiet, subdued, as if the pressure of survival has grown heavy upon it, as if above the growing warmth of the day the cold of winter can be felt waiting to descend.

At my approach a big hawk flies off the low branch of an oak and out over the treetops. Now and again a nuthatch hoots, off somewhere in the woods. Twice I stop and watch an ovenbird. A few feet ahead of me there is a sudden movement in the leaves, and then quiet. When I slip up and examine the spot there is nothing to be found. Whatever passed there has disappeared, quicker than the hand that is quicker than the eye, a shadow fallen into a shadow.

In the afternoon I leave the trail. My walk so far has come perhaps three-quarters of the way around a long zigzagging loop that will eventually bring me back to my starting place. I turn down a small unnamed branch of the creek where I am camped, and I begin the loveliest part of the day. There is nothing here resembling a trail. The best way is nearly always to follow the edge of the stream, stepping from one stone to another. Crossing back and forth over the water, stepping on or over rocks and logs, the way ahead is never clear for more than a few feet. The stream accompanies me down, threading its way under boulders and logs and over little falls and rapids. The rhododendron overhangs it so closely in places that I can go only by stooping. Over the rhododendron are the great dark heads of the hemlocks. The streambanks are ferny and mossy. And through this green tunnel the voice of the stream changes from rock to rock; subdued like all the other autumn voices of the woods, it seems sunk in a deep contented meditation on the sounds of *l*.

The water in the pools is absolutely clear. If it

weren't for the shadows and ripples you would hardly notice that it is water; the fish would seem to swim in the air.
As it is, where there is no leaf floating, it is impossible to
tell exactly where the plane of the surface lies. As I walk up
on a pool the little fish dart every which way out of sight.
And then after I sit still a while, watching, they come out
again. Their shadows flow over the rocks and leaves on the
bottom. Now I have come into the heart of the woods. I am
far from the highway and can hear no sound of it. All
around there is a grand deep autumn quiet, in which a few
insects dream their summer songs. Suddenly a wren sings
way off in the underbrush. A redbreasted nuthatch walks,
hooting, headfirst down the trunk of a walnut. An ovenbird walks out along the limb of a hemlock and looks at
me, curious. The little fish soar in the pool, turning their
clean quick angles, their shadows seeming barely to keep
up. As I lean and dip my cup in the water, they scatter. I
drink, and go on.

When I get back to camp it is only the middle of the
afternoon or a little after. Since I left in the morning I have
walked something like eight miles. I haven't hurried—have
mostly poked along, stopping often and looking around.
But I am tired, and coming down the creek I have got both
feet wet. I find a sunny place, and take off my shoes and
socks and set them to dry. For a long time then, lying
propped against the trunk of a tree, I read and rest and
watch the evening come.

All day I have moved through the woods, making as
little noise as possible. Slowly my mind and my nerves have
slowed to a walk. The quiet of the woods has ceased to be
something that I observe; now it is something that I am a
part of. I have joined it with my own quiet. As the twilight
draws on I no longer feel the strangeness and uneasiness of
the evening before. The sounds of the creek move through

my mind as they move through the valley, unimpeded and clear.

When the time comes I prepare supper and eat, and then wash kettle and cup and spoon and put them away. As far as possible I get things ready for an early start in the morning. Soon after dark I go to bed, and I sleep well.

I wake long before dawn. The air is warm and I feel rested and wide awake. By the light of a small candle lantern I break camp and pack. And then I begin the steep climb back to the car.

The moon is bright and high. The woods stands in deep shadow, the light falling soft through the openings of the foliage. The trees appear immensely tall, and black, gravely looming over the path. It is windless and still; the moonlight pouring over the country seems more potent than the air. All around me there is still that constant low singing of the insects. For days now it has continued without letup or inflection, like ripples on water under a steady breeze. While I slept it went on through the night, a shimmer on my mind. My shoulder brushes a low tree overhanging the path and a bird that was asleep on one of the branches startles awake and flies off into the shadows, and I go on with the sense that I am passing near to the sleep of things.

In a way this is the best part of the trip. Stopping now and again to rest, I linger over it, sorry to be going. It seems to me that if I were to stay on, today would be better than yesterday, and I realize it was to renew the life of that possibility that I came here. What I am leaving is something to look forward to.

The Unforeseen
Wilderness

That the world is stable and its order fixed is perhaps the most persistent human delusion. How many errors have been made on the assumption that what was *is?* To a young child the house he lives in is permanent and unchanging, an eternal verity. But it is clear to the man who keeps the house that if it is treated as an eternal verity it will soon perish altogether. Against the constant jeopardy of decay there is the necessity of constant renewal. And there are, of course, the maxims to the effect that you cannot go home again, or step into the same river twice.

I knew all that as well, I suppose, as any other man of my age. But as soon as I was confronted with the new experience of the Red River Gorge I immediately fell into the old error, assuming that the place partook of the nature of its maps—that, for instance, from what I knew I could predict what I would learn, or that my experience could be made to go according to a plan. Like a good engineer, I wanted to foresee what I was going to do and then do it.

But perhaps the first lesson we have to learn, or re-learn, from a wilderness is that it does not live and change according to a plan, but by freely accommodating what happens to it. The wild creatures do not go to some appointed place such as a kitchen or a restaurant to eat, but eat what they find where they find it. The bends and bars and pools of the river are made in response to obstructions and openings.

To a river, as to any natural force, an obstruction is merely an opportunity. For the river's nature is to flow; it is not just spatial in dimension, but temporal as well. All things must yield to the impulse of the water *in time,* if not today then tomorrow or in a thousand years. If its way is obstructed then it goes around the obstruction or under it or over it and, flowing past it, wears it away. Men may dam it and say that they have made a lake, but it will still be a river. It will keep its nature and bide its time, like a caged wild animal alert for the slightest opening. In time it will have its way; the dam like the ancient cliffs will be carried away piecemeal in the currents.

The engineer's assumption that the nature of a place is fixed and can be altered according to plan is an illusion, as has been too often shown when planned "improvements" have produced wholly unforeseen disasters. But the engineer's illusion, in our time, is an illusion backed by enormous powers of technology and politics and wealth, and an illusion so empowered preserves itself by becoming an institution. It has a much longer life than the illusions of persons, and before it dies it may do, and usually does, long-term damage. The engineering illusion has produced damage, as in the strip mines of Eastern Kentucky, that will require a geologic era to correct.

To a modern engineer, entering a landscape with bulldozers, power shovels, dynamite, and the other tools of his trade, the blueprint must seem as absolute as the will of God. A kindred, if smaller, illusion brought the pioneer plowman onto the steep slopes: the manifest destiny of a plowman was to plow; the tool, the human possibility, was the point of reference, not the nature of the place. When the dam has silted up and a valley is destroyed for the foreseeable future, or when the plowed-up topsoil has washed away and the watershed is ruined, it is too late. The plans have been undone by natural processes that were not foreseen or taken into account. But it is the business of natural processes to produce consequences, and the first law of ecology is that justice is *always* done—though not necessarily to those who deserve it. Ecological justice, in fact, falls most often on later generations, or on the people who live downwind or downstream.

But the man who goes into the wilderness on foot, stripped of all the devices of the illusion of fixed order, finds his assumptions to be much shorter lived. Afoot, cut off from the powers by which men change things, he has made himself vulnerable to change. Whether he intends it or not, the wilderness receives him as a student. And what it begins to teach him is how to live beyond his expectations; if he returns often and stays long perhaps it will teach him to live *without* expectations. It will teach him the wisdom of taking no thought for the morrow—not because taking thought is a bad idea, but because it is not possible; he doesn't know what thought tomorrow will require.

The lessons are everywhere. He can't avoid them. The weather and the mood of the woods have changed since his last trip. The stepping-stones on which he crossed the creek a month ago are now washed away. The pebbles and small stones of the stream bed have moved and changed, and in their changing he feels the changing of the boulders and the cliffs. If the weather on his last trip was so pleasant as to have stayed in his mind, an enticement to come back, he may be discouraged this trip to have to contend with sweltering heat, or with a cold rain. But the elusive ovenbird, that he sort of expected never to see, suddenly appears on a low limb beside the path. Or a pair of grouse erupt in flight almost under his feet, causing his heart to jump out of place—and for the next hundred yards he walks unconsciously on tiptoe, scarcely breathing, alert to what is around him as he has rarely been. Or a turn in the path shows him suddenly a rare flame azalea in bloom. What he planned is not happening, as if by some natural law. He is finding the *life* of the time in what he did not foresee.

No place is to be learned like a textbook or a course in school, and then turned away from forever on the assumption that one's knowledge of it is complete. What is to be known about it is without limit, and it is endlessly changing. Knowing it is therefore like breathing: it can happen, it stays real, only on the condition that it *continue* to happen. As soon as it is recognized that a river—or, for that matter, a home—is not a place but a process, not a fact but an event, there ought to come an immense relief: one can step into the same river twice, one can go home again.

We had spent a hot, hard July afternoon tramping in the Gorge in search of a place we had heard about, and we had failed to find it. The foliage closed in around us like a heavy fog, and we were drenched with sweat and with rainwater from an earlier shower that clung all that humid afternoon to the leaves. From the standpoint of our expectations the afternoon was a total loss, better forgotten. Except that in the midst of that failed search we *happened* on something unforgettable: a little dell in the woods where several streams met, making a pattern like a chicken track. The air opened and grew spacious under great hemlocks and beeches; shafts of sunlight slanted in as thick as the tree trunks; we rested there, and found cool water to drink. It is printed on my memory, a sort of blessing, by the force of its unexpectedness. Though our search failed in its intention, it succeeded in one of its accidents.

One Memorial Day—or as it turned out, one Memorable Day—I started out to canoe the Upper Gorge by myself, putting in below the bridge where Highway 746 crosses the Red. I had previously been down only a little below the mouth of Stillwater Creek, and so I had no idea what I was undertaking.

The river was high, the water about the depth of a paddle blade over the riffles. For a while I went down fast and easy. The current was strong even in the pools, and I was getting what I thought to be a free ride.

I had the river all to myself. As I went down wood ducks rose off the water ahead of me and flew downstream. I saw several water thrushes. I found a phoebe's nest with four fledged young on an overhanging rock face about a foot above the water.

And then I came to the first big rapid about a mile below Stillwater. There the river broke, falling steeply, through a narrow opening between two huge rocks, and above the rocks the slopes rose almost vertically, thickly covered with trees and undergrowth. I tied up first on one side of the river and then the other, and took a long look around.

The uproar of the rapid filled and beat inside my head, seeming to accumulate; I was rapidly becoming unable, as the saying is, to hear myself think. It was as though I had been brought suddenly, ignorant of the proper etiquette, into the presence of a grand and austere personage who had taken my life into his hands. I was losing my confidence and poise. The river was defeating me, and what is more it was making me glad to accept defeat. This rapid was bad, and I knew that it promised worse. I no longer had the faintest shadow of a wish to go any farther. And yet my pride held on to my intentions a while longer, and I carefully considered every possibility of getting through.

After much looking and pondering and looking back I was happy to conclude that there were no arguments at all in favor of going on. Running the rapid seemed a stupid risk for one man, and a portage looked about equally impossible. There was nothing to do but turn around and go out the way I had come in. It took me nearly four hours to make it back to my starting place, wading and pulling the canoe against the swift current. At times the water became too deep to wade, and I would have to swim across, or drift back downstream to where I could wade across. It was something of an ordeal, and I knew at the time that I was in considerable danger: in water like that, plunging under and around big rocks and sunken trees, there are any number of ways to drown.

But the real austerity of the Upper Gorge, and the extremity of my misjudgment in attempting it alone, didn't dawn on me until some weeks later. Mr. Wendell Nickell of West Liberty had taken me down the cliff to the Dog Drowning Hole, perhaps two miles below the rapid where I had turned back on my canoe trip. There had been rain and again the river was swollen; we could hear its clamor while we were still high up on the face of the cliff. When we finally worked our way down to the edge of it we were submerged in its sound. Its great noise, the voice of the whole stream, was so disproportionate to anything we could *see* that, within it, the river seemed to churn past us in silence. It drove down onto the comb of the rocks and was torn apart, buried in white froth, and then it gathered back into the single strand of itself, to be torn apart again.

Dog Drowning Hole indeed! The thought of drowning was native there. One could hardly look at it without knowing how it could tread down the head of a swimmer and hold it, while the great voice drumming there between the cliffs would go on, exuberant and oblivious, unchanged. It was a tenuous margin we stood on, the wall of the Gorge at our backs, and at our feet the let-loose tromping and churning of the Dog Drowning Hole.

And then while we stood there watching, my guide said very casually: "If three men were down in here, and one broke his leg, the other two couldn't carry him out."

I suppose that until somebody has tried it we won't know for sure about that—but I saw his point. As though his words had nudged me finally beyond the frontier of my ignorance, the reality of the Gorge suddenly stood up in all my nerves, and I realized what an edge I had come to on my canoe trip. When I pushed off that morning I passed ahead of my intentions as a driver speeding at night will overdrive his lights. If I had somehow contrived to go on past the rapid where I had turned back, I would have passed beyond what I could imagine, there would have been no foreseeing what might have happened. Before, the Gorge had been a place I understood somewhat as I understood its maps. But now it became a presence that I felt in the roots of my hair and the pit of my stomach, as though something whose existence I had failed to anticipate had come up behind me in the dark and touched the back of my neck.

One way to see the Red River is by canoe. That way one sees it from the perspective of water, having made common cause with it, to be carried by it. Drifting, there comes an intimate sense of how the water has sought its way through the country, and one feels how simple and steadfast is its obedience to the law of gravity, filling and flowing on.

Another way is by foot. Step into the river at the bridge on Highway 746 and wade down through the Gorge to the bridge on Highway 715. You wade because the slopes on either shore are so steep and so thickly overgrown that the best walkway is the bed of the river. And the perspective of the walker is as radically different from that of the boatman as it is from that of the stander on the bank. Walking, you have not merely entered the water; you have entered the course of the stream. You are experiencing not the stream alone nor the land alone, but the contending of the two by which each has been shaped. You are encountering by touch as well as by sight the water of the river and the obstacles it makes its way through or over or under or around. You have put your body into it like a gauge to measure the variations of its depth and the changes of its flow.

There are certain personal considerations to be dealt with at first. You are necessarily wet to the waist from the start, and you know you are *going* to be wet to the waist for hours on end. And there is the strangeness of walking over a surface that you can feel but cannot see; in spite of the use of a walking stick, the most reliable device for detecting submerged boulders and logs turns out to be your shinbone. As soon as these are accepted as normal circumstances you can give your attention to the adventure. And it is an adventure. One of the best.

Canoeing down a flowing stream, no matter in what mood it is done, never quite escapes the impulse of the current. Loitering or stopping, you nevertheless remain answerable to the movement of the water, the necessity to be going on. But walking down the Red, through the roughs of its Upper Gorge, has nothing in common with flowing; the current when it becomes swift enough to be noticeable is not an asset but a difficulty. Walking is slow and considering and deliberate. There is no building in its momentum. Where the canoeist could stop only with some forethought and considerable effort, where he would find it simpler and easier to go on, the walker always finds it easier to stop.

And so walking down through the Upper Gorge, we no sooner become involved in our trip, than we become equally involved in its side trips and diversions. We find phoebes' nests on the rocks—two that are empty, one with two eggs. When we stop and listen we hear warblers singing everywhere. We linger over the rock gardens along the shores, examining their growth of lichens and mosses and liverworts, violets and bluets and rue. The laurel bushes that here and there overhang the banks are in bloom. Once we see a frog clinging to a rock face like a little patch of lichen. On the bed of the river in the shallows we see fish's nests of heaped-up pebbles.

We shed our packs at the mouth of one of the smaller tributary streams and, feeling light and quick-footed without our loads, pass back into the valley wall. The branch enters the river through a deep narrow cut beneath overhanging ledges and the close foliage of rhododendron—a kind of burrow that leads us back and up over preliminary steps in the rock ledges. And then the foliage opens overhead and withdraws on either side. It is a little as though we have emerged on the bottom of a well, but the space is broad and lofty, the proportions those of a great temple. In front of us there is a series of narrow ledges, divided by sheer high falls of the rock. From the top ledge, high up against the sky, a little stream leaps and slides, glittering and spattering, until finally it is gathered again into the tidy stream at our feet. The ledges are all covered and hung with flowers and mosses and ferns. On the other sides of the opening the forest rises tall and densely green. It is the wildest of places, the long casual violence of its making still potent in it. And yet it is pleasing in the way that the greatest architecture is pleasing, as though its shape and proportions were the result of superb calculation. We stand in its shade and its looming gentle quiet, and look. And then we reenter the stream's dark burrow.

Trash. We see plenty of trash—old tires, buckets and bottles and cans, the various plastic conveniences of our disposable civilization, leftovers of what Edward Abbey calls the world's "grossest national product." We see trash that has floated down out of upriver dumps, and trash that has been carried in by campers who would no doubt have got equal enjoyment if they had pitched their tents in the parking lot of a drive-in restaurant. Farther down, where the river begins to be accompanied by foot trails, we will see piles of excrement that might be the sign of some large wild animal were they not surrounded by lavish blossoms of pink toilet paper.

What would it be like to experience the Red River unspoiled by men's abuse and refuse? Perhaps those of us living now will never know. Perhaps we may learn from our errors, in time, and become civilized enough to preserve and care for such places. Perhaps that is an exceedingly small possibility. At any rate, now the traveler in the Gorge will find that to get his experience of it pure he must be continuously editing out the most damning evidence against his species. It is a modern hardship.

And there is an ancient hardship. As motorists we are accustomed to journeys that occur in different places but not in different conditions. A man might drive his car across the Salt Lake Desert and then across Salt Lake City, and the condition of both trips would be that of the auto-mobile; what his predecessors in covered wagons knew of the desert is simply lost to him. Going afoot through the

Upper Gorge, we have reverted to an ancient mode and mentality of travel. We are experiencing the place as a condition. And as the day goes on that condition gets livelier and more assertive. We become weary, the packs heavy, the footwork more and more burdened by the water and the hidden obstacles of the river. We begin looking for a campsite.

Perhaps there are places in the world where Nature has provided comfortable campsites a day's walk apart. In the Red River Gorge Nature had her mind on other work. It is a long time, and a long way, after we have decided to stop before we finally come to a stopping place. But there is a compensation, a sort of justice, in this—not the elusive justice of desert and reward, but the unfailing natural symmetry of cause and effect. The longer and harder the labor has been, the gladder you are to rest, the more intricately satisfying are all the details of the day's end: taking off the pack, changing to dry clothes and shoes and socks, resting, eating, looking around. Sitting and looking around is the best of it. All day we have been in motion ourselves, and now we sit very still and watch the motions of the world: the flight of birds, the stirrings of the wind, the flowing of the river, the darkening of the day. In our weariness and stillness we watch it happen without impatience, with candid interest. It is as gratifying as watching somebody else work.

We have put in a hard day, and we have come to a good place: a smooth sand beach opposite the mouth of Solomon Branch. Towering over us, in the downstream angle between the branch and the river, is a big rust-red point of rock. While we make camp the last of the sunlight glows on this rock and then slowly rises away from it. There seems little likelihood of rain and we decide against the use of shelters, which would be hard to secure there on the open beach anyhow, and simply unroll our beds on the sand. We cook and eat and loaf and talk and finally, with the night cooling on our faces, sleep.

We are awakened a little after daylight by the calling and answering of the phoebes who live on the red cliff above us. We have breakfast, and then loaf around, waiting for the dew to dry off our bedding. Or that is one reason we put off starting. Another is that we have the hardest going still ahead of us, and we know it.

This is the day of the Roughs of the Red. The course of the river becomes choked with tremendous stones—no longer the boulder here and there of other parts of the river, but piles and barricades of boulders. Our day's journey resolves into a series of problems and solutions. We thread our way around a pool too deep to wade, climbing and stooping and straddling and crawling over and around and through a sprawl of big rocks that makes us feel like ants in a gravel pile. We cross swift deep water on stepping-stones the size of automobiles that lie *almost* more than a stride apart. We work our way around one side of a large pool, only to discover that we can't pass that way, and we have to work our way back and try the other side. The way is never clear very far ahead. We keep seeing, just ahead of us, barriers that it seems to us only water could get through. Always in sight around us are the marks of the power of flowing water: the tumbled and sculptured stones, driftlogs lodged in the branches of trees and on the tops of boulders many feet above our heads. We can never quite forget here that we are traveling through the workplace of a great creative force, one of the methods of which is rampage.

A man's way through a wilderness he is familiar with has something of the nature of art; it keeps an abiding reference to knowledge and to previous use. Today we are far removed from men's ways, and are learning something of the way of nature. There are no paths going our way, and as a trail the river has become capricious and deceptive. We go through its stone maze much as the water goes through it, moving easily through the open places, pausing at the barriers to hunt a way through, and then passing, released, relieved, through the opening we have found, going on. Discovering the way for ourselves, we begin to feel that we are not simply *in* the wilderness, but that we are *part* of it, moving within it in direct response to it, moving as it requires us to move and as it moves. Our journey has become one of its processes.

This is a stretch of country that might have been deliberately meant to refute all our idle talk about "the everlasting hills." There are no everlasting hills. There is only everlasting process. Here the hills are clearly being torn down. But this, I keep reminding myself, is not destruction. It is creation. If men, with their souped-up ambitions and their panic-stricken sense of time, should attempt to work on such a scale—and they do—the invariable result would be destruction. But this is a scene, and a result, of the creation—which simply cannot be thought of in man's terms. It is never—except in his limited and selfish view—destructive. It is never going through a period of destruction between something created in the past and something to be created in the future. It is always creating what *is*.

It is our journey, our laborious passage through these works, that has taught us this. Passing down, contriving against obstacles, as the water passes, we have moved outside ourselves into a curious sympathy with what is happening here. We have dealt with it stone by stone. And so we do not now stand apart from it like real estate speculators, saying what a nice place it will be when it is finished. For we know that it *is* finished, just as it was, and as it will be. We know that only a fragment of its substance and its duration is visible to us, and that however tumultuous and chaotic the place may look it is involved in a process that is ever coherent and whole. For the wilderness, which is to say the universe, we have no words. We deal with its stones, its trees, its water. We ask ourselves which will be the best way to go. Our words are for the way we have been.

In the very depths of the Roughs, we find standing in the stream a craggy stone with bluets and liverworts in bloom on it, and a few ferns. It is not large—perhaps six or eight feet in diameter, and standing three or four feet above the surface. What stops us and keeps us standing there, looking, is that it is a complete landscape, a rocky mountain landscape, exquisitely scaled and proportioned and colored, as though contrived and placed there by the most subtle of Japanese gardeners. It is uncannily all of a piece, orderly, impeccable. Like a fine work of art or a neat small farm, it is resonant with the intimation of orders too large and too small to see.

We camp that night at the head of a foot trail that will take us down to the concrete bridge on Highway 715, where we have left a car. To get there in the morning, after our days in the river, will seem a short easy walk. The rough going is all behind us now. As trials go, ours has been mostly a pleasure trip. And yet it has been difficult enough, far enough from roads and paths, to carry us beyond our usual lives into intimate touch, a sort of association, with the wild river. Though we have been gone only two days, and have never been more than a few miles from the paved road, our journey has about it the aura of great distance and long time. I lie down to sleep feeling accomplished and satisfied. I look back on our journey with a great liking. And having been so far outside myself, I find to my relief that I am glad to be back, eager to be going home.

In the morning I wake before daylight, and lie still, looking and listening. The night fades. For a while I hear in the distance the voice of one whippoorwill. And then the day birds.

The Journey's End

Early in 1968 the state's newspapers were taking note of the discovery, in one of the rock houses in the Gorge, of a crude hut built of short split planks overlaying a framework of poles. The hut was hardly bigger than a pup tent, barely large enough, I would say, to accommodate one man and a small stone fireplace. One of its planks bore the carved name: "D. boon." There was some controversy over whether or not it really was built by Daniel Boone. Perhaps it does not matter. But the news of the discovery and of the controversy over it had given the place a certain fame.

The find interested me, for I never cease to regret the scarcity of knowledge of the first explorations of the continent. Some hint, such as the "Boone hut" might provide, of the experience of the Long Hunters would be invaluable. And so one of my earliest visits to the Gorge included a trip to see the hut.

The head of the trail was not yet marked, but once I found the path leading down through the woods it was clear to me that I had already had numerous predecessors. And I had not gone far before I knew their species: scattered more and more thickly along the trail the nearer I got to the site of the hut was the trash that has come to be more characteristic than shoeprints of the race that produced (as I am a little encouraged to remember) such a man as D. boon. And when I came to the rock house itself I found the mouth of it entirely closed, from the ground to the overhanging rock some twenty-five feet above, by a chain-link fence. Outside the fence the ground was littered with polaroid negatives, film spools, film boxes, food wrappers, cigarette butts, a paper plate, a coke bottle.

And inside the fence, which I peered through like a prisoner, was the hut, a forlorn relic overpowered by what had been done to protect it from collectors of mementos, who would perhaps not even know what it was supposed to remind them of. There it was, perhaps a vital clue to our history and our inheritance, turned into a curio. Whether because of the ignorant enthusiasm of souvenir hunters, or because of the strenuous measures necessary to protect it from them, Boone's hut had become a doodad—as had Boone's name, which now stood for a mendacious TV show and a brand of fried chicken.

I did not go back to that place again, not wanting to be associated with the crowd whose vandalism had been so accurately foreseen and so overwhelmingly thwarted. But I did not forget it either, and the memory of it seems to me to bear, both for the Gorge and for ourselves, a heavy premonition of ruin. For are those who propose damming the Gorge, arguing *convenience,* not the same as these who can go no place, not even a few hundred steps to see the hut of D. boon, without the trash of convenience? Are they not the same who will use the proposed lake as a means of transporting the same trash into every isolated cranny that the shoreline will penetrate? I have a vision (I don't know if it is nightmare or foresight) of a time when our children will go to the Gorge and find there a webwork of paved, heavily littered trails passing through tunnels of steel mesh. When people are so ignorant and destructive that they must be divided by a fence from what is vital to them, whether it is their history or their world, they are imprisoned.

On a cold drizzly day in the middle of October I walk down the side of a badly overgrazed ridge into a deep, steep hollow where there remains the only tiny grove of virgin timber still standing in all the Red River country. It is a journey backward through time, from the freeway droning both directions through 1969, across the old ridge denuded by the agricultural policies and practices of the white man's era, and down into such a woods as the Shawnees knew before they knew white men.

Going down, the sense that it is a virgin place comes over you slowly. First you notice what would be the great difficulty of getting in and out, were it not for such improvements as bridges and stairways in the trail. It is this difficulty that preserved the trees, and that even now gives the hollow a feeling of austerity and remoteness. And then you realize that you are passing among poplars and hemlocks of a startling girth and height, the bark of their trunks deeply grooved and moss-grown. And finally it comes to you where you are; the virginity, the uninterrupted wildness, of the place comes to you in a clear strong dose like the first breath of a wind. Here the world is in its pure state, and such men as have been here have all been here in their pure state, for they have destroyed nothing. It has lived whole into our lifetime out of the ages. Its life is a vivid link between us and Boone and the Long Hunters and their predecessors, the Indians. It stands, brooding upon its continuance, in a strangely moving perfection, from the tops of the immense trees down to the leaves of the partridge berries on the ground. Standing and looking, moving on and looking again, I suddenly realize what is missing from nearly all the Kentucky woodlands I have known: the summit, the grandeur of these old trunks that lead the eyes up through the foliage of the lesser trees toward the sky.

At the foot of the climb, over the stone floor of the hollow, the stream is mottled with the gold leaves of the beeches. The water has taken on a vegetable taste from the leaves steeping in it. It has become a kind of weak tea, infused with the essence of the crown of the forest. By spring the fallen leaves on the stream bed will all have been swept away, and the water, filtered once again through the air and the ground, will take back the clear taste of the rock. I drink the cool brew of the autumn.

And then I wander some more among the trees. There is a thought repeating itself in my mind: This is a great Work, this is a great Work. It occurs to me that my head has gone to talking religion, that it is going ahead more or less on its own, assenting to the Creation, finding it good, in the spirit of the first chapters of Genesis. For no matter the age or the hour, I am celebrating the morning of the seventh day. I assent to my mind's assent. It *is* a great Work. It is a *great* Work—begun in the beginning, carried on until now, to be carried on, not by such processes as men make or understand, but by "the kind of intelligence that enables grass seed to grow grass; the cherry stone to make cherries."

Here is the place to remember D. boon's hut. Lay aside all questions of its age and ownership—whether or not he built it, he undoubtedly built others like it in similar places. Imagine it in a cave in a cliff overlooking such a place as this. Imagine it separated by several hundred miles from the nearest white men and by two hundred years from the drone, audible even here, of the parkway traffic. Imagine that the great trees surrounding it are part of a virgin wilderness still nearly as large as the continent, vast rich unspoiled distances quietly peopled by scattered Indian tribes, its ways still followed by buffalo and bear and panther and wolf. Imagine a cold gray winter evening, the wind loud in the branches above the protected hollows. Imagine a man dressed in skins coming silently down off the ridge and along the cliff face into the shelter of the rock house. Imagine his silence that is unbroken as he enters, crawling, a small hut that is only a negligible detail among the stone rubble of the cave floor, as unobtrusive there as the nest of an animal or bird, and as he livens the banked embers of a fire on the stone hearth, adding wood, and holds out his chilled hands before the blaze. Imagine him roasting his supper meat on a stick over the fire while the night falls and the darkness and the wind enclose the hollow. Imagine him sitting on there, miles and months from words, staring into the fire, letting its warmth deepen in him until finally he sleeps. Imagine his sleep.

When I return again it is the middle of December, getting on toward the final shortening, the first lengthening of the days. The year is ending, and my trip too has a conclusive feeling about it. The ends are gathering. The things I have learned about the Gorge, my thoughts and feelings about it, have begun to have a sequence, a pattern. From the start of the morning, because of this sense of the imminence of connections and conclusions, the day has both an excitement and a comfort about it.

As I drive in I see small lots staked off and a road newly graveled in one of the creek bottoms. And I can hear chain saws running in the vicinity of another development on Tunnel Ridge. This work is being done in anticipation of the lake, but I know that it has been hastened by the public-ity surrounding the effort to keep the Gorge unspoiled. I consider the ironic possibility that what I will write for love of it may also contribute to its destruction, enlarging the hearsay of it, bringing in more people to drive the roads and crowd the "points of interest" until they become exact-ly as interesting as a busy street. And yet I might as well leave the place anonymous, for what I have learned here could be learned from any woods and any free-running river.

I pull off the road near the mouth of a hollow I have not yet been in. The day is warm and overcast, but it seems unlikely to rain. Taking only a notebook and a map, I turn away from the road and start out. The woods closes me in. Within a few minutes I have put the road, and where it came from and is going, out of mind. There comes to be a wonderful friendliness, a sort of sweetness I have not known here before, about this day and this solitary walk—as if, having finally understood this country well enough to accept it on its terms, I am in turn accepted. It is as though, in this year of men's arrival on the moon, I have completed my own journey at last, and have arrived, an exult-ant traveler, here on the earth.

I come around a big rock in the stream and two grouse flush in the open not ten steps away. I walk on more quietly, full of the sense of ending and beginning. At any moment, I think, the forest may reveal itself to you in a new way. Some intimate insight, that all you have known has been secretly adding up to, may suddenly open into the clear—like a grouse, that one moment seemed only a part of the forest floor, the next moment rising in flight. Also it may not.

Where I am going I have never been before. And since I have no destination that I know, where I am going is always where I am. When I come to good resting places, I rest. I rest whether I am tired or not because the places are good. Each one is an arrival. I am where I have been going. At a narrow place in the stream I sit on one side and prop my feet on the other. For a while I content myself to be a bridge. The water of heaven and earth is flowing beneath me. While I rest a piece of the world's work is continuing here without my help.

Since I was here last the leaves have fallen. The forest has been at work, dying to renew itself, covering the tracks of those of us who were here, burying the paths and the old campsites and the refuse. It is showing us what to hope for. And that we can hope. And *how* to hope. It will always be a new world, if we will let it be.

The place as it was is gone, and we are gone as we were. We will never be in that place again. Rejoice that it is dead, for having received that death, the place of next year, a new place, is lying potent in the ground like a deep dream.

Somewhere, somewhere behind me that I will not go back to, I have lost my map. At first I am sorry, for on these trips I have always kept it with me. I brood over the thought of it, the map of this place rotting into it along with its leaves and its fallen wood. The image takes hold of me, and I suddenly realize that it is the culmination, the final insight, that I have felt impending all through the day. It is the symbol of what I have learned here, and of the process: the gradual relinquishment of maps, the yielding of knowledge before the new facts and the mysteries of growth and renewal and change. What men know and presume about the earth is part of it, passing always back into it, carried on by it into what they do not know. Even their abuses of it, their diminishments and dooms, belong to it. The tragedy is only ours, who have little time to be here, not the world's whose creation bears triumphantly on and on from the fulfillment of catastrophe to the fulfillment of hepatica blossoms. The thought of the lost map, the map fallen and decaying like a leaf among the leaves, grows in my mind to the force of a cleansing vision. As though freed of a heavy weight, I am light and exultant here in the end and the beginning.

from

The Unsettling of America

V

The Body
and the Earth

But just stop for a minute and think about what
it means to live in a land where 95 percent of the
people can be freed from the drudgery of
preparing their own food.

*James E. Bostic, Jr., Former Deputy
Assistant Secretary of Agriculture
for Rural Development*

Find the shortest, simplest way between the
earth, the hands and the mouth.

Lanza Del Vasto

ON THE CLIFF

The question of human limits, of the proper definition and place of human beings within the order of Creation, finally rests upon our attitude toward our biological
existence, the life of the body in this world. What value and
respect do we give to our bodies? What uses do we have for
them? What relation do we see, if any, between body and
mind, or body and soul? What connections or responsibilities do we maintain between our bodies and the earth?
These are religious questions, obviously, for our bodies are
part of the Creation, and they involve us in all the issues of
mystery. But the questions are also agricultural, for no
matter how urban our life, our bodies live by farming; we
come from the earth and return to it, and so we live in agriculture as we live in flesh. While we live our bodies are
moving particles of the earth, joined inextricably both to

269

the soil and to the bodies of other living creatures. It is hardly surprising, then, that there should be some profound resemblances between our treatment of our bodies and our treatment of the earth.

That humans are small within the Creation is an ancient perception, represented often enough in art that it must be supposed to have an elemental importance. On one of the painted walls of the Lascaux cave (20,000–15,000 B.C.), surrounded by the exquisitely shaped, shaded, and colored bodies of animals, there is the childish stick figure of a man, a huntsman who, having cast his spear into the guts of a bison, is now weaponless and vulnerable, poignantly frail, exposed, and incomplete. The message seems essentially that of the voice out of the whirlwind in the Book of Job: the Creation is bounteous and mysterious, and humanity is only a part of it—not its equal, much less its master.

Old Chinese landscape paintings reveal, among towering mountains, the frail outline of a roof or a tiny human figure passing along a road on foot or horseback. These landscapes are almost always populated. There is no implication of a dehumanized interest in nature "for its own sake." What is represented is a world in which humans belong, but which does not belong to humans in any tidy economic sense; the Creation provides a place for humans, but it is greater than humanity and within it even "great men" are small. Such humility is the consequence of an accurate insight, ecological in its bearing, not a pious deference to "spiritual" value.

Closer to us is a passage from the fourth act of *King Lear*, describing the outlook from one of the Dover cliffs:

> The crows and choughs that wing the midway air
> Show scarce so gross as beetles. Halfway down
> Hangs one that gathers samphire, dreadful trade!
> Methinks he seems no bigger than his head.
> The fishermen that walk upon the beach

> Appear like mice, and yond tall anchoring bark
> Diminished to her cock—her cock, a buoy
> Almost too small for sight.

And this is no mere description of a scenic "view." It is part of a play-within-a-play, a sort of ritual of healing. In it Shakespeare is concerned with the curative power of the perception we are dealing with: by understanding accurately his proper place in Creation, a man may be made whole.

In the lines quoted, Edgar, disguised as a lunatic, a Bedlamite, is speaking to his father, the Earl of Gloucester. Gloucester, having been blinded by the treachery of his false son, Edmund, has despaired and has asked the supposed madman to lead him to the cliff's edge, where he intends to destroy himself. But Edgar's description is from memory; the two are not standing on any such dizzy verge. What we are witnessing is the working out of Edgar's strategy to save his father from false feeling—both the pride, the smug credulity, that led to his suffering and the despair that is its result. These emotions are perceived as madness; Gloucester's blindness is literally the result of the moral blindness of his pride, and it is symbolic of the spiritual blindness of his despair.

Thinking himself on the edge of a cliff, he renounces this world and throws himself down. Though he falls only to the level of his own feet, he is momentarily stunned. Edgar remains with him, but now represents himself as an innocent bystander at the foot of what Gloucester will continue to think is a tall cliff. As the old man recovers his senses, Edgar persuades him that the madman who led him to the cliff's edge was in reality a "fiend." And Gloucester repents his self-destructiveness, which he now recognizes as another kind of pride; a human has no right to destroy what he did not create:

> You ever-gentle gods, take my breath from me.
> Let not my worser spirit tempt me again
> To die before you please.

What Gloucester has passed through, then, is a rite of death and rebirth. In his new awakening he is finally able to recognize his true son. He escapes the unhuman conditions of godly pride and fiendish despair and dies "smilingly" in the truly human estate " 'Twixt two extremes of passion, joy and grief . . ."

Until modern times, we focused a great deal of the best of our thought upon such rituals of return to the human condition. Seeking enlightenment or the Promised Land or the way home, a man would go or be forced to go into the wilderness, measure himself against the Creation, recognize finally his true place within it, and thus be saved both from pride and from despair. Seeing himself as a tiny member of a world he cannot comprehend or master or in any final sense possess, he cannot possibly think of himself as a god. And by the same token, since he shares in, depends upon, and is graced by all of which he is a part, neither can he become a fiend; he cannot descend into the final despair of destructiveness. Returning from the wilderness, he becomes a restorer of order, a preserver. He sees the truth, recognizes his true heir, honors his forebears and his heritage, and gives his blessing to his successors. He embodies the passing of human time, living and dying within the human limits of grief and joy.

ON THE TOWER

Apparently with the rise of industry, we began to romanticize the wilderness—which is to say we began to institutionalize it within the concept of the "scenic." Because of railroads and improved highways, the wilderness was no longer an arduous passage for the traveler, but something to be looked at as grand or beautiful from the high vantages of the roadside. We became viewers of "views." And because we no longer traveled in the wilderness as a matter of course, we forgot that wilderness still circumscribed civilization and persisted in domesticity. We forgot, indeed, that the civilized and the domestic continued to *depend* upon wilderness—that is, upon natural forces within the climate and within the soil that have never in any meaningful sense been controlled or conquered. Modern civilization has been built largely in this forgetfulness.

And as we transformed the wilderness into scenery, we began to feel in the presence of "nature" an awe that was increasingly statistical. We would not become appreciators of the Creation until we had taken its measure. Once we had climbed or driven to the mountain top, we were awed by the view, but it was an awe that we felt compelled to validate or prove by the knowledge of how high we stood and how far we saw. We are invited to "see seven states from atop Lookout Mountain," as if our political boundaries had been drawn in red on the third morning of Creation.

We became less and less capable of sensing ourselves as small within Creation, partly because we thought we could comprehend it statistically, but also because we were becoming creators, ourselves, of a mechanical creation by which we felt ourselves greatly magnified. We built bridges that stood imposingly in titanic settings, towers that stood around us like geologic presences, single machines that could do the work of hundreds of people. Why, after all, should one get excited about a mountain when one can see almost as far from the top of a building, much farther from an airplane, farther still from a space capsule? We have learned to be fascinated by the statistics of magnitude and power. There is apparently no limit in sight, no end, and so it is no wonder that our minds, dizzy with numbers, take refuge in a yearning for infinitudes of energy and materials.

And yet these works that so magnify us also dwarf

us, reduce us to insignificance. They magnify us because we are capable of them. They diminish us because, say what we will, once we build beyond a human scale, once we conceive ourselves as Titans or as gods, we are lost in magnitude; we cannot control or limit what we do. The statistics of magnitude call out like Sirens to the statistics of destruction. If we have built towering cities, we have raised even higher the cloud of megadeath. If people are as grass before God, they are as nothing before their machines.

If we are fascinated by the statistics of magnitude, we are no less fascinated by the statistics of our insignificance. We never tire of repeating the commonizing figures of population and population growth. We are entranced to think of ourselves as specks on the pages of our own overwhelming history. I remember that my high-school biology text dealt with the human body by listing its constituent elements, measuring their quantities, and giving their monetary worth—at that time a little less than a dollar. That was a bit of the typical fodder of the modern mind, at once sensational and belittling—no accidental product of the age of Dachau and Hiroshima.

In our time Shakespeare's cliff has become the tower of a bridge—not the scene of a wakening rite of symbolic death and rebirth, but of the real and final death of suicide. Hart Crane wrote its paradigm, as if against his will, in *The Bridge:*

> Out of some subway scuttle, cell or loft
> A bedlamite speeds to thy parapets,
> Tilting there momentarily, shrill shirt ballooning,
> A jest falls from the speechless caravan.

In Shakespeare, the real Bedlamite or madman is the desperate and suicidal Gloucester. The supposed Bedlamite is in reality his true son, and together they enact an eloquent ritual in which Edgar gives his father a vision of Creation. Gloucester abandons himself to this vision, literally casting himself into it, and is renewed; he finds his life by losing it. Gloucester is saved by a renewal of his sense of the world and of his proper place in it. And this is brought about by an enactment that is communal, both in the sense that he is accompanied in it by his son, who for the time being has assumed the disguise of a madman but the role of a priest, and in the sense that it is deeply traditional in its symbols and meanings. In Crane, on the other hand, the Bedlamite is alone, surrounded by speechlessness, cut off within the crowd from any saving or renewing vision. The height, which in Shakespeare is the traditional place of vision, has become in Crane a place of blindness: the bridge, which Crane intended as a unifying symbol, has become the symbol of a final estrangement.

HEALTH

After I had begun to think about these things, I received a letter containing an account of a more recent suicide. The following sentences from that letter seem both to corroborate Crane's lines and to clarify them:

"My friend ——— jumped off the Golden Gate Bridge two months ago. . . . She had been terribly depressed for years. There was no help for her. None that she could find that was sufficient. She was trying to get from one phase of her life to another, and couldn't make it. She had been terribly wounded as a child. . . . Her wound could not be healed. She destroyed herself."

The letter had already asked, "How does a human pass through youth to maturity without 'breaking down'?" And it had answered: "help from tradition, through ceremonies and rituals, rites of passage at the most difficult stages."

My correspondent went on to say: "Healing, it seems to me, is a necessary and useful word when we talk about agriculture." And a few paragraphs later he wrote:

"The theme of suicide belongs in a book about agriculture . . ."

I agree. But I am also aware that many people will find it exceedingly strange that these themes should enter so forcibly into this book. It will be thought that I am off the subject. And so I want to take pains to show that I am *on* the subject—and on it, moreover, in the only way most people have of getting on it: by way of the issue of their own health. Indeed, it is when one approaches agriculture from any *other* issue than that of health that one may be said to be off the subject.

The difficulty probably lies in our narrowed understanding of the word *health*. That there is some connection between how we feel and what we eat, between our bodies and the earth, is acknowledged when we say that we must "eat right to keep fit" or that we should eat "a balanced diet." But by health we mean little more than how we feel. We are healthy, we think, if we do not feel any pain or too much pain, and if we are strong enough to do our work. If we become unhealthy, then we go to a doctor who we hope will "cure" us and restore us to health. By health, in other words, we mean merely the absence of disease. Our health professionals are interested almost exclusively in preventing disease (mainly by destroying germs) and in curing disease (mainly by surgery and by destroying germs).

But the concept of health is rooted in the concept of wholeness. To be healthy is to be whole. The word *health* belongs to a family of words, a listing of which will suggest how far the consideration of health must carry us: *heal, whole, wholesome, hale, hallow, holy*. And so it is possible to give a definition to health that is positive and far more elaborate than that given to it by most medical doctors and the officers of public health.

If the body is healthy, then it is whole. But how can it be whole and yet be dependent, as it obviously is, upon other bodies and upon the earth, upon all the rest of Creation in fact? It becomes clear that the health or wholeness of the body is a vast subject, and that to preserve it calls for a vast enterprise. Blake said that "Man has no Body distinct from his Soul . . ." and thus acknowledged the convergence of health and holiness. In that, all the convergences and dependences of Creation are surely implied. Our bodies are also not distinct from the bodies of other people, on which they depend in a complexity of ways from biological to spiritual. They are not distinct from the bodies of plants and animals, with which we are involved in the cycles of feeding and in the intricate companionships of ecological systems and of the spirit. They are not distinct from the earth, the sun and moon, and the other heavenly bodies.

It is therefore absurd to approach the subject of health piecemeal with a departmentalized band of specialists. A medical doctor uninterested in nutrition, in agriculture, in the wholesomeness of mind and spirit is as absurd as a farmer who is uninterested in health. Our fragmentation of this subject cannot be our cure, because it is our disease. The body cannot be whole alone. Persons cannot be whole alone. It is wrong to think that bodily health is compatible with spiritual confusion or cultural disorder, or with polluted air and water or impoverished soil. Intellectually, we know that these patterns of interdependence exist; we understand them better now perhaps than we ever have before; yet modern social and cultural patterns contradict them and make it difficult or impossible to honor them in practice.

To try to heal the body alone is to collaborate in the destruction of the body. Healing is impossible in loneliness; it is the opposite of loneliness. Conviviality is healing. To be healed we must come with all the other creatures to the feast of Creation. Together, the above two descriptions of suicides suggest this very powerfully. The setting of both is urban, amid the gigantic works of modern humanity. The fatal sickness is despair, a wound that cannot be healed because it is encapsulated in loneliness, surrounded by speechlessness. Past the scale of the human, our works do not liberate us—they confine us. They cut off access to the wilderness of Creation where we must go to be reborn—to receive the awareness, at once humbling and exhilarating, grievous and joyful, that we are a part of Creation, one with all that we live from and all that, in turn, lives from us. They destroy the communal rites of passage that turn us toward the wilderness and bring us home again.

THE ISOLATION OF THE BODY

Perhaps the fundamental damage of the specialist system—the damage from which all other damages issue—has been the isolation of the body. At some point we began to assume that the life of the body would be the business of grocers and medical doctors, who need take no interest in the spirit, whereas the life of the spirit would be the business of churches, which would have at best only a negative interest in the body. In the same way we began to see nothing wrong with putting the body—most often somebody else's body, but frequently our own—to a task that insulted the mind and demeaned the spirit. And we began to find it easier than ever to prefer our own bodies to the bodies of other creatures and to abuse, exploit, and otherwise hold in contempt those other bodies for the greater good or comfort of our own.

The isolation of the body sets it into direct conflict with everything else in Creation. It gives it a value that is destructive of every other value. That this has happened is paradoxical, for the body was set apart from the soul in order that the soul should triumph over the body. The aim is stated in Shakespeare's Sonnet 146 as plainly as anywhere:

> Poor soul, the center of my sinful earth,
> Lord of these rebel powers that thee array,
> Why dost thou pine within and suffer dearth,
> Painting thy outward walls so costly gay?
> Why so large cost, having so short a lease,
> Dost thou upon thy fading mansion spend?
> Shall worms, inheritors of this excess,
> Eat up thy charge? Is this thy body's end?
> Then, soul, live thou upon thy servant's loss,
> And let that pine to aggravate thy store;
> Buy terms divine in selling hours of dross;
> Within be fed, without be rich no more.
> So shalt thou feed on death, that feeds on men,
> And death once dead, there's no more dying then.

The soul is thus set against the body, to thrive at the body's expense. And so a spiritual economy is devised within which the only law is competition. If the soul is to live in this world only by denying the body, then its relation to worldly life becomes extremely simple and superficial. Too simple and superficial, in fact, to cope in any meaningful or useful way with the world. Spiritual value ceases to have any worldly purpose or force. To fail to employ the body in this world at once for its own good and the good of the soul is to issue an invitation to disorder of the most serious kind.

What was not foreseen in this simple-minded economics of religion was that it is not possible to devalue the body and value the soul. The body, cast loose from the soul, is on its own. Devalued and cast out of the temple, the body does not skulk off like a sick dog to die in the bushes. It sets up a counterpart economy of its own, based also on the law of competition, in which it devalues and exploits the spirit. These two economies maintain themselves at each other's expense, living upon each other's loss, collaborating without cease in mutual futility and absurdity.

You cannot devalue the body and value the soul—or value anything else. The prototypical act issuing from this division was to make a person a slave and then instruct him in religion—a "charity" more damaging to the master than to the slave. Contempt for the body is invariably manifested in contempt for other bodies—the bodies of slaves, laborers, women, animals, plants, the earth itself. Relationships with all other creatures become competitive and exploitive rather than collaborative and convivial. The world is seen and dealt with, not as an ecological community, but as a stock exchange, the ethics of which are based on the tragically misnamed "law of the jungle." This "jungle" law is a basic fallacy of modern culture. The body is degraded and saddened by being set in conflict against the Creation itself, of which all bodies are members, therefore members of each other. The body is thus sent to war against itself.

Divided, set against each other, body and soul drive each other to extremes of misapprehension and folly. Nothing could be more absurd than to despise the body and yet yearn for its resurrection. In reaction to this supposedly religious attitude, we get, not reverence or respect for the body, but another kind of contempt: the desire to comfort and indulge the body with equal disregard for its health. The "dialogue of body and soul" in our time is being carried on between those who despise the body for the sake of its resurrection and those, diseased by bodily extravagance and lack of exercise, who nevertheless desire longevity above all things. These think that they oppose each other, and yet they could not exist apart. They are locked in a conflict that is really their collaboration in the destruction of soul and body both.

What this conflict has done, among other things, is to make it extremely difficult to set a proper value on the life of the body in this world—to believe that it is good, howbeit short and imperfect. Until we are able to say this and know what we mean by it, we will not be able to live our lives in the human estate of grief and joy, but repeatedly will be cast outside in violent swings between pride and despair. Desires that cannot be fulfilled in health will keep us hopelessly restless and unsatisfied.

COMPETITION

By dividing body and soul, we divide both from all else. We thus condemn ourselves to a loneliness for which the only compensation is violence—against other creatures, against the earth, against ourselves. For no matter the distinctions we draw between body and soul, body and earth, ourselves and others—the connections, the dependences, the identities remain. And so we fail to contain or control our violence. It gets loose. Though there are categories of violence, or so we think, there are no categories of victims. Violence against one is ultimately violence against all. The willingness to abuse other bodies is the willingness to abuse one's own. To damage the earth is to damage your children. To despise the ground is to despise its fruit; to despise the fruit is to despise its eaters. The wholeness of health is broken by despite.

If competition is the correct relation of creatures to one another and to the earth, then we must ask why exploitation is not more successful than it is. Why, having lived so long at the expense of other creatures and the earth, are we not healthier and happier than we are? Why does modern society exist under constant threat of the same suffering, deprivation, spite, contempt, and obliteration that it has imposed on other people and other creatures? Why do the health of the body and the health of the earth decline together? And why, in consideration of this decline of our worldly flesh and household, our "sinful earth," are we not healthier in spirit?

It is not necessary to have recourse to statistics to see that the human estate is declining with the estate of nature, and that the corruption of the body is the corruption of the soul. I know that the country is full of "leaders" and experts of various sorts who are using statistics to prove the opposite: that we have more cars, more superhighways, more TV sets, motorboats, prepared foods, etc., than any people ever had before—and are therefore better off than any people ever were before. I can see the burgeoning of this "consumer economy" and can appreciate some of its attractions and comforts. But that economy has an inside and an outside; from the outside there are other things to be seen.

I am writing this in the north-central part of Kentucky on a morning near the end of June. We have had rain for two days, hard rain during the last several hours. From where I sit I can see the Kentucky River swiftening and rising, the water already yellow with mud. I know that inside this city-oriented consumer economy there are many people who will never see this muddy rise and many who will see it without knowing what it means. I know also that there are many who will see it, and know what it means, and not care. If it lasts until the weekend there will be people who will find it as good as clear water for motorboating and waterskiing.

In the past several days I have seen some of the worst-eroded corn fields that I have seen in this country in my life. This erosion is occurring on the cash-rented farms of farmers' widows and city farmers, absentee owners, the doctors and businessmen who buy a farm for the tax breaks or to have "a quiet place in the country" for the weekends. It is the direct result of economic and agricultural policy; it might be said to *be* an economic and agricultural policy. The signs of the "agridollar," big-business fantasy of the Butz mentality are all present: the absenteeism, the temporary and shallow interest of the land-renter, the row-cropping of slopes, the lack of rotation, the plowed-out waterways, the rows running up and down the hills. Looked at from the field's edge, this is ruin, criminal folly, moral idiocy. Looked at from Washington, D.C., from inside the "economy," it is called "free enterprise" and "full production."

And around me here, as everywhere else I have been in this country—in Nebraska, Iowa, Indiana, New York, New England, Tennessee—the farmland is in general decline: fields and whole farms abandoned, given up with their scars unmended, washing away under the weeds and bushes; fine land put to row crops year after year, without rest or rotation; buildings and fences going down; good houses standing empty, unpainted, their windows broken.

And it is clear to anyone who looks carefully at any crowd that we are wasting our bodies exactly as we are wasting our land. Our bodies are fat, weak, joyless, sickly, ugly, the virtual prey of the manufacturers of medicine and cosmetics. Our bodies have become marginal; they are growing useless like our "marginal" land because we have less and less use for them. After the games and idle flourishes of modern youth, we use them only as shipping cartons to transport our brains and our few employable muscles back and forth to work.

As for our spirits, they seem more and more to comfort themselves by buying things. No longer in need of the exalted drama of grief and joy, they feed now on little shocks of greed, scandal, and violence. For many of the churchly, the life of the spirit is reduced to a dull preoccupation with getting to Heaven. At best, the world is no more than an embarrassment and a trial to the spirit, which is otherwise radically separated from it. The true lover of God must not be burdened with any care or respect for His works. While the body goes about its business of destroying the earth, the soul is supposed to lie back and wait for Sunday, keeping itself free of earthly contaminants. While the body exploits other bodies, the soul stands aloof, free from sin, crying to the gawking bystanders: "I am not enjoying it!" As far as this sort of "religion" is concerned, the body is no more than the lusterless container of the soul, a mere "package," that will nevertheless light up in eternity, forever cool and shiny as a neon cross. This separation of the soul from the body and from the world is no disease of the fringe, no aberration, but a fracture that runs through the mentality of institutional religion like a geologic fault. And this rift in the mentality of religion continues to characterize the modern mind, no matter how secular or worldly it becomes.

But I have not stated my point exactly enough. This rift is not *like* a geologic fault; it *is* a geologic fault. It is a flaw in the mind that runs inevitably into the earth. Thought affects or afflicts substance neither by intention nor by accident, but because, occurring in the Creation that is unified and whole, it must; there is no help for it.

The soul, in its loneliness, hopes only for "salvation." And yet what is the burden of the Bible if not a sense of the mutuality of influence, rising out of an essential unity, among soul and body and community and world? These are all the works of God, and it is therefore the work of virtue to make or restore harmony among them. The world is certainly thought of as a place of spiritual trial, but it is also the confluence of soul and body, word and flesh, where thoughts must become deeds, where goodness is to be enacted. This is the great meeting place, the narrow passage where spirit and flesh, word and world, pass into each other. The Bible's aim, as I read it, is not the freeing of the

spirit from the world. It is the handbook of their interaction. It says that they cannot be divided; that their mutuality, their unity, is inescapable; that they are not reconciled in division, but in harmony. What else can be meant by the resurrection of the body? The body should be "filled with light," perfected in understanding. And so everywhere there is the sense of consequence, fear and desire, grief and joy. What is desirable is repeatedly defined in the tensions of the sense of consequence. False prophets are to be known "by their fruits." We are to treat others as we would be treated; thought is thus barred from any easy escape into aspiration or ideal, is turned around and forced into action. The following verses from Proverbs are not very likely the original work of a philosopher-king; they are overheard from generations of agrarian grandparents whose experience taught them that spiritual qualities become earthly events:

> I went by the field of the slothful, and by the vineyard of the man void of understanding;
> And, lo, it was all grown over with thorns, and nettles had covered the face thereof, and the stone wall thereof was broken down.
> Then I saw, and considered it well. I looked upon it, and received instruction.
> Yet a little sleep, a little slumber, a little folding of the hands to sleep:
> So shall thy poverty come as one that traveleth; and thy want as an armed man.

CONNECTIONS

I do not want to speak of unity misleadingly or too simply. Obvious distinctions can be made between body and soul, one body and other bodies, body and world, etc. But these things that appear to be distinct are nevertheless caught in a network of mutual dependence and influence that is the substantiation of their unity. Body, soul (or mind or spirit), community, and world are all susceptible to each other's influence, and they are all conductors of each other's influence. The body is damaged by the bewilderment of the spirit, and it conducts the influence of that bewilderment into the earth, the earth conducts it into the community, and so on. If a farmer fails to understand what health is, his farm becomes unhealthy; it produces unhealthy food, which damages the health of the community. But this is a network, a spherical network, by which each part is connected to every other part. The farmer is a part of the community, and so it is as impossible to say exactly where the trouble began as to say where it will end. The influences go backward and forward, up and down, round and round, compounding and branching as they go. All that is certain is that an error introduced anywhere in the network ramifies beyond the scope of prediction; consequences occur all over the place, and each consequence breeds further consequences. But it seems unlikely that an error can ramify endlessly. It spreads by way of the connections in the network, but sooner or later it must also begin to break them. We are talking, obviously, about a circulatory system, and a disease of a circulatory system tends first to impair circulation and then to stop it altogether.

Healing, on the other hand, complicates the system by opening and restoring connections among the various parts—in this way restoring the ultimate simplicity of their union. When all the parts of the body are working together, are under each other's influence, we say that it is whole; it is healthy. The same is true of the world, of which our bodies are parts. The parts are healthy insofar as they are joined harmoniously to the whole.

What the specialization of our age suggests, in one example after another, is not only that fragmentation is a disease, but that the diseases of the disconnected parts are similar or analogous to one another. Thus they memorialize their lost unity, their relation persisting in their disconnection. Any severance produces two wounds that are, among other things, the record of how the severed parts once fitted together.

The so-called identity crisis, for instance, is a disease that seems to have become prevalent after the disconnection of body and soul and the other piecemealings of the modern period. One's "identity" is apparently the immaterial part of one's being—also known as psyche, soul, spirit, self, mind, etc. The dividing of this principle from the body and from any particular worldly locality would seem reason enough for a crisis. Treatment, it might be thought, would logically consist in the restoration of these connections: the lost identity would find itself by recognizing physical landmarks, by connecting itself responsibly to practical circumstances; it would learn to stay put in the body to which it belongs and in the place to which preference or history or accident has brought it; it would, in short, find itself in finding its work. But "finding yourself," the pseudo-ritual by which the identity crisis is supposed to be resolved, makes use of no such immediate references. Leaving aside the obvious, and ancient, realities of doubt and self-doubt, as well as the authentic madness that is often the result of cultural disintegration, it seems likely that the identity crisis is a conventional illusion, one of the genres of self-indulgence. It can be an excuse for irresponsibility or a fashionable mode of self-dramatization. It is the easiest form of self-flattery—a way to construe procrastination as a virtue—based on the romantic assumption that "who I really am" is better in some fundamental way than the available evidence would suggest.

The fashionable cure for this condition, if I understand the lore of it correctly, has nothing to do with the assumption of responsibilities or the renewal of connections. The cure is "autonomy," another illusory condition, suggesting that the self can be self-determining and independent without regard for any determining circumstance or any of the obvious dependences. This seems little more than a jargon term for indifference to the opinions and feelings of other people. There is, in practice, no such thing as autonomy. Practically, there is only a distinction between responsible and irresponsible dependence. Inevitably failing this impossible standard of autonomy, the modern self-seeker becomes a tourist of cures, submitting his quest to the guidance of one guru after another. The "cure" thus preserves the disease.

It is not surprising that this strange disease of the spirit—the self's loss of the self—should have its counterpart in an anguish of the body. One of the commonplaces of modern experience is dissatisfaction with the body—not as one has allowed it to become, but as it naturally is. The hardship is perhaps greater here because the body, unlike the self, is substantial and cannot be supposed to be inherently better than it was born to be. It can only be thought inherently worse than it *ought* to be. For the appropriate standard for the body—that is, health—has been replaced, not even by another standard, but by very exclusive physical *models*. The concept of "model" here conforms very closely to the model of the scientists and planners: it is an exclusive, narrowly defined ideal which affects destructively whatever it does not include.

Thus our young people are offered the ideal of health only by what they know to be lip service. What they are made to feel forcibly, and to measure themselves by, is the exclusive desirability of a certain physical model. Girls are taught to want to be leggy, slender, large-breasted, curly-haired, unimposingly beautiful. Boys are instructed to be "athletic" in build, tall but not too tall, broad-shouldered, deep-chested, narrow-hipped, square-jawed, straight-nosed, not bald, unimposingly handsome. Both sexes should look what passes for "sexy" in a bathing suit. Neither, above all, should look old.

Though many people, in health, are beautiful, very few resemble these models. The result is widespread suffering that does immeasurable damage both to individual persons and to the society as a whole. The result is another absurd pseudo-ritual, "accepting one's body," which may take years or may be the distraction of a lifetime. Woe to the man who is short or skinny or bald. Woe to the man with a big nose. Woe, above all, to the woman with small breasts or a muscular body or strong features; Homer and Solomon might have thought her beautiful, but she will see her own beauty only by a difficult rebellion. And like the crisis of identity, this crisis of the body brings a helpless dependence on cures. One spends one's life dressing and "making up" to compensate for one's supposed deficiencies. Again, the cure preserves the disease. And the putative healer is the guru of style and beauty aid. The sufferer is by definition a customer.

SEXUAL DIVISION

To divide body and soul, or body and mind, is to inaugurate an expanding series of divisions—not, however, an *infinitely* expanding series, because it is apparently the nature of division sooner or later to destroy what is divided; the principle of durability is unity. The divisions issuing from the division of body and soul are first sexual and then ecological. Many other divisions branch out from those, but those are the most important because they have to do with the fundamental relationships—with each other and with the earth—that we all have in common.

To think of the body as separate from the soul or as soulless, either to subvert its appetites or to "free" them, is to make an object of it. As a thing, the body is denied any dimension or rightful presence or claim in the mind. The concerns of the body—all that is comprehended in the term *nurture*—are thus degraded, denied any respected place among the "higher things" and even among the more exigent practicalities.

The first sexual division comes about when nurture is made the exclusive concern of women. This cannot happen until a society becomes industrial; in hunting and gathering and in agricultural societies, men are of necessity also involved in nurture. In those societies there usually have been differences between the work of men and that of women. But the necessity here is to distinguish between sexual difference and sexual division.

In an industrial society, following the division of body and soul, we have at the "upper" or professional level a division between "culture" (in the specialized sense of religion, philosophy, art, the humanities, etc.) and "practicality," and both of these become increasingly abstract. Thinkers do not act. And the "practical" men do not work with their hands, but manipulate the abstract quantities and values that come from the work of "workers." Workers are simplified or specialized into machine parts to do the wage-work of the body, which they were initially permitted to think of as "manly" because for the most part women did not do it.

Women traditionally have performed the most confining—though not necessarily the least dignified—tasks of nurture: housekeeping, the care of young children, food preparation. In the urban-industrial situation the confinement of these traditional tasks divided women more and more from the "important" activities of the new economy. Furthermore, in this situation the traditional nurturing role of men—that of provisioning the household, which in an agricultural society had become as constant and as complex as the women's role—became completely abstract; the man's duty to the household came to be simply to provide money. The only remaining *task* of provisioning—purchasing food—was turned over to women. This determination that nurturing should become *exclusively* a concern of women served to signify to both sexes that neither nurture nor womanhood was very important.

But the assignment to women of a kind of work that was thought both onerous and trivial was only the beginning of their exploitation. As the persons exclusively in charge of the tasks of nurture, women often came into sole charge of the household budget; they became family purchasing agents. The time of the household barterer was past. Kitchens were now run on a cash economy. Women had become customers, a fact not long wasted on the salesmen, who saw that in these women they had customers of a new and most promising kind. The modern housewife was isolated from her husband, from her school-age children, and from other women. She was saddled with work from which much of the skill, hence much of the dignity, had been withdrawn. She did not know what her husband did at work, or after work, and she knew that her life was passing in his regardlessness and in his absence. Such a woman was ripe for a sales talk: this was the great commercial insight of modern times. Such a woman must be told—or subtly made to understand—that she must not be a drudge, that she must not let her work affect her looks, that she must not become "unattractive," that she must always be fresh, cheerful, young, shapely, and pretty. All her sexual and mortal fears would thus be given voice, and she would be made to reach for money. What was implied was always the question that a certain bank finally asked outright in a billboard advertisement: "Is your husband losing interest?"

Motivated no longer by practical needs, but by loneliness and fear, women began to identify themselves by what they bought rather than by what they did. They bought labor-saving devices which worked, as most modern machines have tended to work, to devalue or replace the skills of those who used them. They bought manufactured foods, which did likewise. They bought any product that offered to lighten the burdens of housework, to be "kind to hands," or to endear one to one's husband. And they furnished their houses, as they made up their faces and selected their clothes, neither by custom nor invention, but by the suggestion of articles and advertisements in "women's magazines." Thus housewifery, once a complex discipline acknowledged to be one of the bases of culture and economy, was reduced to the exercise of purchasing power. (She did continue to do "housework," of course. But we must ask what this had come to mean. The industrial economy had changed the criterion of housekeeping from thrift to convenience. Thrift was a complex standard, requiring skill, intelligence, and moral character, and private thrift was rightly considered a public value. Once thrift was destroyed as a value, housekeeping became simply a corrupt function of a corrupt economy: its public "value" lay in the wearing out or using up of commodities.) The housewife's only remaining productive capacity was that of reproduction. But even as a mother she remained a consumer,* subjecting herself to an all-presuming doctor and again to written instructions calculated to result

---

* This was written before the era of commercial child production. A woman may now "work" as a brood animal and sell her offspring. This cottage industry is a grand advance for liberty, since it frees some women from impecuniousness and others from sterility—the rule being that one has the right to be freed from any objectionable condition by any means. It is also the most significant expansion of commerce since the Emancipation Proclamation.

in the purchase of merchandise. Breast-feeding of babies became unfashionable, one suspects, because it was the last form of home production; no way could be found to persuade a woman to purchase her own milk. All these "improvements" involved a radical simplification of mind that was bound to have complicated, and ironic, results. As housekeeping became simpler and easier, it also became more boring. A woman's work became less accomplished and less satisfying. It became easier for her to believe that what she did was not important. And this heightened her anxiety and made her even more avid and even less discriminating as a consumer. The cure not only preserved the disease, it compounded it.

There was, of course, a complementary development in the minds of men, but there is less to say about it. The man's mind was not simplified by a degenerative process, but by a kind of coup: as soon as he separated working and living and began to work away from home, the practical considerations of the household were excerpted from his mind all at once.

In modern marriage, then, what was once a difference of work became a division of work. And in this division the household was destroyed as a practical bond between husband and wife. It was no longer a condition, but only a place. It was no longer a circumstance that required, dignified, and rewarded the enactment of mutual dependence, but the site of mutual estrangement. Home became a place for the husband to go when he was not working or amusing himself. It was the place where the wife was held in servitude.

A sexual difference is not a wound, or it need not be; a sexual division is. And it is important to recognize that this division—this destroyed household that now stands between the sexes—is a wound that is suffered inescapably by both men and women. Sometimes it is assumed that the estrangement of women in their circumscribed "women's world" can only be for the benefit of men. But that interpretation seems to be based on the law of competition that is modeled in the exploitive industrial economy. This law holds that for everything that is exploited or oppressed there must be something else that is proportionately improved; thus, men must be as happy as women are unhappy.

There is no doubt that women have been deformed by the degenerate housewifery that is now called their "role"—but not, I think, for any man's benefit. If women are deformed by their role, then, insofar as the roles are divided, men are deformed by theirs. Degenerate housewifery is indivisible from degenerate husbandry. There is no escape. This is the justice that we are learning from the ecologists: you cannot damage what you are dependent upon without damaging yourself. The suffering of women is noticed now, is noticeable now, because it is not given any considerable status or compensation. If we removed the status and compensation from the destructive exploits we classify as "manly," men would be found to be suffering as much as women. They would be found to be suffering for the same reason: they are in exile from the communion of men and women, which is their deepest connection with the communion of all creatures.

For example: a man who is in the traditional sense a *good* farmer is husbandman and husband, the begetter and conserver of the earth's bounty, but he is also midwife and motherer. He is a nurturer of life. His work is domestic; he is bound to the household. But let "progress" take such a man and transform him into a technologist of production (that is, sever his bonds to the household, make useless or pointless or "uneconomical" his impulse to conserve and to

nurture), and it will have made of him a creature as deformed, and as pained, as it has notoriously made of his
wife.

THE DISMEMBERMENT OF THE HOUSEHOLD

We are familiar with the concept of the disintegral
life of our time as a dismembered cathedral, the various
concerns of culture no longer existing in reference to each
other or within the discipline of any understanding of their
unity. It may also be conceived, and its strains more immediately felt, as a dismembered household. Without the
household—not just as a unifying ideal, but as a practical
circumstance of mutual dependence and obligation, requiring skill, moral discipline, and work—husband and wife
find it less and less possible to imagine and enact their marriage. Without much in particular that they can *do* for each
other, they have a scarcity of practical reasons to be together. They may "like each other's company," but that is a
reason for friendship, not for marriage. Aside from affection for any children they may have and their abstract legal
and economic obligations to each other, their union has to
be empowered by sexual energy alone.

Perhaps the most dangerous, certainly the most
immediately painful, consequence of the disintegration of
the household is this isolation of sexuality. The division of
sexual energy from the functions of household and community that it ought both to empower and to grace is
analogous to that other modern division between hunger
and the earth. When it is no longer allied by proximity and
analogy to the nurturing disciplines that bound the household to the cycles of fertility and the seasons, life and
death, then sexual love loses its symbolic or ritualistic
force, its deepest solemnity and its highest joy. It loses its

sense of consequence and responsibility. It becomes "autonomous," to be valued only for its own sake, therefore frivolous, therefore destructive—even of itself. Those who speak of sex as "recreation," thinking to claim for it "a new place," only acknowledge its displacement from Creation.

The isolation of sexuality makes it subject to two influences that dangerously oversimplify it: the lore of sexual romance and capitalist economics. By "sexual romance" I mean the sentimentalization of sexual love that for generations has been the work of popular songs and stories. By means of them, young people have been taught a series of extremely dangerous falsehoods:

> 1. That people in love ought to conform to the fashionable models of physical beauty, and that to be unbeautiful by these standards is to be unlovable.
> 2. That people in love are, or ought to be, young—even though love is said to last "forever."
> 3. That marriage is a solution—whereas the most misleading thing a love story can do is to end "happily" with a marriage, not because there is no such thing as a happy marriage, but because marriage cannot be happy except by being *made* happy.
> 4. That love, alone, regardless of circumstances, can make harmony and resolve serious differences.
> 5. That "love will find a way" and so finally triumph over any kind of practical difficulty.
> 6. That the "right" partners are "made for each other," or that "marriages are made in Heaven."
> 7. That lovers are "each other's all" or "all the world to each other."
> 8. That monogamous marriage is therefore logical and natural, and "forsaking all others" involves no difficulty.

Believing these things, a young couple could not be more cruelly exposed to the abrasions of experience—or better prepared to experience marriage as another of those grim and ironic modern competitions in which the victory of one is the defeat of both.

As experience frets away gullibility, the exclusiveness of the sentimental ideal gives way to the possessiveness of sexual capitalism. Failing, as they cannot help but fail, to be each other's all, the husband and wife become each other's only. The sacrament of sexual union, which in the time of the household was a communion of workmates, and afterward tried to be a lovers' paradise, has now become a kind of marketplace in which husband and wife represent each other as sexual property. Competitiveness and jealousy, imperfectly sweetened and disguised by the illusions of courtship, now become governing principles, and they work to isolate the couple inside their marriage. Marriage becomes a capsule of sexual fate. The man must look on other men, and the woman on other women, as threats. This seems to have become particularly damaging to women; because of the progressive degeneration and isolation of their "role," their worldly stock in trade has increasingly had to be "their" men. In the isolation of the resulting sexual "privacy," the disintegration of the community begins. The energy that is the most convivial and unifying loses its communal forms and becomes divisive. This dispersal was nowhere more poignantly exemplified than in the replacement of the old ring dances, in which all couples danced together, by the so-called ballroom dancing, in which each couple dances alone. A significant part of the etiquette of ballroom dancing is, or was, that the exchange of partners was accomplished by a "trade." It is no accident that this capitalization of love and marriage was followed by a divorce epidemic—and by fashions of dancing in which each one of the dancers moves alone.

The disintegration of marriage, which completes the disintegration of community, came about because the encapsulation of sexuality, meant to preserve marriage from competition, inevitably *enclosed* competition. The principle that fenced everyone else out fenced the couple in; it became a sexual cul-de-sac. The model of economic competition proved as false to marriage as to farming. As with other capsules, the narrowness of the selective principle proved destructive of what it excluded, and what it excluded was essential to the life of what it enclosed: the nature of sexuality itself. Sexual romance cannot bear to acknowledge the generality of instinct, whereas sexual capitalism cannot acknowledge its particularity. But sexuality appears to be *both* general and particular. One cannot love a particular woman, for instance, unless one loves womankind—if not all women, at least other women. The capsule of sexual romance leaves out this generality, this generosity of instinct; it excludes Aphrodite and Dionysus. And it fails for that reason. Though sexual love can endure between the same two people for a long time, it cannot do so on the basis of this pretense of the exclusiveness of affection. The sexual capitalist—that is, the disillusioned sexual romantic—in reaction to disillusion makes the opposite oversimplification; one acknowledges one's spouse as one of a general, necessarily troublesome kind or category.

Both these attitudes look on sexual love as ownership. The sexual romantic croons, "You be-long to me." The sexual capitalist believes the same thing but has stopped crooning. Each holds that a person's sexual property shall be sufficient unto him or unto her, and that the morality of that sufficiency is to be forever on guard against expropriation. Within the capsule of marriage, as in that of economics, one intends to exploit one's property and to protect it. Once the idea of property becomes abstract or economic, both these motives begin to rule over it. They are, of course, contradictory; all that one can really protect is one's "right" or intention to exploit. The proprieties and privacies used to encapsulate marriage may have come from the tacit recognition that exploitive sex, like exploitive economics, is a very dirty business. One makes a secret of the sexuality of one's marriage for the same reason that one posts "Keep Out/Private Property" on one's strip mine. The tragedy, more often felt than acknowledged, is that what is exploited becomes undesirable.

The protective capsule becomes a prison. It becomes a household of the living dead, each body a piece of incriminating evidence. Or a greenhouse excluding the neighbors and the weather for the sake of some alien and unnatural growth. The marriage shrinks to a dull vigil of duty and legality. Husband and wife become competitors necessarily, for their only freedom is to exploit each other or to escape.

It is possible to imagine a more generous enclosure—a household welcoming to neighbors and friends; a garden open to the weather, between the woods and the road. It is possible to imagine a marriage bond that would bind a woman and a man not only to each other, but to the community of marriage, the amorous communion at which all couples sit: the sexual feast and celebration that joins them to all living things and to the fertility of the earth, and the sexual responsibility that joins them to the human past and the human future. It is possible to imagine marriage as a grievous, joyous human bond, endlessly renewable and renewing, again and again rejoining memory and passion and hope.

FIDELITY

But it is extremely difficult, now, to imagine marriage in terms of such dignity and generosity, and this difficulty is explained by the failure of these possessive and competitive forms of sexual love that have been in use for so long. This failure raises unavoidably the issue of fidelity:

What is it, and what does it mean—in marriage, and also, since marriage is a fundamental relationship and metaphor, in other relationships?

No one can be glad to have this issue so starkly raised, for any consideration of it now must necessarily involve one's own bewilderment. We are apparently near the end of a degenerative phase of an evolutionary process—a long way from any large-scale regeneration. For that reason it is necessary to be hesitant and cautious, respectful of the complexity and importance of the problem. Marriage is not going to change because somebody thinks about it and recommends an "answer"; it can change only as its necessities are felt and as its circumstances change.

The idea of fidelity is perverted beyond redemption by understanding it as a grim, literal duty enforced only by willpower. This is the "religious" insanity of making a victim of the body a victory of the soul. Self-restraint that is so purely negative is self-hatred. And one cannot be good, anyhow, just by not being bad. To be faithful merely out of duty is to be blinded to the possibility of a better faithfulness for better reasons.

It is reasonable to suppose, if fidelity is a virtue, that it is a virtue with a purpose. A purposeless virtue is a contradiction in terms. Virtue, like harmony, cannot exist alone; a virtue must lead to harmony between one creature and another. To be good for nothing is just that. If a virtue has been thought a virtue long enough, it must be assumed to have practical justification—though the very longevity that proves its practicality may obscure it. That seems to be what happened with the idea of fidelity. We heard the words "forsaking all others" repeated over and over again for so long that we lost the sense of their practical justification. They assumed the force of superstition: people came to be faithful in marriage not out of any understanding of the meaning of faith or of marriage, but out of the same fear of obscure retribution that made one careful not to break a mirror or spill the salt. Like other superstitions, this one was weakened by the scientific, positivist intellectuality of modern times and by the popular "sophistication" that came with it. Our age could be characterized as a manifold experiment in faithlessness, and if it has as yet produced no effective understanding of the practicalities of faith, it has certainly produced massive evidence of the damage and disorder of its absence.

It is possible to open this issue of the practicality of fidelity by considering that the modern age was made possible by the freeing, and concurrently by the cheapening, of energy. It can be said, of course, that the modern age was made possible by technologies that *control* energy and thus make it usable at an unprecedented rate. But such control is at best extremely limited: the devices by which industrial and military energies are used control them only momentarily; their moment of usefulness sets them loose in the world as social, ecological, and geological *forces*. We can use these energies only as explosives; we can control the rate, intensity, and time of combustion, but our effective control ends with the use of the small amount of the released energy that we are able to harness. Past that, the effects are on their own, to compound themselves as they will. In modern times we have never been able to subject our use of energy to a sense of responsibility anywhere near complex enough to be equal to its effects.

It may be that the principle of sexual fidelity, once it is again fully understood, will provide us with as good an example as we can find of the responsible use of energy. Sexuality is, after all, a form of energy, one of the most powerful. If we see sexuality as energy, then it becomes impossible to see sexual fidelity as merely a "duty," a virtue for the sake of virtue, or a superstition. If we made a superstition of fidelity, and thereby weakened it, by thinking of it as purely a moral or spiritual value, then perhaps we can restore its strength by recovering an awareness of its practicality.

At the root of culture must be the realization that uncontrolled energy is disorderly—that in nature all energies move in forms; that, therefore, in a human order energies must be *given* forms. It must have been plain at the beginning, as cultural degeneracy has made it plain again and again, that one can be indiscriminately sexual but not indiscriminately responsible, and that irresponsible sexuality would undermine any possibility of culture since it implies a hierarchy based purely upon brute strength, cunning, regardlessness of value and of consequence. Fidelity can thus be seen as the necessary discipline of sexuality, the practical definition of sexual responsibility, or the definition of the moral limits within which such responsibility can be conceived and enacted. The forsaking of all others is a keeping of faith, not just with the chosen one, but with the ones forsaken. The marriage vow unites not just a woman and a man with each other; it unites each of them with the community in a vow of sexual responsibility toward all others. The whole community is married, realizes its essential unity, in each of its marriages.*

Another use of fidelity is to preserve the possibility of devotion against the distractions of novelty. What marriage offers—and what fidelity is meant to protect—is the possibility of moments when what we have chosen and

---

*Marital fidelity, that is, involves the public or institutional as well as the private aspect of marriage. One is married to marriage as well as to one's spouse. But one is married also to something vital of one's own that does not exist before the marriage: one's given word. It now seems to me that the modern misunderstanding of marriage involves a gross misunderstanding and underestimation of the seriousness of giving one's word, and of the dangers of breaking it once it is given. Adultery and divorce now must be looked upon as instances of that disease of word-breaking, which our age justifies as "realistic" or "practical" or "necessary," but which is tattering the invariably single fabric of speech and trust.

what we desire are the same. Such a convergence obviously cannot be continuous. No relationship can continue very long at its highest emotional pitch. But fidelity prepares us for the *return* of these moments, which give us the highest joy we can know: that of union, communion, atonement (in the root sense of at-one-ment). The principle is stated in these lines by William Butler Yeats (by "the world" he means the world after the Fall):

> Maybe the bride-bed brings despair,
> For each an imagined image brings
> And finds a real image there;
> Yet the world ends when these two things,
> Though several, are a single light . . .

To forsake all others does not mean—because it *cannot* mean—to ignore or neglect all others, to hide or be hidden from all others, or to desire or love no others. To live in marriage is a responsible way to live in sexuality, as to live in a household is a responsible way to live in the world. One cannot enact or fulfill one's love for womankind or mankind, or even for all the women or men to whom one is attracted. If one is to have the power and delight of one's sexuality, then the generality of instinct must be resolved in a responsible relationship to a particular person. Similarly, one cannot live in the world; that is, one cannot become, in the easy, generalizing sense with which the phrase is commonly used, a "world citizen." There can be no such thing as a "global village." No matter how much one may love the world as a whole, one can live fully in it only by living responsibly in some small part of it. Where we live and who we live there with define the terms of our relationship to the world and to humanity. We thus come again to the paradox that one can become whole only by the responsible acceptance of one's partiality.

But to encapsulate these partial relationships is to entrap and condemn them in their partiality; it is to endan-

ger them and to make them dangerous. They are enlivened
and given the possibility of renewal by the double sense of
particularity and generality: one lives in marriage *and* in
sexuality, at home *and* in the world. It is impossible, for instance, to conceive that a man could despise women and
yet love his wife, or love his own place in the world and yet
deal destructively with other places.

HOME LAND AND HOUSE HOLD

What I have been trying to do is to define a pattern
of disintegration that is at once cultural and agricultural. I
have been groping for connections—that I think are indissoluble, though obscured by modern ambitions—between
the spirit and the body, the body and other bodies, the
body and the earth. If these connections do necessarily exist, as I believe they do, then it is impossible for material
order to exist side by side with spiritual disorder, or vice
versa, and impossible for one to thrive long at the expense
of the other; it is impossible, ultimately, to preserve ourselves apart from our willingness to preserve other creatures, or to respect and care for ourselves except as we respect and care for other creatures; and, most to the point of
this book, it is impossible to care for each other more or
differently than we care for the earth.

This last statement becomes obvious enough when
it is considered that the earth is what we all have in common, that it is what we are made of and what we live from,
and that we therefore cannot damage it without damaging
those with whom we share it. But I believe it goes farther
and deeper than that. There is an uncanny *resemblance* between our behavior toward each other and our behavior
toward the earth. Between our relation to our own sexuality and our relation to the reproductivity of the earth, for
instance, the resemblance is plain and strong and apparent-

ly inescapable. By some connection that we do not recognize, the willingness to exploit one becomes the willingness to exploit the other. The conditions and the means of exploitation are likewise similar.

The modern failure of marriage that has so estranged the sexes from each other seems analogous to the "social mobility" that has estranged us from our land, and the two are historically parallel. It may even be argued that these two estrangements are very close to being one, both of them having been caused by the disintegration of the household, which was the formal bond between marriage and the earth, between human sexuality and its sources in the sexuality of Creation. The importance of this practical bond has not been often or very openly recognized in our tradition; in modern times it has almost disappeared under the burden of adverse fashion and economics. It is necessary to go far back to find it clearly exemplified.

To my mind, one of the best examples that we have is in Homer's *Odyssey*. Nowhere else that I know are the connections between marriage and household and the earth so fully and so carefully understood.

At the opening of the story Odysseus, after a twenty-year absence, is about to begin the last leg of his homeward journey. The sole survivor of all his company of warriors, having lived through terrible trials and losses, Odysseus is now a castaway on the island of the goddess Kalypso. He is Kalypso's lover but also virtually her prisoner. At night he sleeps with Kalypso in her cave; by day he looks across the sea toward Ithaka, his home, and weeps. Homer does not stint either feeling—the delights of Kalypso's cave, where the lovers "revel and rest softly, side by side," or the grief and longing of exile.

But now Zeus commands Kalypso to allow Odysseus to depart; she comes to tell him that he is free to go. And yet it is a tragic choice that she offers him: he must

choose between her and Penélopê, his wife. If he chooses
Kalypso, he will be immortal, but remain in exile; if he
chooses Penélopê, he will return home at last, but will die
in his time like other men:

> If you could see it all, before you go—
> all the adversity you face at sea—
> you would stay here, and guard this house, and be
> immortal—though you wanted her forever,
> that bride for whom you pine each day.
> Can I be less desirable than she is?
> Less interesting? Less beautiful? Can mortals
> compare with goddesses in grace and form?

And Odysseus answers:

> My quiet Penélopê—how well I know—
> would seem a shade before your majesty,
> death and old age being unknown to you,
> while she must die. Yet, it is true, each day
> I long for home . . .

This is, in effect, a wedding ritual much like our
own, in which Odysseus forsakes all others, in renouncing
the immortal womanhood of the goddess, and renews his
pledge to the mortal terms of his marriage. But unlike our
ritual, this one involves an explicit loyalty to a home. Odysseus' far-wandering through the wilderness of the sea is not
merely the return of a husband; it is a journey home. And a
great deal of the power as well as the moral complexity of
The Odyssey rises out of the richness of its sense of home.

By the end of Book XXIII, it is clear that the action
of the narrative, Odysseus' journey from the cave of Kalypso to the bed of Penélopê, has revealed a structure that is at
once geographical and moral. This structure may be
graphed as a series of diminishing circles centered on one of
the posts of the marriage bed. Odysseus makes his way
from the periphery toward that center.

All around, this structure verges on the sea, which is

the wilderness, ruled by the forces of nature and by the gods. In spite of the excellence of his ship and crew and his skill in navigation, a man is alien there. Only when he steps ashore does he enter a human order. From the shoreline of his island of Ithaka, Odysseus makes his way across a succession of boundaries, enclosed and enclosing, with the concentricity of a blossom around its pistil, a human pattern resembling a pattern of nature. He comes to his island, to his own lands, to his town, to his household and house, to his bedroom, to his bed.

As he moves toward this center he moves also through a series of recognitions, tests of identity and devotion. By these, his homecoming becomes at the same time a restoration of order. At first, having been for a while uncertain of his whereabouts, he recognizes his homeland by the conformation of the countryside and by a certain olive tree. He then becomes the guest of his swineherd, Eumaios, and tests his loyalty, though Eumaios will not be permitted to recognize his master until the story approaches its crisis. In the house of Eumaios, Odysseus meets and makes himself known to his son, Telémakhos. As he comes, disguised as a beggar, into his own house, he is recognized by Argus, his old hunting dog. That night, as the guest of Penélopê, who does not yet know who he is, he is recognized by his aged nurse, Eurýkleia, who sees a well-remembered scar on his thigh as she is bathing his feet.

He is scorned and abused as a vagabond by the band of suitors who, believing him dead, have been courting his wife, consuming his meat and wine, desecrating his household, and plotting the murder of his son. Penélopê proposes a trial by which the suitors will compete for her: she will become the bride of whichever one can string the bow of her supposedly dead husband and shoot an arrow through the aligned helve-sockets of twelve axe heads. The suitors fail. Odysseus performs the feat easily and is thereby recognized as "the great husband" himself. And then, with the help of the swineherd, the cowherd, and Teléma-khos, he proceeds to trap the suitors and slaughter them all without mercy. To so distinguished a commentator as Richmond Lattimore, their punishment "seems excessive." But granting the acceptability of violent means to a warrior such as Odysseus, this outcome seems to me appropriate to the moral terms of the poem. It is made clear that the punishment is not merely the caprice of a human passion: Odysseus enacts the will of the gods; he is the agent of a divine judgment. The suitors' sin is their utter contempt for the domestic order that the poem affirms. They do not respect or honor the meaning of the household, and in *The Odyssey* this meaning is paramount.

It is therefore the recognition of Odysseus by Penél-opê that is the most interesting and the most crucial. By the time Odysseus' vengeance and his purification of the house are complete, Penélopê is the only one in the household who has not acknowledged him. It is only reasonable that she should delay this until she is absolutely certain. After all, she has waited twenty years; it is not to be expected that she would be less than cautious now. Her faith has been equal and more than equal to his, and now she proves his equal also in cunning. She tells Eurýkleia to move their bed outside their bedroom and to make it up for Odysseus there. Odysseus' rage at hearing that identifies him beyond doubt, for she knew that only Odysseus would know—it is their "pact and pledge" and "secret sign"—that the bed could not be moved without destroying it. He built their bedroom with his own hands, and an old olive tree, as he says,

> grew like a pillar on the building plot,
> and I laid out our bedroom round that tree . . .
> . . . I lopped off the silvery leaves and branches,
> hewed and shaped that stump from the roots up
> into a bedpost . . .

She acknowledges him then, and only then does she give herself to his embrace.

> Now from his heart into his eyes the ache
> of longing mounted, and he wept at last,
> his dear wife, clear and faithful in his arms,
> longed for
> as the sunwarmed earth is longed for by a swimmer
> spent in rough water where his ship went down . . .

And so in the renewal of his marriage, the return of Odysseus and the restoration of order are complete. The order of the kingdom is centered on the marriage bed of the king and queen, and that bed is rooted in the earth. The figure last quoted makes explicit at last the long-hinted analogy between Odysseus' fidelity to his wife and his fidelity to his homeland. In Penélopê's welcoming embrace his two fidelities become one.

For Odysseus, then, marriage was not merely a legal bond, nor even merely a sacred bond, between himself and Penélopê. It was part of a complex practical circumstance involving, in addition to husband and wife, their family of both descendants and forebears, their household, their community, and the sources of all these lives in memory and tradition, in the countryside, and in the earth. These things, wedded together in his marriage, he thought of as his home, and it held his love and faith so strongly that sleeping with a goddess could not divert or console him in his exile.

In Odysseus' return, then, we see a complete marriage and a complete fidelity. To reduce marriage, as we have done, to a mere contract of sexual exclusiveness is at once to degrade it and to make it impossible. That is to take away its dignity and its potency of joy, and to make it only a pitiful little duty—not a union, but a division and a solitude.

The Odyssey's understanding of marriage as the vital link which joins the human community and the earth

is obviously full of political implication. In this it will remind us of the Confucian principle that "The government
of the state is rooted in family order." But *The Odyssey*
goes further than the Confucian texts, it seems to me, in its
understanding of agricultural value as the foundation of
domestic order and peace.

I have considered the poem so far as describing a
journey from the non-human order of the sea wilderness to
the human order of the cleansed and reunited household.
But it is also a journey between two kinds of human value;
it moves from the battlefield of Troy to the terraced fields
of Ithaka, which, through all the years and great deeds of
Odysseus' absence, the peasants have not ceased to farm.

The Odyssey begins in the world of *The Iliad,* a
world which, like our own, is war-obsessed, preoccupied
with "manly" deeds of exploitation, anger, aggression, pil-
lage, and the disorder, uprootedness, and vagabondage
that are their result. At the end of the poem, Odysseus
moves away from the values of that world toward the values of domesticity and peace. He restores order to his
household by an awesome violence, it is true. But that finished and the house purified, he re-enters his marriage, the
bedchamber and the marriage bed rooted in the earth.
From there he goes into the fields.

The final recognition scene occurs between Odysseus and his old father, Laërtês:

> Odysseus found his father in solitude
> spading the earth around a young fruit tree.
>
> He wore a tunic, patched and soiled, and leggings—
> oxhide patches, bound below his knees
> against the brambles . . .

The point is not stated—the story is moving so evenly now
toward its conclusion that it will not trouble to remind us
that the man thus dressed is a *king*—but it is clear that

Laërtês has survived his son's absence and the consequent grief and disorder *as a peasant*. Although Odysseus jokes about his father's appearance, the appropriateness of what he is doing is never questioned. In a time of disorder he has returned to the care of the earth, the foundation of life and hope. And Odysseus finds him in an act emblematic of the best and most responsible kind of agriculture: an old man caring for a young tree.

But the homecoming of Odysseus is still not complete. During his wanderings, he was instructed by the ghost of the seer Teirêsias to perform what is apparently to be a ritual of atonement. As the poem ends he still has this before him. Carrying an oar on his shoulder, he must walk inland until he comes to a place where men have no knowledge of the sea or ships, where a passerby will mistake his oar for a winnowing fan. There he must "plant" his oar in the ground and make a sacrifice to the sea god, Poseidon. Home again, he must sacrifice to all the gods. Like those people of the Biblical prophecy who will "beat their swords into plowshares, and their spears into pruning hooks" and not "learn war any more," Odysseus will not know rest until he has carried the instrument of his sea wanderings inland and planted it like a tree, until he has seen the symbol of his warrior life as a farming tool. But after his atonement has been made, a gentle death will come to him when he is weary with age, his countrymen around him "in blessed peace."

The Odyssey, then, is in a sense an anti-*Iliad*, posing against the warrior values of the other epic—the glories of battle and foreign adventuring—an affirmation of the values of domesticity and farming. But at the same time *The Odyssey* is too bountiful and wise to set these two kinds of value against each other in any purity or exclusiveness of opposition. Even less does it set into such opposition the two kinds of experience. The point seems to be that these apparently opposed experiences are linked together. The higher value may be given to domesticity, but this cannot be valued or understood alone. Odysseus' fidelity and his homecoming are as moving and instructive as they are precisely because they are the result of *choice*. We know—as Odysseus undoubtedly does also— the extent of his love for Penélopê because he can return to her only by choosing her, at the price of death, over Kalypso. We feel and understand, with Odysseus, the value of Ithaka as a homeland, because bound inextricably to the experience of his return is the memory of his absence, of his long wandering at sea, and even of the excitement of his adventures. The prophecy of the peaceful death that is to come to him is so deeply touching because the poem has so fully realized the experiences of discord and violent death. The farm life of the island seems so sweet and orderly because we know the dark wilderness of natural force and mystery within which the fields are cleared and lighted.

THE NECESSITY OF WILDNESS

Domestic order is obviously threatened by the margin of wilderness that surrounds it. Marriage may be destroyed by instinctive sexuality; the husband may choose to remain with Kalypso or the wife may run away with godlike Paris. And the forest is always waiting to overrun the fields. These are real possibilities. They must be considered, respected, even feared.

And yet I think that no culture that hopes to endure can afford to destroy them or to set up absolute safeguards against them. Invariably the failure of organized religions, by which they cut themselves off from mystery and therefore from sanctity, lies in the attempt to impose an absolute division between faith and doubt, to make belief perform as knowledge; when they forbid their prophets to go into the wilderness, they lose the possibility of renewal. And the most dangerous tendency in modern society, now rapidly emerging as a scientific-industrial ambition, is the tendency toward encapsulation of human order—the severance, once and for all, of the umbilical cord fastening us to the wilderness or the Creation. The threat is not only in the totalitarian desire for absolute control. It lies in the willingness to ignore an essential paradox: the natural forces that so threaten us are the same forces that preserve and renew us.

An enduring agriculture must never cease to consider and respect and preserve wildness. The farm can exist only within the wilderness of mystery and natural force. And if the farm is to last and remain in health, the wilderness must survive within the farm. That is what agricultural fertility *is:* the survival of natural process in the human order. To learn to preserve the fertility of the farm, Sir Albert Howard wrote, we must study the forest.

Similarly the instinctive sexuality within which marriage exists must somehow be made to thrive within marriage. To divide one from the other is to degrade both and ultimately to destroy marriage.

Fidelity to human order, then, if it is fully responsible, implies fidelity also to natural order. Fidelity to human order makes devotion possible. Fidelity to natural order preserves the possibility of choice, the possibility of the renewal of devotion. Where there is no possibility of choice, there is no possibility of faith. One who returns home—to one's marriage and household and place in the world—desiring anew what was previously chosen, is neither the world's stranger nor its prisoner, but is at once in place and free.

The relation between these two fidelities, inasmuch as they sometimes appear to contradict one another, cannot help but be complex and tricky. In our present stage of cultural evolution, it cannot help but be baffling as well. And yet it is only the double faith that is adequate to our need. If we are to have a culture as resilient and competent in the face of necessity as it needs to be, then it must somehow involve within itself a ceremonious generosity toward the wilderness of natural force and instinct. The farm must yield a place to the forest, not as a wood lot, or even as a necessary agricultural principle, but as a sacred grove—a place where the Creation is let alone, to serve as instruction, example, refuge; a place for people to go, free of work and presumption, to let themselves alone. And marriage must recognize that it survives because of, as well as in spite of, Kalypso and Paris and the generosity of instinct that they represent. It must give some ceremonially acknowledged place to the sexual energies that now thrive outside all established forms, in the destructive freedom of moral ignorance or disregard. Without these accommodations we will remain divided: some of us will continue to destroy the world for purely human ends, while others, for the sake of nature, will abandon the task of human order.

What forms or revisions of forms may be adequate to this double faith, I do not know. Cultural solutions are organisms, not machines, and they cannot be invented deliberately or imposed by prescription. Perhaps all that one can do is to clarify as well as possible the needs and pressures that bear upon the process of cultural evolution. I am certain, however, that no satisfactory solution can come from considering marriage alone or agriculture alone. These are our basic connections to each other and to the earth, and they tend to relate analogically and to be reciprocally defining: our demands upon the earth are determined by our ways of living with one another; our regard for one another is brought to light in our ways of using the earth. And I am certain that neither can be changed for the better in the experimental, prescriptive ways we have been using. Ways of life change only in living. To live by expert advice is to abandon one's life.

"FREEDOM" FROM FERTILITY

The household is the bond of marriage that is most native to it, that grows with it and gives it substantial being in the world. It is the practical condition within which husband and wife can enact devotion and loyalty to each other. The motive power of sexual love is thus joined directly to constructive work and is given communal and ecological value. Without the particular demands and satisfactions of the making and keeping of a household, the sanctity and legality of marriage remain abstract, in effect theoretical, and its sexuality becomes a danger. Work is the health of love. To last, love must enflesh itself in the materiality of the world—produce food, shelter, warmth or shade, surround itself with careful acts, well-made things. This, I think, is what Millen Brand means in *Local Lives* when he speaks of the "threat" of love—"so that perhaps acres of earth and its stones are needed and drawn-out work and monotony/to balance that danger . . ."

Marriage and the care of the earth are each other's disciplines. Each makes possible the enactment of fidelity toward the other. As the household has become increasingly generalized as a function of the economy and, as a consequence, has become increasingly "mobile" and temporary, these vital connections have been weakened and finally broken. And whatever has been thus disconnected has become a ground of exploitation for some breed of salesman, specialist, or expert.

A direct result of the disintegration of the household is the division of sexuality from fertility and their virtual takeover by specialists. The specialists of human sexuality are the sexual clinicians and the pornographers, both of whom subsist on the increasing possibility of sex between people who neither know nor care about each other. The specialists of human fertility are the evangelists, technicians, and salesmen of birth control, who subsist upon our failure to see any purpose or virtue in sexual discipline. In this, as in our use of every other kind of energy, our inability to contemplate any measure of restraint or forbearance has been ruinous. Here the impulse is characteristically that of the laboratory scientist: to encapsulate sexuality by separating it absolutely from the problems of fertility.

This division occurs, it seems to me, in a profound cultural failure: the loss of any sense that sexuality and fertility might exist together compatibly in this world. We have lost this possibility because we do not understand, because we cannot bear to consider, the meaning of restraint. (At the root of this failure is probably another sexual division: the assignment to women of virtually all responsibility for sexual discipline.) The sort of restraint I am talking about is illustrated in a recent *National Geographic* article about the people of Hunza in northern Pakistan. The author is a woman, Sabrina Michaud, and she is talking with a Hunza woman in her kitchen:

"'What have you done to have only one child?' she asks me. Her own children range from 12 to 30 years of age, and seem evenly spaced, four to five years apart. 'We leave our husband's bed until each child is weaned,' she explains simply. But this natural means of birth control has declined, and population has soared."

The woman's remark is thus passed over and not returned to; but if I understand the significance of this paragraph, it is of great importance. The decline of "this natural means of birth control" seems to have been contemporaneous with the coming of roads and "progress" and the opening up of a previously isolated country. What is of interest is that in their isolation in arid, narrow valleys surrounded by the stone and ice of the Karakoram Mountains, these people had practiced sexual restraint as a form of birth control. They had neither our statistical expertise nor our doom-prophets of population growth; it just happened that, placed geographically as they were, they lived always in sight of their agricultural or ecological limits, and they made a competent response.

We have been unable to see the difference between this kind of restraint—a cultural response to an understood practical limit—and the obscure, self-hating, self-congratulating Victorian self-restraint, of which our attitudes and technologies of sexual "freedom" are merely the equally obscure other side. This so-called freedom fragments us and turns us more vehemently and violently than before against our own bodies and against the bodies of other people.

For the care or control of fertility, both that of the earth and that of our bodies, we have allowed a technology of chemicals and devices to replace entirely the cultural means of ceremonial forms, disciplines, and restraints. We have gathered up the immense questions that surround the coming of life into the world and reduced them to simple problems for which we have manufactured and marketed simple solutions. An infertile woman and an infertile field both receive a dose of chemicals, at the calculated risk of undesirable consequences, and are thus equally reduced to the status of productive machines. And for unwanted life—sperm, ova, embryos, weeds, insects, etc.—we have the same sort of ready remedies, for sale, of course, and characteristically popularized by advertisements that speak much of advantages but little of problems.

The result is that we are bringing up a generation of young people who feel that they are "free from worry" about fertility. The pharmacist or the doctor will look after the fertility of the body, and the farming experts and agribusinessmen will look after the fertility of the earth. This is to short-circuit human culture at its source. It is, in effect, to remove from consciousness the two fundamental issues of human life. It permits two great powers to be regarded and used as if they were unimportant.

More serious is the resort to "authorized" modes of direct violence. In land use, this is the permanent diminishment or destruction of fertility as an allowable cost of production, as in strip-mining or in the sort of agriculture that good farmers have long referred to also as "mining." This use of technological means cuts across all issues of health and culture for the sake of an annual quota of production.

The human analogue is in the "harmless" and "simple" surgeries of permanent sterilization, which are now being promoted by a propaganda of extreme oversimplification. The publicity on this subject is typically evangelical in tone and simplistically moral; the operations are recommended like commercial products by advertisings complete with exuberant testimonials of satisfied customers and appeals to the prospective customer's maturity, sexual pride, and desire for "freedom"; and the possible physical and psychological complications are played down, misrepresented, not mentioned at all, or simply not known. It is altogether possible that the operations will be performed by doctors as perfunctory, simplistic, presumptuous, and uninforming as the public literature.

I am fully aware of the problem of overpopulation, and I do not mean to say that birth control is unnecessary. What I do mean to say is that any means of birth control is a serious matter, both culturally and biologically, and that sterilization is the most serious of all: to give up fertility is a major change, as important as birth, puberty, marriage, or death.

The great changes having to do with a woman's fertility—puberty, childbirth, and menopause—have, like sexual desire, the unarguable sanction of biological determinism. They belong to a kind of natural tradition. As a result, they are not only endurable, but they belong to a process—the life process or the Wheel of Life—that we have learned to affirm with some understanding. We know, among other things, that this process includes tragedy and survives it, even triumphs over it. The same applies to the occasions of a man's fertility, although not so formidably, a man being less involved, physically, in the *predicament* of fertility and consciously involved in it only if he wants to be. Nevertheless, he comes to fertility and, if he is a moral person, to the same issues of responsibility that it poses for women.

One of the fundamental interests of human culture is to impose this responsibility, to subject fertility to moral will. Culture articulates needs and forms for sexual restraint and involves issues of value in the process of mating. It is possible to imagine that the resulting tension creates a distinctly human form of energy, highly productive of works of the hands and the mind. But until recently there was no division between sexuality and fertility, because none was possible.

This division was made possible by modern technology, which subjected human fertility, like the fertility of the earth, to a new kind of will: the technological will, which may not *necessarily* oppose the moral will, but which has not only tended to do so, but has tended to replace it. Simply because it became possible—and simultaneously profitable—we have cut the cultural ties between sexuality and fertility, just as we have cut those between eating and farming. By "freeing" food and sex from worry, we have also set them apart from thought, responsibility, and the issue of quality. The introduction of "chemical additives" has tended to do away with the issue of taste or preference; the specialist of sex, like the specialist of food, is dealing with a commodity, which he can measure but cannot value.

What is horrifying is not only that we are relying so exclusively on a technology of birth control that is still experimental, but that we are using it *casually,* in utter cultural nakedness, unceremoniously, without sufficient understanding, and as a substitute for cultural solutions—exactly as we now employ the technology of land use. And to promote these means without cultural and ecological insight, as merely a way to divorce sexuality from fertility, pleasure from responsibility—or to *sell* them that way for ulterior "moral" motives—is to try to cure a disease by another disease. That is only a new battle in the old war between body and soul—as if we were living in front of a chorus of the most literal fanatics chanting: "If thy right eye offend thee, pluck it out! If thy right hand offend thee, cut it off!"

The technologists of fertility exercise the powers of gods and the social function of priests without community ties or cultural responsibilities. The clinicians of sex change the lives of people—as the clinicians of agriculture change the lives of places and communities—to whom they are strangers and whom they do not know. These specialists thrive in a profound cultural rift, and they are always accompanied by the exploiters who mine that rift for gold. The pornographer exploits sexual division. And working the similar division between us and our land we have the "agribusinessmen," the pornographers of agriculture.

FERTILITY AS WASTE

But there is yet another and more direct way in which the isolation of the body has serious agricultural effects. That is in our society's extreme oversimplification of the relation between the body and its food. By regarding it as merely a consumer of food, we reduce the function of the body to that of a conduit which channels the nutrients of the earth from the supermarket to the sewer. Or we make it a little factory which transforms fertility into pollution—to the enormous profit of "agribusiness" and to the impoverishment of the earth. This is another technological and economic interruption of the cycle of fertility.

Much has already been said here about the division between the body and its food in the productive phase of the cycle. It is the alleged wonder of the Modern World that so many people take energy from food in which they have invested no energy, or very little. Ninety-five percent of our people, boasted the former deputy assistant secretary of agriculture, are now free of the "drudgery" of food production. The meanings of that division, as I have been trying to show, are intricate and degenerative. But that is only half of it. Ninety-five percent (at least) of our people are also free of any involvement or interest in the maintenance phase of the cycle. As their bodies take in and use the nutrients of the soil, those nutrients are transformed into what we are pleased to regard as "wastes"—and are duly wasted.

This waste also has its cause in the old "religious" division between body and soul, by which the body and its products are judged offensive. Once, living with this offensiveness was considered a condemnation, and that was bad enough. But modern technology "saved" us with the flush toilet and the water-borne sewage system. These devices deal with the "wastes" of our bodies by simply removing them from consideration. The irony is that this technological purification of the body requires the pollution of the rivers and the starvation of the fields. It makes the alleged offensiveness of the body truly and inescapably offensive and blinds an entire society to the knowledge that these "offensive wastes" are readily purified in the topsoil—that, indeed, from an ecological point of view, these are not wastes and are not offensive, but are valuable agricultural products essential both to the health of the land and to that of the "consumers."

Our system of agriculture, by modeling itself on economics rather than biology, thus removes food from the *cycle* of its production and puts it into a finite, linear process that in effect destroys it by transforming it into waste. That is, it transforms food into fuel, a form of energy that is usable only once, and in doing so it transforms the body into a consumptive machine.

It is strange, but only apparently so, that this system of agriculture is institutionalized, not in any form of rural life or culture, but in what we call our "urban civilization." The cities subsist in competition with the country; they live upon a one-way movement of energies out of the country-side—food and fuel, manufacturing materials, human labor, intelligence, and talent. Very little of this energy is ever returned. Instead of gathering these energies up into coherence, a cultural consummation that would not only return to the countryside what belongs to it, but also give back generosities of learning and art, conviviality and order, the modern city dissipates and wastes them. Along with its glittering "consumer goods," the modern city produces an equally characteristic outpouring of garbage and pollution—just as it produces and/or collects unemployed, unemployable, and otherwise wasted people.

Once again it must be asked, if competition is the appropriate relationship, then why, after generations of this inpouring of rural wealth, materials, and humanity into the cities, are the cities and the countryside in equal states of disintegration and disrepair? Why have the rural and urban communities *both* fallen to pieces?

HEALTH AND WORK

The modern urban-industrial society is based on a series of radical disconnections between body and soul, husband and wife, marriage and community, community and the earth. At each of these points of disconnection the collaboration of corporation, government, and expert sets up a profit-making enterprise that results in the further dismemberment and impoverishment of the Creation.

Together, these disconnections add up to a condition of critical ill health, which we suffer in common—not just with each other, but with all other creatures. Our economy is based upon this disease. Its aim is to separate us as far as possible from the sources of life (material, social, and spiritual), to put these sources under the control of corporations and specialized professionals, and to sell them to us at the highest profit. It fragments the Creation and sets the fragments into conflict with one another. For the relief of the suffering that comes of this fragmentation and conflict, our economy proposes, not health, but vast "cures" that further centralize power and increase profits: wars, wars on crime, wars on poverty, national schemes of medical aid, insurance, immunization, further industrial and economic "growth," etc.; and these, of course, are followed by more regulatory laws and agencies to see that our health is protected, our freedom preserved, and our money well spent. Although there may be some "good intention" in this, there is little honesty and no hope.

Only by restoring the broken connections can we be healed. Connection *is* health. And what our society does its best to disguise from us is how ordinary, how commonly attainable, health is. We lose our health—and create profitable diseases and dependences—by failing to see the direct connections between living and eating, eating and working, working and loving. In gardening, for instance, one works with the body to feed the body. The work, if it is knowledgeable, makes for excellent food. And it makes one hungry. The work thus makes eating both nourishing and joyful, not consumptive, and keeps the eater from getting fat and weak. This is health, wholeness, a source of delight. And such a solution, unlike the typical industrial solution, does not cause new problems.

The "drudgery" of growing one's own food, then, is not drudgery at all. (If we make the growing of food a drudgery, which is what "agribusiness" does make of it, then we also make a drudgery of eating and of living.) It is—in addition to being the appropriate fulfillment of a practical need—a sacrament, as eating is also, by which we enact and understand our oneness with the Creation, the conviviality of one body with all bodies. This is what we learn from the hunting and farming rituals of tribal cultures.

As the connections have been broken by the fragmentation and isolation of work, they can be restored by restoring the wholeness of work. There is work that is isolating, harsh, destructive, specialized or trivialized into meaninglessness. And there is work that is restorative, convivial, dignified and dignifying, and pleasing. Good work is not just the maintenance of connections—as one is now said to work "for a living" or "to support a family"—but the *enactment* of connections. It *is* living, and a way of living; it is not support for a family in the sense of an exterior brace or prop, but is one of the forms and acts of love.

To boast that now "95 percent of the people can be freed from the drudgery of preparing their own food" is possible only to one who cannot distinguish between these kinds of work. The former deputy assistant secretary cannot see work as a vital connection; he can see it only as a trade of time for money, and so of course he believes in doing as little of it as possible, especially if it involves the use of the body. His ideal is apparently the same as that of a real-estate agency which promotes a rural subdivision by advertising "A homelife of endless vacation." But the society that is so glad to be free of the drudgery of growing and preparing food also boasts a thriving medical industry to which it is paying $500 per person per year. And that is only the down payment.

We embrace this curious freedom and pay its exorbitant cost because of our hatred of bodily labor. We do not want to work "like a dog" or "like an ox" or "like a horse"—that is, we do not want to use ourselves as beasts. This as much as anything is the cause of our disrespect for farming and our abandonment of it to businessmen and experts. We remember, as we should, that there have been agricultural economies that used people as beasts. But that cannot be remedied, as we have attempted to do, by using people as machines, or by not using them at all.

Perhaps the trouble began when we started using animals disrespectfully: as "beasts"—that is, as if they had no more feeling than a machine. Perhaps the destructiveness of our use of machines was prepared in our willingness to abuse animals. That it was never necessary to abuse animals in order to use them is suggested by a passage in *The Horse in the Furrow,* by George Ewart Evans. He is speaking of how the medieval ox teams were worked at the plow: ". . . the ploughman at the handles, the team of oxen—yoked in pairs or four abreast—and the driver who walked alongside with his goad." And then he says: "It is also worth noting that in the Welsh organization . . . the counterpart of the driver was termed *y geilwad* or the *caller.* He walked *backwards* in front of the oxen singing to them as they worked. Songs were specially composed to suit the rhythm of the oxen's work . . ."

That seems to me to differ radically from our present customary use of any living thing. The oxen were not used as beasts or machines, but as fellow creatures. It may be presumed that this work used people the same way. It is possible, then, to believe that there is a kind of work that does not require abuse or misuse, that does not use anything as a substitute for anything else. We are working well when we use ourselves as the fellow creatures of the plants, animals, materials, and other people we are working with. Such work is unifying, healing. It brings us home from pride and from despair, and places us responsibly within the human estate. It defines us as we are: not too good to work with our bodies, but too good to work poorly or joylessly or selfishly or alone.

VI

The Making of a
Marginal Farm

One day in the summer of 1956, leaving home for school, I stopped on the side of the road directly above the house where I now live. From there you could see a mile or so across the Kentucky River Valley, and perhaps six miles along the length of it. The valley was a green trough full of sunlight, blue in its distances. I often stopped here in my comings and goings, just to look, for it was all familiar to me from before the time my memory began: woodlands and pastures on the hillsides; fields and croplands, wooded slew-edges and hollows in the bottoms; and through the midst of it the tree-lined river passing down from its head-waters near the Virginia line toward its mouth at Carroll-ton on the Ohio.

Standing there, I was looking at land where one of my great-great-great-grandfathers settled in 1803, and at the scene of some of the happiest times of my own life, where in my growing-up years I camped, hunted, fished, boated, swam, and wandered—where, in short, I did whatever escaping I felt called upon to do. It was a place where I had happily been, and where I always wanted to be. And I remember gesturing toward the valley that day and saying to the friend who was with me: "That's all I need."

I meant it. It was an honest enough response to my recognition of its beauty, the abundance of its lives and possibilities, and of my own love for it and interest in it. And in the sense that I continue to recognize all that, and feel that what I most need is here, I can still say the same thing.

And yet I am aware that I must necessarily mean differently—or at least a great deal more—when I say it now. Then I was speaking mostly from affection, and did not know, by half, what I was talking about. I was speaking of a place that in some ways I knew and in some ways cared for, but did not live in. The differences between knowing a place and living in it, between cherishing a place and living responsibly in it, had not begun to occur to me. But they are critical differences, and understanding them has been perhaps the chief necessity of my experience since then.

I married in the following summer, and in the next seven years lived in a number of distant places. But, largely because I continued to feel that what I needed was here, I could never bring myself to want to live in any other place. And so we returned to live in Kentucky in the summer of 1964, and that autumn bought the house whose roof my friend and I had looked down on eight years before, and with it "twelve acres more or less." Thus I began a profound change in my life. Before, I had lived according to expectation rooted in ambition. Now I began to live according to a kind of destiny rooted in my origins and in my life. One should not speak too confidently of one's "destiny;" I use the word to refer to causes that lie deeper in history and character than mere intention or desire. In buying the little place known as Lanes Landing, it seems to me, I began to obey the deeper causes.

We had returned so that I could take a job at the University of Kentucky in Lexington. And we expected to live pretty much the usual academic life: I would teach and write; my "subject matter" would be, as it had been, the few square miles in Henry County where I grew up. We bought the tiny farm at Lanes Landing, thinking that we would use it as a "summer place," and on that understanding I began, with the help of two carpenter friends, to make some necessary repairs on the house. I no longer remember exactly how it was decided, but that work had hardly begun when it became a full-scale overhaul.

By so little our minds had been changed: this was not going to be a house to visit, but a house to live in. It was as though, having put our hand to the plow, we not only did not look back, but could not. We renewed the old house, equipped it with plumbing, bathroom, and oil furnace, and moved in on July 4, 1965.

Once the house was whole again, we came under the influence of the "twelve acres more or less." This acreage included a steep hillside pasture, two small pastures by the river, and a "garden spot" of less than half an acre. We had, besides the house, a small barn in bad shape, a good large building that once had been a general store, and a small garage also in usable condition. This was hardly a farm by modern standards, but it was land that could be used, and it was unthinkable that we would not use it. The land was not good enough to afford the possibility of a cash income, but it would allow us to grow our food—or most of it. And that is what we set out to do.

In the early spring of 1965 I had planted a small orchard; the next spring we planted our first garden. Within the following six or seven years we reclaimed the pastures, converted the garage into a henhouse, rebuilt the barn, greatly improved the garden soil, planted berry bushes, acquired a milk cow—and were producing, except for hay and grain for our animals, nearly everything that we ate: fruit, vegetables, eggs, meat, milk, cream, and butter. We built an outbuilding with a meat room and a food-storage cellar. Because we did not want to pollute our land and water with sewage, and in the process waste nutrients that should be returned to the soil, we built a composting privy. And so we began to attempt a life that, in addition to whatever else it was, would be responsibly agricultural. We used no chemical fertilizers. Except for a little rotenone, we used no insecticides. As our land and our food became healthier, so did we. And our food was of better quality than any that we could have bought.

We were not, of course, living an idyll. What we had done could not have been accomplished without difficulty and a great deal of work. And we had made some mistakes and false starts. But there was great satisfaction, too, in restoring the neglected land, and in feeding ourselves from it.

Meanwhile, the forty-acre place adjoining ours on the downriver side had been sold to a "developer," who planned to divide it into lots for "second homes." This project was probably doomed by the steepness of the ground and the difficulty of access, but a lot of bulldozing—and a lot of damage—was done before it was given up. In the fall of 1972, the place was offered for sale and we were able to buy it.

We now began to deal with larger agricultural problems. Some of this new land was usable; some would have to be left in trees. There were perhaps fifteen acres of hillside that could be reclaimed for pasture, and about two and a half acres of excellent bottomland on which we would grow alfalfa for hay. But it was a mess, all of it badly neglected, and a considerable portion of it badly abused by the developer's bulldozers. The hillsides were covered with thicket growth; the bottom was shoulder high in weeds; the diversion ditches had to be restored; a bulldozed gash meant for "building sites" had to be mended; the barn needed a new foundation, and the cistern a new top; there were no fences. What we had bought was less a farm than a reclamation project—which has now, with a later purchase, grown to seventy-five acres.

While we had only the small place, I had got along very well with a Gravely "walking tractor" that I owned, and an old Farmall A that I occasionally borrowed from my Uncle Jimmy. But now that we had increased our acreage, it was clear that I could not continue to depend on a borrowed tractor. For a while I assumed that I would buy a tractor of my own. But because our land was steep, and there was already talk of a fuel shortage—and because I liked the idea—I finally decided to buy a team of horses instead. By the spring of 1973, after a lot of inquiring and looking, I had found and bought a team of five-year-old sorrel mares. And—again by the generosity of my Uncle Jimmy, who has never thrown any good thing away—I had enough equipment to make a start.

Though I had worked horses and mules during the time I was growing up, I had never worked over ground so steep and problematical as this, and it had been twenty years since I had worked a team over ground of any kind. Getting started again, I anticipated every new task with uneasiness, and sometimes with dread. But to my relief and delight, the team and I did all that needed to be done that year, getting better as we went along. And over the years since then, with that team and others, my son and I have carried on our farming the way it was carried on in my boyhood, doing everything with our horses except baling the hay. And we have done work in places and in weather in which a tractor would have been useless. Experience has shown us—or re-shown us—that horses are not only a satisfactory and economical means of power, especially on such small places as ours, but are probably *necessary* to the most conservative use of steep land. Our farm, in fact, is surrounded by potentially excellent hillsides that were maintained in pasture until tractors replaced the teams.

Another change in our economy (and our lives) was accomplished in the fall of 1973 with the purchase of our first wood-burning stove. Again the petroleum shortage was on our minds, but we also knew that from the pasture-clearing we had ahead of us we would have an abundance of wood that otherwise would go to waste— and when that was gone we would still have our permanent wood lots. We thus expanded our subsistence income to include heating fuel, and since then have used our furnace only as a "backup system" in the coldest weather and in our absences from home. The horses also contribute significantly to the work of fuel-gathering; they will go easily into difficult places and over soft ground or snow where a truck or a tractor could not move.

As we have continued to live on and from our place, we have slowly begun its restoration and healing. Most of the scars have now been mended and grassed over, most of the washes stopped, most of the buildings made sound; many loads of rocks have been hauled out of the fields and used to pave entrances or fill hollows; we have done perhaps half of the necessary fencing. A great deal of work is still left to do, and some of it—the rebuilding of fertility in the depleted hillsides—will take longer than we will live. But in doing these things we have begun a restoration and a healing in ourselves.

I should say plainly that this has not been a "paying proposition." As a reclamation project, it has been costly both in money and in effort. It seems at least possible that, in any other place, I might have had little interest in doing any such thing. The reason I have been interested in doing it here, I think, is that I have felt implicated in the history, the uses, and the attitudes that have depleted such places as ours and made them "marginal."

I had not worked long on our "twelve acres more or less" before I saw that such places were explained almost as much by their human history as by their nature. I saw that they were not "marginal" because they ever were unfit for human use, but because in both culture and character *we* had been unfit to use them. Originally, even such steep slopes as these along the lower Kentucky River Valley were deep-soiled and abundantly fertile; "jumper" plows and generations of carelessness impoverished them. Where yellow clay is at the surface now, five feet of good soil may be gone. I once wrote that on some of the nearby uplands one walks as if "knee-deep" in the absence of the original soil. On these steeper slopes, I now know, that absence is shoulder-deep.

That is a loss that is horrifying as soon as it is imagined. It happened easily, by ignorance, indifference, "a little folding of the hands to sleep." It cannot be remedied in human time; to build five feet of soil takes perhaps fifty or sixty thousand years. This loss, once imagined, is potent with despair. If a people in adding a hundred and fifty years to itself subtracts fifty thousand from its land, what is there to hope?

And so our reclamation project has been, for me, less a matter of idealism or morality than a kind of self-preservation. A destructive history, once it is understood as such, is a nearly insupportable burden. Understanding it is a disease of understanding, depleting the sense of efficacy and paralyzing effort, unless it finds healing work. For me that work has been partly of the mind, in what I have written, but that seems to have depended inescapably on work of the body and of the ground. In order to affirm the values most native and necessary to me—indeed, to affirm my own life as a thing decent in possibility—I needed to know in my own experience that this place did not have to be abused in the past, and that it can be kindly and conservingly used now.

With certain reservations that must be strictly borne in mind, our work here has begun to offer some of the needed proofs.

Bountiful as the vanished original soil of the hillsides may have been, what remains is good. It responds well—sometimes astonishingly well—to good treatment. It never should have been plowed (some of it never should have been cleared), and it never should be plowed again. But it can be put in pasture without plowing, and it will support an excellent grass sod that will in turn protect it from erosion, if properly managed and not overgrazed.

Land so steep as this cannot be preserved in row crop cultivation. To subject it to such an expectation is simply to ruin it, as its history shows. Our rule, generally, has been to plow no steep ground, to maintain in pasture only such slopes as can be safely mowed with a horse-drawn mower, and to leave the rest in trees. We have increased the numbers of livestock on our pastures gradually, and have carefully rotated the animals from field to field, in order to avoid overgrazing. Under this use and care, our hillsides have mended and they produce more and better pasturage every year.

As a child I always intended to be a farmer. As a young man, I gave up that intention, assuming that I could not farm and do the other things I wanted to do. And then I became a farmer almost unintentionally and by a kind of necessity. That wayward and necessary becoming—along with my marriage, which has been intimately a part of it—is the major event of my life. It has changed me profoundly from the man and the writer I would otherwise have been.

There was a time, after I had left home and before I came back, when this place was my "subject matter." I meant that too, I think, on the day in 1956 when I told my friend, "That's all I need." I was regarding it, in a way too easy for a writer, as a mirror in which I saw myself. There was obviously a sort of narcissism in that—and an inevitable superficiality, for only the surface can reflect.

In coming home and settling on this place, I began to *live* in my subject, and to learn that living in one's subject is not at all the same as "having" a subject. To live in the place that is one's subject is to pass through the surface. The simplifications of distance and mere observation are thus destroyed. The obsessively regarded reflection is broken and dissolved. One sees that the mirror was a blinder; one can now begin to see where one is. One's relation to one's subject ceases to be merely emotional or esthetical, or even merely critical, and becomes problematical, practical, and responsible as well. Because it must. It is like marrying your sweetheart.

Though our farm has not been an economic success, as such success is usually reckoned, it is nevertheless beginning to make a kind of economic sense that is consoling and hopeful. Now that the largest expenses of purchase and repair are behind us, our income from the place is beginning to run ahead of expenses. As income I am counting the value of shelter, subsistence, heating fuel, and money earned by the sale of livestock. As expenses I am counting maintenance, newly purchased equipment, extra livestock feed, newly purchased animals, reclamation work, fencing materials, taxes, and insurance.

If our land had been in better shape when we bought it, our expenses would obviously be much smaller. As it is, once we have completed its restoration, our farm will provide us a home, produce our subsistence, keep us warm in winter, and earn a modest cash income. The significance of this becomes apparent when one considers that most of this land is "unfarmable" by the standards of conventional agriculture, and that most of it was producing nothing at the time we bought it.

And so, contrary to some people's opinion, it *is* possible for a family to live on such "marginal" land, to take a bountiful subsistence and some cash income from it, and, in doing so, to improve both the land and themselves. (I believe, however, that, at least in the present economy, this should not be attempted without a source of income other than the farm. It is now extremely difficult to pay for the best of farmland by farming it, and even "marginal" land has become unreasonably expensive. To attempt to make a living from such land is to impose a severe strain on land and people alike.)

I said earlier that the success of our work here is subject to reservations. There are only two of these, but both are serious.

The first is that land like ours—and there are many acres of such land in this country—can be conserved in use only by competent knowledge, by a great deal more work than is required by leveler land, by a devotion more particular and disciplined than patriotism, and by ceaseless watchfulness and care. All these are cultural values and resources, never sufficiently abundant in this country, and now almost obliterated by the contrary values of the so-called "affluent society."

One of my own mistakes will suggest the difficulty. In 1974 I dug a small pond on a wooded hillside that I wanted to pasture occasionally. The excavation for that pond—as I should have anticipated, for I had better reason than I used—caused the hillside to slump both above and below. After six years the slope has not stabilized, and more expense and trouble will be required to stabilize it. A small hillside farm will not survive many mistakes of that order. Nor will a modest income.

The true remedy for mistakes is to keep from making them. It is not in the piecemeal technological solutions that our society now offers, but in a change of cultural (and economic) values that will encourage in the whole population the necessary respect, restraint, and care. Even more important, it is in the possibility of settled families and local communities, in which the knowledge of proper means and methods, proper moderations and restraints, can be handed down, and so accumulate in place and stay alive; the experience of one generation is not adequate to inform and control its actions. Such possibilities are not now in sight in this country.

The second reservation is that we live at the lower end of the Kentucky River watershed, which has long been intensively used, and is increasingly abused. Strip mining, logging, extractive farming, and the digging, draining, roofing, and paving that go with industrial and urban "development," all have seriously depleted the capacity of the watershed to retain water. This means not only that floods are higher and more frequent than they would be if the watershed were healthy, but that the floods subside too quickly, the watershed being far less a sponge, now, than it is a roof. The floodwater drops suddenly out of the river, leaving the steep banks soggy, heavy, and soft. As a result, great strips and blocks of land crack loose and slump, or they give way entirely and disappear into the river in what people here call "slips."

The flood of December 1978, which was unusually high, also went down extremely fast, falling from banktop almost to pool stage within a couple of days. In the aftermath of this rapid "drawdown," we lost a block of bottomland an acre square. This slip, which is still crumbling, severely damaged our place, and may eventually undermine two buildings. The same flood started a slip in another place, which threatens a third building. We have yet another building situated on a huge (but, so far, very gradual) slide that starts at the river and, aggravated by two state highway cuts, goes almost to the hilltop. And we have serious river bank erosion the whole length of our place.

What this means is that, no matter how successfully we may control erosion on our hillsides, our land remains susceptible to a more serious cause of erosion that we cannot control. Our river bank stands literally at the cutting edge of our nation's consumptive economy. This, I think, is true of many "marginal" places—it is true, in fact, of many places that are not marginal. In its consciousness, ours is an upland society; the ruin of watersheds, and what that involves and means, is little considered. And so the land is heavily taxed to subsidize an "affluence" that consists, in reality, of health and goods stolen from the unborn.

Living at the lower end of the Kentucky River watershed is what is now known as "an educational experience"—and not an easy one. A lot of information comes with it that is severely damaging to the reputation of our people and our time. From where I live and work, I never have to look far to see that the earth does indeed pass away. But however that is taught, and however bitterly learned, it is something that should be known, and there is a certain good strength in knowing it. To spend one's life farming a piece of the earth so passing is, as many would say, a hard lot. But it is, in an ancient sense, the human lot. What saves it is to love the farming.